In Search of a New Logic for Marketing

Foundations of Contemporary Theory

Christian Grönroos

BICENTENNIAL
1807
WILEY
2007
BICENTENNIAL

John Wiley & Sons, Ltd

Email (for orders and customer service enquiries): cs-books@wiley.co.uk
Visit our Home Page on www.wiley.com

Other Wiley Editorial Offices

John Wiley & Sons Inc., 111 River Street, Hoboken, NJ 07030, USA

Jossey-Bass, 989 Market Street, San Francisco, CA 94103-1741, USA

Wiley-VCH Verlag GmbH, Boschstr. 12, D-69469 Weinheim, Germany

John Wiley & Sons Australia Ltd, 33 Park Road, Milton, Queensland 4064, Australia

John Wiley & Sons (Asia) Pte Ltd, 2 Clementi Loop #02-01, Jin Xing Distripark, Singapore 129809

John Wiley & Sons Canada Ltd, 6045 Freemont Blvd, Mississauga, ONT, Canada L5R 4J3

Wiley also publishes its books in a variety of electronic formats. Some content that appears in print
may not be available in electronic books.

Library of Congress Cataloging in Publication Data

Grönroos, Christian, 1947–
  In search of a new logic for marketing : foundations of contemporary theory / Christian
Grönroos.
    p. cm.
  Includes bibliographical references and index.
  ISBN-13: 978-0-470-06127-5 (cloth : alk. paper)
  ISBN-10: 0-470-06127-8 (cloth : alk. paper)
  ISBN-13: 978-0-470-06129-9 (pbk. : alk. paper)
  ISBN-10: 0-470-06129-4 (pbk. : alk. paper)   1. Marketing.   I. Title.
  HF5415.G755 2007
  658.8001—dc22

                                                                          2006032096

British Library Cataloguing in Publication Data

A catalogue record for this book is available from the British Library

ISBN-10: 0-470-06127-8 (HB)
ISBN-13: 978-0-470-06127-5 (HB)
ISBN-10: 0-470-06129-4 (PB)
ISBN-13: 978-0-470-06129-9 (PB)

Typeset in 10/14pt Kunstler by Integra Software Services Pvt. Ltd, Pondicherry, India
Printed and bound in Great Britain by Antony Rowe Ltd, Chippenham, Wiltshire
This book is printed on acid-free paper responsibly manufactured from sustainable forestry in which
at least two trees are planted for each one used for paper production.

Contents

Preface

Just when I am about to turn 60 I realize that I have spent half of my life looking for an alternative marketing logic to the one I was taught in business school in the 1960s. Ten years after I began my business school studies I was, purely by accident, made aware of the existence of services and quite soon after that I came to the conclusion, or suspicion at least, that marketing based on a service logic could provide a better foundation for a marketing theory than the goods-based mainstream marketing. Services have always been relational, but when relationship marketing emerged as an explicitly articulated field, the truth of this conclusion became even more evident. The business and marketing environment was changing and, by and large, customers were becoming more informed and more demanding. In principle, firms marketing to consumer markets and firms marketing to business markets face the same challenges. The introduction of the Internet and the development of information technologies have supported these trends. To maintain their competitiveness, firms have had to actively add more elements to their customer interfaces, such as information and advice, installation, repair and maintenance, and they have had to turn hidden service features such as complaints handling and invoicing systems into actively managed customer-focused services. Traditionally, a quickly and fairly resolved quality problem or service failure or the production of an always correct and easily under-standable invoice have remained hidden services for the customers, because these activities are managed and executed as administrative or legal routines with a limited or no customer focus involved. From the customers' perspective, if these tasks are not properly implemented, the result is a nuisance rather than support. Complaints handling and invoicing are only two examples of a whole host of hidden services.

Until recently, service and relationship marketing have developed as sepa-rate fields, not interfering with mainstream marketing with its marketing mix management approach. Previously, it was important to establish service marketing and relationship marketing as legitimate marketing fields. The possible usefulness for marketing in general of the logic underpinning service marketing, and its extension into relationship marketing, was not discussed. However, finally, this has become an international topic.

In view of the ongoing development in the marketing environment, mainstream marketing has less to offer firms. Marketing as a discipline and as a practice is in crisis (see the analysis in Chapter 1, Marketing – A Discipline in Crisis). According to the *marketing concept*, firms' decisions and activities should be geared towards the needs and wants of customers, thereby relating the firms to their customers. In other words, they should support the customers' everyday activities and processes. To use the *promise concept*, marketing should make promises to customers about available solutions and provide promise fulfilment through the provision of solutions that in a satisfactory manner meet the expectations created by the promises that have been made. In this way, successful *customer management* takes place. However, in its new environment, marketing has become preoccupied with promise making, customer acquisition and the generation of new business. In this process, marketing has become overly tactical and has had difficulties renewing itself. At the same time, by and large, promise keeping and the creation of customer loyalty have become the responsibility of other organizational functions.

In principle, the renewal of marketing can follow either of two paths. Marketing as a discipline and as a practice can limit itself to getting customers and creating new business, and let marketing theory be developed accordingly. If this path is chosen, marketing should be developed as a separate organizational function with the goal of making customers aware of existing solutions and persuading customers to consider a firm's products in some decisive way as better than those of the competition. This would, however, make marketing geared towards promise making and, to use a branding terminology, the creation of brand awareness, whereas promise keeping and brand fulfilment and the creation of brand image would be beyond its scope. Marketing would continue to be mostly tactically engaged in only a part of customer management. The major part of customer management, i.e. making sure that the customers are satisfied and that customer loyalty is developing, would remain in the hands of other organizational functions. The requirement of the marketing concept would not be fulfilled. In my opinion, this would not benefit our discipline.

The alternative path to follow is to develop marketing so that it can take responsibility for the whole process of customer management. As long as a standardized product was the only thing customers were looking for and the only thing needed to create satisfaction and loyalty, mainstream marketing managed this responsibility quite well. To create marketing today so that it can reassume total responsibility for customer management, attitudinal, structural and managerial changes have to take place. For example, marketing cannot be limited to a predetermined set of decision-making areas and it cannot remain the responsibility of one separate organizational function only. Compared to the first alternative, the challenges for marketing both as a discipline and as a practice are huge.

In my opinion, following the first path to develop marketing will marginalize marketing as a business practice even more. Marketing and marketers will become increasingly less relevant to top management, customers and shareholders alike. Marketing as a discipline may survive, but it will become increasingly tactical and less interesting for students. In spite of the challenge of the second path to develop marketing, in my view, it provides the only way of restoring marketing's importance for customer management and reinstating its role in corporate decision-making. Here the development of service and relationship marketing concepts and models and the emergence of their underpinning logic provide one foundation for renewing marketing. With the growing interest in a service-dominant logic, it is only natural to analyse whether the logic of service and relationship marketing can provide a useful foundation for a contemporary marketing theory.

In this book, I have collected nine of my scientific articles on service marketing and relationship marketing, originally published between 1978 and 2006. Four articles on service marketing form Part One and four articles on relationship marketing form Part Two. In addition, an introduction and an analysis of the state of marketing form the introductory section, and the ninth article together with an extensive conclusion on the development of a foundation for a contemporary marketing theory form the third concluding part. It is, of course, my view of how marketing in general could benefit from the logic that has emerged in service and relationship marketing. Moreover, my research has constantly and from the outset been geared towards the *Nordic School* of marketing thought (see the discussion of the Nordic School in the introduction). This, of course, influences my scientific approach and my approach to studying the field.

Acknowledgements

There is a large group of people, academics as well as business practitioners, to whom I owe a great deal. Thank you all for your help. As it is impossible to mention everyone to whom I am grateful, I will have to acknowledge by name only a few people who have had a decisive impact on my thoughts and my career. There are six people whom I want to mention first, namely, Kurt Kääriäinen who unexpectedly phoned me to invite me to give a speech on theoretical aspects of the marketing of services and made me aware of the existence of services, Lars Lindqvist who urged me to drop everything else I was exploring as possible topics for a doctoral thesis and concentrate on service marketing, Evert Gummesson who, in the 1970s, was a doctoral student as equally devoted to studying service marketing as I was and with whom I, over the years, have compared thoughts and shared views on mainstream marketing, service marketing, relationship marketing and life itself, William George, co-chairperson of the American Marketing Association's first special conference on the marketing of services who as unexpectedly as Kurt phoned me from the USA one day to invite me to submit a paper for that conference and thereby involved me in an international network much earlier than otherwise would have been possible, and Alf-Erik Lerviks, my thesis supervisor, who accepted and supported my research, in spite of my totally new and previously unheard-of topic, my treatment of mainstream marketing which most academics considered heretical and unacceptable, and my, at that time, highly unconventional scientific approach. Finally, I am indebted to Gösta Mickwitz, who was professor of marketing and economics at Hanken Swedish School of Economics Finland and the University of Helsinki, and my mentor. He taught me to think laterally and look for solutions outside the limits set by the prevailing opinion. I am extremely grateful to all of them.

Colleagues at business schools and universities I am affiliated with have in various ways helped me in my research and in advancing my career. In particular, I want to thank Lars Lindqvist, Tore Strandvik, Veronica Liljander, Annika Ravald, Maria Holmlund, Kirsti Lindberg-Repo, and the late Henrik Calonius at my main university affiliation, Hanken Swedish School of Economics, in Finland, and Stephen Brown and Mary Jo Bitner as well as Lawrence Crosby, who has left academia for a successful career in business, at Arizona State University in Tempe, which I consider my second home, and also Hervé Corvellec and Jan Persson at Lund University's Campus Helsingborg in Sweden, to the best of my knowledge the only academic institution where a trans-disciplinary academic programme in service science from undergraduate and graduate to doctoral studies is offered.

I also want to thank Bo Edvardsson, and Uolevi Lehtinen as well as Jarmo Lehtinen and Kaj Storbacka, who both are pursuing successful academic and business careers, and also David Ballantyne, Leonard Berry, David Bowen, Roderick Brodie, Pierre Eiglier, Ray Fisk, William George, the late Eric Langeard, Christopher Lovelock, Robert Lusch, Parsu Parasuraman, Roland Rust, Benjamin Schneider, Lynn Shostack and Stephen Vargo. In addition, there are a huge number of business practitioners who in many ways have supported me in my work. My thanks go to all of you.

Sarah Booth and Anneli Anderson at John Wiley & Sons, Ltd have provided me with excellent support throughout the process of preparing this book. Thank you very much. Last but not least, I would like to acknowledge the support I have received throughout this endeavour from my wife Viveca and my children and grandchildren.

Christian Grönroos
Tölö, Finland
January 16, 2007

Introduction
I Did It My Way

How It All Began

It all began with a phone call thirty years ago. In March 1976, a former colleague of mine called me and asked if I could give a theoretical presentation on the marketing of services at a public seminar later that spring. The consultancy firm he worked for had just finished a study of marketing in the hospitality industry in Finland. After a moment of hesitation, I had the good sense to accept. I had never heard of a field called marketing of services, but apparently nobody else in academia in Finland had done so either. This was the beginning of a thirty-year journey in search of a new logic for marketing that still continues. At that time I was looking for an interesting topic for a doctoral thesis that would have the potential to make a noticeable contribution to the marketing field. At that time I was also writing a tentative research proposal on the marketing of education. The hospitality services seminar was cancelled – the time for service marketing was yet to come – but my eyes had been opened to a wide-open marketing field to be explored and I had included a section on the marketing of services in my research proposal. Without Kurt Kääriäinen, now the owner of a successful consultancy firm, who made that phone call, and Lars Lindqvist, then a fellow doctoral student of mine and now a professor of marketing in Finland, who, when he and I walked to have lunch after a research seminar later that spring when my education marketing proposal had been turned down, urged me to work on the piece on service marketing and drop the rest, I would probably never have become interested in services. When walking back from lunch, I had already decided to follow Lars's advice.

In January 1979, I defended my doctoral thesis on the marketing of services. The year before, I had already published my first article on this topic in an international scholarly journal. This article is included in this volume as the first article on service marketing ('A Service-Orientated Approach to Marketing of Services').

From the beginning, I used the expression 'service marketing'. In my view, I was not studying marketing for a fragmented field of very different types of services, but rather the underpinning logic of service as a phenomenon. For my initial literature review, I first discovered John Rathmell's book *Marketing in the Service Sector* (1974) and Aubrey Wilson's book on professional services (1972). Rathmell observed that when attempting to understand services 'definitions, classifications, data, and concepts are lacking, noncomparable, or unreal from a marketing perspective' and concluded that 'as one attempts to integrate marketing terms, concepts, and practices with firms, institutions, and professions having their own traditions, customs, and practices which are quite foreign to conventional marketing (and much older), the linkage appears awkward and even improper'. His views were convincingly supported by my initial empirical studies on several service industries. Rathmell's observations and my own first empirical analyses made me, from the outset, believe that service marketing required a totally new logic.

However, very early, I boldly came to a tentative conclusion that this new logic and the principles and concepts of service marketing that followed from it also would fit marketing at large, regardless of whether the core of a firm's offering is a service or a physical product. At a nationwide research conference in 1977, together with seven other doctoral students from different universities and business schools, I presented my proposal for a doctoral thesis in a session chaired by the most senior marketing professor in Finland. Towards the end of my presentation orally – I had had the good sense not to put it in writing at least – I drew the conclusion that the principles and concepts for service marketing that I was developing could be a new foundation for marketing in general. Of course, on the spot, I was declared insane. A doctoral student should be humble, or at least not express his thoughts in the wrong places. In his concluding remarks, the chairman made the comment that five of the eight research proposals were good as they were and two had to be somewhat refocused, but the eighth doctoral student would never make it to a PhD. I, and probably everyone else there as well, knew whom he meant.

In 1977, another ground-breaking publication appeared, namely Lynn Shostack's article, 'Breaking Free from Product Marketing', which supported my view that a new logic was called for. After another nationwide research conference in Finland in 1978, where Philip Kotler, answering a question about Shostack's article, stated that he did not agree with her and 'if marketing fails in a service firm, it is not because there is something wrong with marketing, but because it is badly implemented', a young PhD asked me whether after this I dared continue my pursuit of new service-focused principles for marketing. I answered him that I do, and I did.

In 1976, I met Evert Gummesson, then a somewhat more senior doctoral student than I was, at a seminar in Sweden. He, too, was looking for a new logic for marketing, albeit in a professional services context. We very quickly realized that we were pursuing the same ideas, and moreover, that most people in academia did not understand us very much, whereas practitioners responsible for marketing in service firms in our research almost invariably saw the potential for them. The following year, I met Pierre Eiglier and Eric Langeard at a workshop on services in France and found two more academics looking for service-focused principles for marketing. I was very much influenced by their research as well (see, for example, Eiglier and Langeard 1975 and 1976).

In view of the international research traditions in marketing, my approach was often not considered very scientific. I relied on qualitative data, case studies in several service industries and conceptual development instead of development of hypotheses from an existing body of knowledge and rigorous hypothesis testing. However, as I was of the opinion that a new logic and new principles and concepts were needed for service marketing, I could not see how I could test hypotheses without knowing what to test. I did not accept the existing body of marketing knowledge as a starting point, so, much like Evert Gummesson in Sweden and Pierre Eiglier and Eric Langeard in France, I set out to develop a conceptual body of knowledge first. Moreover, in my opinion, *quantum leaps* in a field do not follow from theory testing but from conceptual work and theory generation.

I probably broke every rule for academic research in my field but one, which of course is something a sensible doctoral student should not do. The one rule I tried not to break was to be logical in whatever I did. I did try to do a survey, but when I realized that the respondents, who for obvious reasons had the existing goods marketing logic in their minds, could not understand my questions very well, I decided to turn to an interpretative case study approach and qualitative interviews instead. Regardless of what existing research traditions and colleagues in academia suggested, I just could not force myself to do things which I thought were unproductive or downright stupid. In the end, my stubbornness paid off. When writing an article about my career as a service marketing researcher for a collection of essays by scholars who had contributed to the field since the 1970s or 1980s (Fisk, Grove and John 2000), I tried to characterize myself as a researcher. I found no better way of doing it than by quoting Frank Sinatra: *I Did It My Way*.

The Nordic School of Marketing Thought

When attending the American Marketing Association's first special conference on the marketing of services in 1980, both Evert Gummesson and I realized that our approaches to developing service marketing knowledge as well as our approaches to doing research differed greatly from the view of how scholarly research in the field should be done. Generally, the scholarly audience in North America considered our ideas interesting and perhaps even thought-provoking, but nobody, with a few notable exceptions, really seemed to know what to do with them. Our case study approach was considered interesting anecdotal evidence at best by most North American researchers. And to paraphrase Rathmell, albeit the other way around, from a conventional marketing body of knowledge point of view: 'our marketing terms, concepts and practices . . . were quite foreign and the linkage to conventional marketing appeared awkward and even improper'. We got the impression that we did not honour the existing marketing 'truths' such as the marketing mix management paradigm enough. And indeed we did not. Rather, we considered them to be straitjackets that should be avoided so that they did not hinder the development of service-oriented marketing concepts and models. Of course, this did not mean that many of the elements of conventional marketing, such as marketing communication, pricing, segmentation and targeting, would not be useful in a service context.

However, our approaches to the field were considered interesting enough, so we were invited to attend the second AMA special conference in 1982 and I was even asked to give a keynote speech. Before the conference, in my sauna in Helsinki, I suggested that although we were the only two from the Nordic countries at the moment, we represented a distinctly different approach to service marketing research and we should perhaps label that approach in some way. We decided to use the label *The Nordic School of Service Marketing*. Today this would be called branding. In my keynote speech before the still almost predominantly North American audience, I introduced the Nordic School by making the point that the thoughts and research results I was going to share with the audience were based on the Nordic School research tradition. During the 1980s, the number of Nordic School researchers grew and quite quickly this school of thought was internationally recognized as one of three research traditions in the field (Berry and Parasuraman 1993).

My research has constantly and consistently been based on this research tradition and all nine articles included in this volume are 'Nordic School publications', and they form part of the development of not only a logic for service marketing

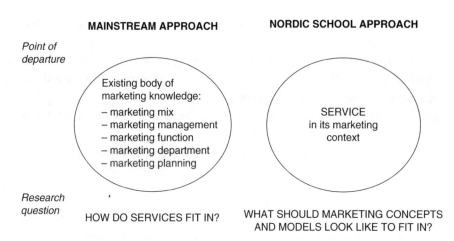

MAINSTREAM APPROACH **NORDIC SCHOOL APPROACH**

Point of departure

Existing body of marketing knowledge:
 – marketing mix
 – marketing management
 – marketing function
 – marketing department
 – marketing planning

SERVICE
in its marketing
context

Research question HOW DO SERVICES FIT IN? WHAT SHOULD MARKETING CONCEPTS
AND MODELS LOOK LIKE TO FIT IN?

Figure 1 The Nordic School approach to studying services as compared with the mainstream approach

and relationship marketing but for marketing in general. To understand the development of the Nordic School view of service marketing, it is important that one keeps one thing in mind: contrary to a mainstream approach to service marketing research, where the starting point was existing, goods-based marketing models, the researchers took the *phenomenon* of service in its marketing context as a starting point, and asked themselves, 'What should marketing look like to fit this phenomenon?' (Figure 1). In this way, existing marketing models that had been developed, based on a different logic, did not become a straitjacket for the development of service marketing.

According to the Nordic School research tradition, *theory generation* is considered more important and more productive to the development of a field than *theory testing*. However, there are two aspects of this to bear in mind:

1. Theory generation and theory testing are not considered totally different scientific avenues; theory generation may also include elements of theory testing.
2. Over the years, as a more solid body of knowledge has been established, pure theory testing also becomes important and interesting.

Some other general aspects of this research tradition are as follows (see Grönroos and Gummesson 1985):

1. Research is not constrained by established norms regarding what marketing is or what makes research scientific.
2. Research is often oriented towards action research, case studies and qualitative research, but, when appropriate, not ignoring surveys and quantitative methods.

3. In the beginning, research is normative and pragmatic, but striving to combine basic research with applied research.
4. It involves an interest in internal marketing as an integral part of marketing.
5. Many characteristics of services and customer relations of service firms fit business-to-business marketing contexts as well.
6. Interactions and relationships rather than exchange are considered the focus of marketing and marketing research.
7. Processes are considered the main and most discriminating characteristic of services:

    (i)   services are activities and processes;
    (ii)   service processes (often called service 'production and delivery') and service consumption are simultaneously occurring processes;
    (iii) consumers participate as co-producers in the service processes and influence the processes and their outcomes as well as each other;
    (iv)   services are to some extent intangible.

8. Buying and consuming services are considered integrated processes which from a marketing point of view cannot be kept apart.
9. Marketing and other organizational functions cannot be kept apart but have to be integrated around a customer focus:

    (i)   market-oriented management rather than marketing management;
    (ii)   service management rather than purely service marketing.

Implicit in the tenets of the Nordic School approach is a view that services as processes are inherently relational and a relationship notion is always present, and even though it was never explicitly put forward, value for customers is considered to emerge in the customers' activities and processes, not in the firm's designing and planning processes, a view that later was labelled *value-in-use*. Moreover, because customers are part of the service processes and influence the flow of the processes and their outcomes, they are not only co-producers but also co-creators of value for themselves.

Aim and Organization of the Book

This volume consists of nine of my articles published in scholarly journals over a period of almost thirty years and an introductory chapter followed by an analysis of the state of the marketing discipline and, finally, a concluding chapter. Four articles published between 1978 and 1998 are on service marketing, four articles published between 1990 and 2004 are on relationship marketing. Finally, the ninth article, published in 2006, and the concluding chapter present an analysis of how a new logic for marketing could form the foundation of a contemporary marketing theory. In view of these and other publications on service marketing and relationship marketing and the ongoing discussion about a service-dominant logic for marketing (see, for example, Vargo and Lusch 2004, and Lusch and Vargo 2006), it seems only natural to take service and relationship marketing as the starting point for the development of a new marketing logic. The analysis and arguments in this volume are predominantly, but not totally, based on the Nordic School research tradition.

The following articles are included in this book:

A Service-Orientated Approach to Marketing of Services. *European Journal of Marketing*, vol. 12, no. 8, 1978, pp. 588–601.

An Applied Service Marketing Theory. *European Journal of Marketing*, vol. 16, no. 7, 1982, pp. 30–41.

A Service Quality Model and its Marketing Implications. *European Journal of Marketing*, vol. 18, no. 4, 1984, pp. 36–44.

Marketing Services: The Case of a Missing Product. *Journal of Business & Industrial Marketing*, vol. 13, no. 4–5, 1998, pp. 322–338.

Relationship Approach to Marketing in Service Contexts: The Marketing and Organizational Behavior Interface. *Journal of Business Research*, vol. 20, no. 1, January 1990, pp. 3–11.

Quo Vadis, Marketing? Toward a Relationship Marketing Paradigm. *Journal of Marketing Management*, vol. 10, no. 5, 1994, pp. 347–360.

Relationship Marketing: Challenges for the Organization. *Journal of Business Research*, vol. 46, no. 3, 1999, pp. 327–335.

The Relationship Marketing Process: Communication, Interaction, Dialogue, Value. *Journal of Business & Industrial Marketing*, vol. 19, no. 2, 2004, pp. 99–113.

Adopting a Service Logic for Marketing. *Marketing Theory*, vol. 6, no. 3, 2006, pp. 317–333.

From the very beginning, the search for a new logic to replace the goods logic of the mainstream marketing mix management paradigm is evident in the articles. However, in the first three articles on service marketing, services as a marketing object are clearly contrasted with goods and it is claimed that services and goods are different. This looks contradictory, but there is a quite natural reason for this. In order to be accepted by marketing academia, which in the 1970s and 1980s was totally dominated by followers of the goods-based marketing mix management paradigm, emphasizing differences between goods and services and pointing out that the new field of research did not interfere with the mainstream were ways of breaking ground for something new. It was actually with the emerging interest in relationship marketing towards the end of the 1980s that it became evident that service-based concepts could be relevant for manufacturers of goods as well. In the articles, this can be seen quite clearly. During the 1990s it was sometimes stated that all businesses are service businesses (compare, for example, Webster 1992), but only from the year 2000 onwards did an explicit discussion of the possibility that goods-producing firms could be better off by adopting frameworks, models and concepts based on a service logic appear in the literature (see Grönroos 2000, and Vargo and Lusch 2004).

The four articles on service marketing constitute Part One of the book, and the four articles on relationship marketing constitute Part Two. The ninth article on 'adopting a service logic for marketing' belongs to the concluding part.

Already, the first three articles on service marketing, published in 1978, 1982 and 1984, include all the central elements of the service logic. In the first article (1978) (Chapter 2), the ideas that in services in a marketing context production and consumption cannot be kept apart and that customers not only consume services but also perform as *co-producers* are discussed. Two consequences for marketing are pointed out, namely, 'the consumers are actively taking part in shaping the service offering' (p. 596), and 'producing and marketing are very interactive processes . . . Both activities are simultaneously performed by the same persons in a service company' (p. 591). The internal challenges are also discussed: 'it is important to be aware of the *internal marketing task of service firms*, i.e., a service must first be successfully marketed to the personnel, so that the employees accept the service offering and thoroughly engage in performing their marketing duties' (p. 594). In this article from 1978 the notion of *value-in-use* is also present, without using this expression and without explicitly pointing it out: 'It is, of course, reasonable to consider both goods and services to be bought by consumers in order to give some service or value satisfaction' (p. 590). As customers are co-producers of services which give them value, they are also *co-creators of value*. Observe that it is stated that not only services but also goods render service to the consumer, an argument that during the past few years has become central in the discussion of the relevance of a service-dominant logic for marketing (see Vargo and Lusch 2004).

In the second article from 1982 (Chapter 3), the division of the marketing process into a traditional part and an interactive marketing part is discussed and it is concluded that '[interactive marketing] is concerned with what happens in the interface between production and consumption' (pp. 32–33). Based on previous work by Eiglier and Langeard (1976), an interactive marketing resource model is also developed. This resource model includes contact personnel, physical and technical resources and customers and, as an outcome of the service process, also includes perceived service quality with its three dimensions: *technical* quality of the outcome, *functional* quality of the service process and *image*. 'There are buyer–seller interactions involving a range of resources and the management of these resources and interactions does have an impact on the consumers' preferences and future buying behaviour' (p. 36). The elements of the perceived service quality model, which is further developed in the third article (1984) (Chapter 4), were first introduced in this second article.

Moreover, in the 1982 article, without using the term 'relationship marketing' a relational approach to marketing is explicitly argued for:

> Marketing is, of course, a dynamic process, where the marketer should not only be interested in getting customers, i.e., in sales, but also in keeping customers i.e., in resales and enduring customer contacts. This means that marketing activities must be performed throughout the process where the service firm is in contact with its consumers. (p. 39)

In the article on service marketing on 'the case of a missing product' (1998) (Chapter 5), the concept of *process consumption* is introduced to describe how services are consumed as compared to physical goods that are outcomes of a production process.

> A central part of service marketing is based on the fact that consumption of a service is *process consumption* rather than *outcome consumption*, where the consumer or user perceives the production process as part of the service consumption, not just the outcome of that process as in traditional marketing of physical goods. (p. 322)

There is also a discussion of the *service marketing triangle* which, in addition to the employees, also includes technology and knowledge as well as the customer and the customer's time as resources in the service process. This model which draws on the earlier research on traditional, interactive and internal marketing as well as on the interactive marketing resource model presented in the 1978 and 1982 articles was originally introduced in an article from 1996, not included in this volume (Grönroos 1996).

In the articles on relationship marketing, the service foundation of the relational approach typical for the Nordic School research tradition is evident. In the first article (1990), relationship marketing is defined as follows: 'Marketing is to establish, maintain, enhance and commercialize customer relationships (often but not necessarily always long-term relationships) so that the objectives of the parties involved are met. This is done by a mutual exchange and fulfilment of promises' (p. 5). In later articles and other publications this definition is slightly modified, but the basic idea remains the same. This definition and the use of the promise concept as a key marketing concept had been introduced in an earlier article the year before (Grönroos 1989). In the 2007 edition of my book *Service Management and Marketing* (Grönroos 2007), relationship marketing is defined as follows: 'Marketing is to identify and establish, maintain and enhance, and when necessary terminate relationships with customers (and other parties) so that the objectives regarding economic and other variables of all parties are met. This is achieved through a mutual making and fulfillment of promises.' In the 1990 article (Chapter 6), the tenet of relationship marketing is described rather categorically as follows:

> Marketing can be considered revolving around relationships, some of which are like single transactions, narrow in scope and not involving much or any social relationship (e.g., marketing soap or breakfast cereals). Other relationships, on the other hand, are broader in scope and may involve even substantial social contacts and be continuous and enduring in nature (e.g., marketing financial and hospitality services). (p. 3)

In a later article not included in this volume (Grönroos 1997), it is concluded that not all customers can be expected to be in a *relational mode* and interested in engaging in a relationship with a firm. Customers can also be in *transactional modes* and move from one mode to another. Hence, although relationships exist latently, they cannot always be used as a basis for marketing. The customers will not always react in a positive way. Moreover, as recent research shows, it is not always profitable for firms to pursue a relational strategy (Reinartz and Kumar 2002; Ryals 2005). However, latent relationships always exist, and when appropriate from both the firm's and its customers' point of view, firms can use them as a basis for a relational marketing strategy.

In the second article on relationship marketing (1994) (Chapter 7), a critical analysis of the marketing mix management approach, which still today is the mainstream paradigm, is conducted. It is concluded that it is internally oriented and, paraphrasing the product orientation–marketing orientation dichotomy, this approach to marketing is labelled 'product oriented'. In contemporary marketing situations there are often a large number of *part-time marketers* (Gummesson 1991), i.e., employees whose main task is something else than marketing but who often on a regular basis interact with customers. As Gummesson (1991) notes, frequently the marketing specialists of the marketing departments, the full-time marketers, do not have direct contact with the firm's customers and are not present when marketing-like efforts are required to make them inclined to continue buying from the firm. In addition, he observes that the part-time marketers normally outnumber the full-time marketers several times. And, moreover, 'often they [the part-time marketers] are the only marketers around' (Grönroos 1984, p. 352). This article concludes with an analysis of a relational approach to marketing and a discussion of how such an approach fits contemporary marketing contexts.

In the third relationship marketing article (1999) (Chapter 8), the consequences for marketing of a relational approach are analysed and eight propositions, called viewpoints, are put forward. They include, for example, the content and offering of marketing, organizing for marketing, marketing planning and budgeting principles to be used in relationship marketing. The final proposition is related to the term to be used for the phenomenon of customer management, for which the term 'marketing' has been used for the past one hundred years or so. The problems that quite obviously are related to the term 'marketing' are discussed. This is an issue which was briefly touched upon already in the second article (1994): 'Some firms have solved this problem [creating an interest among employees in being part-time marketers] not only by downscaling or altogether terminating their marketing departments but also *by banning the use of the term marketing*' (p. 356; emphasis added).

In the fourth article on relationship marketing (2004) (Chapter 9), a dynamic process model of relationship marketing tying marketing to customers' value creation is presented. This model includes three continuous and parallel processes: (1) a *planned communication process*; (2) an *interaction process*; and (3) a *value process*. It is observed that

> Although communication efforts such as sales negotiations and personally addressed letters may look relational, just planning and managing marketing communication through distinct communication media, even as a two-way process, is not relationship marketing. Only the integration of the planned communication and the interaction

process into one strategy that is systematically implemented creates relationship marketing. In such a case customers' perceived value of the relationship is developing favorably. (p. 105)

Finally, in the ninth article (2006) (Chapter 10), and the concluding chapter 'Towards a Contemporary Marketing Theory', a synthesis of the eight articles, and of course of other publications as well, is developed. In the article the need to adopt a service logic in contemporary marketing is analysed. As a conclusion, it is stated that when directly integrating consumption and usage in a marketing framework and taking into account how most customer interfaces today have grown far beyond a standardized product only, marketing based on a service logic becomes the norm, whereas a goods logic can be used successfully only in the special case of simple customer interfaces where the customers are not looking for more than standardized goods. In the conclusion four propositions including eleven sub-propositions for the development of a marketing theory based on a service logic are presented and a *promises management* definition for a contemporary marketing theory using the process-oriented promise concept instead of the marketing mix metaphor is put forward.

References

Berry, L.L. and Parasuraman, A. (1993) 'Building a New Academic Field – The Case of Service Marketing', *Journal of Retailing*, 69(1): 13–60.

Eiglier, P. and Langeard, E. (1975) 'Une approche nouvelle du marketing des services', *Revue Française de Gestion*, 2(November): 97–114.

Eiglier, P. and Langeard, E. (1976) *Principe de politique marketing pour les enterprises de service*, Working Paper. Institut d'Administration des Enterprises, Université d'Aix-Marseille.

Fisk, R.P, Grove, S.J. and John, J. (eds) (2000) *Services Marketing Self-Portraits: Introspections, Reflections, and Glimpses from the Experts*. Chicago: American Marketing Association, pp. 71–108.

Grönroos, C. (1989) 'Defining Marketing: A Market-Oriented Approach', *European Journal of Marketing*, 23(1): 52–60.

Grönroos, C. (1996) 'Relationship Marketing Logic', *The Asia-Australia Marketing Journal*, 4(1): 7–18.

Grönroos, C. (1997) 'Value-Driven Relational Marketing: From Products to Resources and Competencies', *Journal of Marketing Management*, 13(5): 407–419.

Grönroos, C. (2000) *Service Management and Marketing: A Customer Relationship Management Approach*. Chichester: John Wiley & Sons, Ltd.

Grönroos, C. (2007) *Service Management and Marketing: Customer Management in Service Competition*. Chichester: John Wiley & Sons, Ltd.

Grönroos, C. and Gummesson, E. (1985) 'The Nordic School of Services: An Introduction', in Grönroos, C. and Gummesson, E. (eds) *Service Marketing: Nordic School Perspectives*, Series R2. Stockholm: University of Stockholm, pp. 6–11.

Gummesson, E. (1991) 'Marketing Revisited: The Crucial Role of the Part-Time Marketer', *European Journal of Marketing*, 25(2): 60–67.

Lusch, R.F. and Vargo, S.L. (eds) (2006) *The Service-Dominant Logic of Marketing. Dialog, Debate, and Directions*. Armonk, NY: M.E. Sharpe.

Rathmell, J.M. (1974) *Marketing in the Service Sector*. Cambridge, MA: Winthrop Publishers.

Reinartz, W. and Kumar, V. (2002) 'The Mismanagement of Customer Loyalty', *Harvard Business Review*, 80(July–September): 4–12.

Ryals, L. (2005) 'Making Customer Relationship Management Work: The Measurement and Profitable Management of Customer Relationships', *Journal of Marketing*, 69(October): 252–261.

Shostack, G.L. (1977) 'Breaking Free from Product Marketing', *Journal of Marketing*, 41(April): 73–80.

Vargo, S.L. and Lusch, R.F. (2004) 'Evolving to a New Dominant Logic for Marketing', *Journal of Marketing*, 68(January): 1–17.

Webster Jr., F.E. (1992) 'The Changing Role of Marketing in the Corporation', *Journal of Marketing*, 56(October): 1–17.

Wilson, A. (1972) *The Marketing of Professional Services*, London: McGraw-Hill.

1
Marketing – A Discipline in Crisis

The development of the fields of service marketing and relationship marketing in general and especially according to the Nordic School of marketing thought clearly demonstrates how the scope and content and hence the whole nature of marketing are changing. The highly structured approach of mainstream marketing with its inside-out focus on marketing mix management and the 4P model (McCarthy 1960), consisting of a narrow set of decision-making variables, increasingly becomes a straitjacket for the development of marketing theory and practice alike. Almost regardless of industry and of whether the core of an offering is a service or a physical product or something else, the interface between a firm and its customers and the number and variety of customer touchpoints in that interface have grown far beyond the simplistic customer interfaces on which mainstream marketing is based.

Research has not only shown that marketing has to renew itself to be able to handle growing and multi-faceted customer interfaces, but also that it has to be developed so that, when appropriate, it can allow long-term relationships with customers to develop and to be nurtured. Rigid frameworks and transaction-oriented models will not make this renewal possible. Moreover, they also make mainstream marketing overly tactical and do not allow for strategic considerations. Marketing itself lacks the possibility to be strategic, but, in addition, the way marketing has developed has also cut the strings between marketing planning and strategic planning at the corporate level. As McGovern *et al.* observe, 'in too many companies marketing is poorly linked to strategy' (2004, p. 72). The tactical orientation has removed innovativeness from marketing and prevents marketing from being adaptive to changes in the environment (Day and Montgomery 1999, p. 3).

During the past quarter of a century, most of a firm's business functions and processes have undergone a substantial change. Through automation, process re-engineering, total quality management, just-in-time logistics and other business restructuring efforts, manufacturing and operations, logistics and warehousing, deliveries and many other processes have been developed and improved in such dramatic ways that someone who knew how these functions and processes looked fifty years ago would not believe their eyes today. Moreover, through the introduction of computerized systems, information technology, extranets and intranets and through downsizing, re-engineering and outsourcing, management and administrative routines and processes have also changed. Meanwhile, when coming back to his job a marketer who has spent the past fifty years on the moon would feel quite comfortable. Except for the introduction of a few new communication and distribution channels, no fundamental structural changes and innovations have taken place. Furthermore, marketing productivity lags behind the productivity of other functions. As reported by Sheth and Sisodia (1995), from 1947 to the mid-1990s, manufacturing and operations costs have decreased from 50 to 30 per cent of total costs, and during the same period management and administrative costs have decreased from 30 to 20 per cent of total costs. Meanwhile, marketing's share of total costs has increased substantially between the 1940s and the 1990s. No major improvement in the relative productivity of marketing has occurred since that time.

In a lead section on the need for a 'marketing renaissance' in a 2005 issue of the *Journal of Marketing*, distinguished marketing professors, albeit all but one from North America, voice their concerns regarding the status of marketing theory (Marketing Renaissance, 2005). The problems of mainstream marketing are clearly recognized, but all the articles seem to be restricted by conventional marketing thinking and frameworks. Very few innovative suggestions are made. However, in one article, Stephen Brown describes how prominent top management team members representing large firms discussed the importance of the customer to the firm. When discussing how to handle the relation between the firms and their customers, they do not mention marketing at all as an important actor in customer management (Brown 2005). Brown reports: 'Notably, none of the executives mentioned marketing as being responsible for the customer' (2005, p. 3). He also notes that marketing and sales seem to have a major role in 'making promises to customers and generating new business', whereas 'the keeping of promises and building customer loyalty is typically considered the responsibility of others in the enterprise' (2005, p. 3). These observations that customer management is considered an issue for other organizational functions than marketing and that marketers are given responsibility only for the tactical tasks of persuading customers to buy should be a serious warning signal for mainstream marketers, academics and practitioners alike, to wake up and throw away their blinders and, provided that they already have started, continue looking for a new marketing logic. While others take over the responsibility for interpreting customers' thoughts, preferences and expectations and turning them into strategic and tactical customer management, marketing's basic framework keeps the marketers' thoughts and actions within the borders set by the 4 Ps of the marketing mix. Mainstream marketing continues to be oriented towards doing something *to* customers, instead of seeing customers as people *with whom* something is done. This conclusion made by Dixon and Blois (1983) over two decades ago is still very much valid. As a consequence of this, development marketing has become less relevant for top management and corporate decision-making and hence also for shareholders. An unfortunate additional consequence is that marketing has become increasingly less relevant for customers as well.

A stream of studies and reports from the USA as well as from Europe demonstrates that marketing's impact on the thoughts and decisions of top management has been declining and the customers' voice has become less important in corporate decision-making. Gradually marketing is losing its credibility and the marketing function is in decline (see, for example, Webster Jr., Malter and Ganesan 2005). Although this is not the case for every firm everywhere, nevertheless it looks like a trend. Increasingly marketing professionals seems to be less represented on the board of directors and even on top management teams. According to McGovern *et al.*'s large study of US firms (2004), less than 10 per cent of the board's time is spent discussing marketing and customer-related issues. In another US poll, almost half of CEOs interviewed make the point that marketing organizations need improvement (*Chief Executive*, 2004). This view is echoed in a European study by McKinsey, which indicates that over 50 per cent of CEOs interviewed have a negative impression of their marketers (Cassidy, Freeling and Kiewell 2005). Another study from the USA demonstrates that chief marketing executives do not last long (Welch 2004).

Mainstream marketing seems to have pushed marketing into a vicious circle: because of its frameworks and models, marketing has become overly preoccupied with tactical issues and become less strategic, which makes top management less interested in listening to marketers and more inclined to turn to others to make strategic decisions regarding customer management, which in turn makes marketing even less strategic and more tactical.

The facts that marketing is the only business function that has remained untouched by major structural and managerial changes and that marketing's productivity has constantly diminished clearly demonstrate that marketing, still dominated by conventional frameworks and models, is doing a remarkably bad job in taking responsibility for customer management. Mainstream marketing is preoccupied with the wrong activities and is utilizing wrong and less effective resources, or is at least only partly doing the right things. In 1998, Ian Gordon put it like this: 'Busy attending the practice of marketing, marketers may not have noticed that marketing is, for all its practical purposes, dead . . . Marketing rarely achieves its promise of differentiating and developing enduring, competitively superior value.' (Gordon, 1998). Seven years earlier, Regis McKenna concludes, in a discussion of the decline in North America of advertising, the flagship of conventional marketing, that 'the underlying reason behind [this decline] . . . is advertising's dirty little secret: it serves no useful purpose . . . Advertising misses the fundamental point of marketing – adaptability, flexibility and responsiveness.' (McKenna, 1991). Undoubtedly, this is to take it to the extreme, but the point is well taken.

The productivity of marketing cannot be improved within the existing frameworks and structures. As long as marketing's major responsibility is customer acquisition and promise-making, the costs of marketing will continue to grow, and its effectiveness will continue to go down. Taking the Internet and interactive and mobile communications media in use and turning to direct marketing channels and event marketing have offered no real innovative and structurally new improvements. The development of brand management and adopting a branding terminology in marketing is only more of the same, in some situations making conventional marketing more effective perhaps, but offering no innovative new avenues for customer management. Marketing as a discipline is in crisis. And marketing as a business practice responsible for customer management is losing credibility.

Because marketers, alongside salespeople, should be the ones who know best how to translate customers' preferences and expectations into corporate strategies and customer management programmes and activities, they should be the ones who take responsibility for customer management. However, in strategic decision-making, due to the marginalization of marketing and its lack of innovativeness, the voice of the customers is interpreted by people who by and large through training and experience are often less customer-focused than marketers should be. However, as long as the marketers are hostages of outdated and too narrow frameworks for thinking and doing, marketing's vicious circle will continue to spin in a direction which is unfortunate for marketers and customers alike, and in the final analysis for the firm and its shareholders as well.

In the three parts of this book that follow a service-based logic for marketing is explored: service marketing (Part One) and its extension into relationship marketing (Part Two) and a concluding analysis of a service logic as a foundation for a contemporary marketing theory (Part Three).

References

Brown, S.W. (2005) 'When Executives Speak, We Should Listen and Act Differently', *Journal of Marketing*, 69(October): 2–4.

Cassidy, F., Freeling, A. and Kiewell, D. (2005) 'A Credibility Gap for Marketers', Research Brief. *McKinsey Quarterly*, 2.

CEOs Are Not Happy With Their Marketing (2004) *Chief Executive*, 201, August/September, www.chiefexecutive.net/depts/ceowatch/201a.htm

Day, G. and Montgomery, D. (1999) 'Charting New Directions for Marketing', *Journal of Marketing*, 63(Special Issue): 3–13.

Dixon, D.F. and Blois, K. (1983) 'Some Limitations of the 4Ps as a Paradigm for Marketing', Paper Presented at Marketing Education Group Annual Conference, Cranfield Institute of Technology, UK, July.

Gordon, I. (1998) *Relationship Marketing*, John Wiley & Sons, Toronto: p. 1.

'Marketing Renaissance: Opportunities and Imperatives for Improving Marketing Thought, Practice, and Infrastructure' (2005) *Journal of Marketing*, 69(October): 1–25.

McCarthy, E.J. (1960) *Basic Marketing: A Managerial Approach*. Homewood, IL: Irwin.

McGovern, G.J., Court, D., Quelch, J.A. and Crawford, B. (2004) 'Bringing Customers into the Boardroom', *Harvard Business Review*, 82(November): 70–80.

McKenna, R. (1991) *Relationship Marketing. Successful Strategies for the Age of the Customer*. Addison-Wesley, Reading, MA: p. 13.

Sheth, J.N. and Sisodia, R.S. (1995) 'Improving Marketing's Productivity', in *Marketing Encyclopedia*, Lincolnwood, IL: NTC Business Books, pp. 217–237.

Webster Jr., F.E., Malter, A.J. and Ganesan, S. (2005) 'The Decline and Dispersion of Marketing Competence', *MIT Sloan Management Review*, 46(4): 35–43.

Welch, G. (2004) 'CMO Tenure: Slowing Down the Revolving Door', Blue Paper, July, www.spencerstuart.com/research/articles/744/

Part One
Articles on Service Marketing

2

A Service-Orientated Approach to Marketing of Services

The Problem

Service companies are less marketing-orientated than firms which are marketing physical goods, according to reports on service marketing[1]. Some prominent Swedish firms have recently, after several meetings in 1975 and 1976, reported that there are severe marketing problems in the service sector in comparison with goods marketing[2]. The main difference between marketing goods and services was found to be the difficulty of developing a concrete, tangible service offering. Most marketing problems discussed by the service companies came out of this conclusion.

It has even been said that service marketing has failed[3]. The research which I have been conducting among companies in several service industries in Sweden and in Finland has confirmed the view that marketing services is a difficult task. Moreover, it has also been said that the existing marketing literature has little aid to offer companies in service industries. This view should not be surprising. Marketing literature and research almost completely take their examples from goods industries. Therefore, the problems relevant to this area of business have been investigated very thoroughly indeed. Marketing scholars have, however, been very little interested in the problems of firms in service industries. Examples of the marketing problems and the marketing planning situation of these industries are very seldom discussed by researchers or treated in marketing texts.

Grönroos, C. A Service-Orientated Approach to Marketing of Services, *European Journal of Marketing* 1978; **12**(8): 588–601. Reproduced by permission of Emerald Group Publishing, Limited.

The service sector has thus been forgotten to a great extent[4]. The re-defining of the product concept seems to be the only radical development of service marketing. Products became goods and services indicating that services are by no means without interest. However, this may have been quite fatal. It seems as if marketing scholars have been tempted to deal with service marketing and goods marketing using the same concepts, models, and frames of reference. As marketing focusing on the problems of companies producing physical goods has been developed to a high degree of sophistication, marketers seem to have come to believe that this progress would be a gain to service firms as well. Many writers do, however, point out that service marketing must differ from goods marketing, but, nevertheless, no radical effort to develop a marketing theory, or even some marketing concepts, for service firms aiming at solving their problems seems to have been made[5]. I think that companies in the service industries deserve a better treatment by marketing scholars.

The Purpose of this Article

A good deal of the marketing problems of service companies may be caused by the lack of a theory of its own for service marketing. The purpose of the present article is to discuss this matter and to suggest a hypothetical framework for an important part of such a theory, i.e., the marketing mix planning. Some empirical evidence supporting the hypotheses will also be accounted for.

The most severe problems of service marketing are, in my opinion, to be found in connection with the planning of a marketing mix. I believe that this part of marketing planning is the main victim of the goods-orientation in marketing research. In this context I am mainly concentrating on *the development of a concrete service offering as part of a service marketing mix planning process*, whereas the marketing variables not to be considered part of the offering—the 'product' of service firms—are not discussed in any detail. Moreover, I am mainly interested in marketing services to consumer markets.

Marketing of Services—The Marketing Myopia of Today

The Service Marketing Confusions

There are, in my opinion, at least three confusions of service marketing, which can to a great extent be blamed for the situation of service marketing. I believe that marketing of services can be labelled the marketing myopia of today. Yet the proportion of GNP coming from the service industries, and the proportion of all employees working in this sector of business, are approaching 50% in most developed societies, and the percentage is in fact over 50% in the most developed ones.

These confusions of service marketing are (1) the faltering service concept, (2) the opinion that everybody is in service, and (3) the view that marketing research helping companies in goods industries would help service firms equally well.

The service concept itself is confusing. No distinction is made between services as objects of marketing and services as marketing variables, i.e., as means of competition when marketing goods. Such a distinction must, in my opinion, definitely be made. Marketing of services concerns services in the first sense of the concept. The service is the *object* of marketing, i.e., *the company is selling the service as the core of its market offering.* When services are treated as a means of competition, the core of the selling proposition is a physical good, not a service. Then it is not service marketing, and the planning situation can be coped with by means of the traditional concepts and models of marketing literature.

The faltering service concept may well be a result of the idea of a goods-service continuum. All offerings may, it is said, be described by the continuum with pure goods at one extreme and pure services at the other, and with most offerings falling somewhere between these points[6]. This continuum concept mixes the two service concepts separated above. From a marketing planning point-of-view the continuum does not exist, or at least it is highly misguiding to the marketer. It gives the impression that every offering basically is the same, and can be planned in a similar manner applying the same planning instruments. In my opinion an offering concerns either goods, with or without service support (transport, maintenance, repair, etc.), or services, which may be pure services or services which make it possible to use goods or which are accompanied by goods (car rental, hotel, inclusive tours, etc.).

The same company may, of course, be engaged in both goods marketing and service marketing. Every firm must, however, in every planning situation, analyse the planning problem, and try to find out whether it is developing a service offering or a goods offering. A definite borderline between these two kinds of offerings cannot be drawn in a goods-service continuum. The problem must be solved *in situ* by the marketer.

Sometimes combinations of equally important goods and service elements are marketed. This marketing planning situation, systems selling, is, however, out of the scope of the present article.

Is Everybody Really in Service?

It has become popular to consider all marketing to be service marketing. Consumers, it is said, are not buying goods or services, but the value satisfaction of offerings[7]. Consequently, there are no goods industries or service industries, but industries with varying degrees of service components, and, thus, everybody is in service[8].

This seems to be another confusion of service marketing. The present marketing literature normally maintains that there is nothing like marketing of goods and marketing of services, but there is just marketing of goods (and services). So it also, although not on the same grounds, supports the view that everybody is in the same sort of business. Yet companies in the service sector still seem to be in trouble with their marketing.

It is, of course, reasonable to consider both goods and services to be bought by consumers in order to give some service or value satisfaction. And companies marketing physical goods would certainly many times be better off by concentrating more on the needs of the consumers and less on the tangible good itself in their marketing planning. Every consumer can perhaps be said to be in service, but certainly not every enterprise. To state that every industry is a service industry would indicate, from a marketing planning point-of-view, that the planning situation, and the tools, concepts, and models used are the same for service companies as for firms marketing goods. But, the marketing planning situation is, in my opinion, different when marketing services than when marketing physical goods.

If the marketing planning situation differs between service industries and goods industries, which I think it does, *the planning instruments developed to assist in solving the problems of goods industries may well not be applicable when planning service marketing.* However, it is most frequently said that the concepts and models used by companies in goods industries can equally well be applied by service firms. I think that there is enough empirical evidence to prove this opinion to be wrong and just another confusion of service marketing. A theory of service marketing is needed. The traditional marketing does not offer service companies appropriate planning tools.

Characteristics of Services

I do not intend to add a definition of my own to the range of more or less unsatisfactory definitions already existing. I believe that it is quite impossible to find one final definition. One can, for instance, use a rather traditional one suggested by Judd in the 1960's:

> 'Marketed Services—A market transaction by an enterprise of an entrepreneur where the object of the market transaction is *other than* the transfer of ownership (or title, if nay) of a tangible commodity.'[9]

In my opinion, it would be more fruitful to find out in what respects services differ from goods, and to examine the implications for marketing planning caused by the characteristics of services.

Several characteristics can be found, but I am here going to stress only three, which I think are vital to service marketing planning. Perhaps the most important characteristic of a service is its *intangibility*. The customer cannot feel, taste, smell, or see a service before he buys it. One cannot make a thorough evaluation of a service. However, such an evaluation seems often to be desirable for most consumers, so they evaluate what they can: the interior of a restaurant, the appearance of the air hostesses, the behaviour of the bank clerks[10].

Of course, it is not always easy to evaluate physical goods either, but the point is that they can be physically evaluated, i.e., there is something tangible to evaluate. Services cannot be evaluated as such, so they must be transformed to concrete offerings, which can be evaluated and compared to those of the competitors. If the firm does not manage this process, the customers will, in an unguided manner, pick out tangible attributes which *are* the service in the customers' mind.

Another essential characteristic of services is the *production/consumption interaction* in most service businesses. Services cannot be separated from the producer, and the producer and the seller are the same organisation[11]. A service is considered to be consumed as it is produced. Thus, producing and marketing are very interactive processes, too. Both activities are simultaneously performed by the same persons in a service company. Moreover, the inseparability of services is said to make only direct distribution possible. In fact, no normal distribution could be possible, as there is nothing tangible to distribute using the usual channels of distribution[12].

A third characteristic of services is the *lack of ownership and transaction of ownership* when dealing with services. One does not own anything, when one has purchased a service. One is only given the right to use things, and as symbols of the lack of ownership one may get tickets, certificates, value coupons, etc.

As a summary, it seems obvious that services do differ from goods as objects of marketing. Therefore, services cannot be treated like goods in a marketing planning context. *A new service marketing mix concept is needed.*

Weaknesses of the Traditional Goods-orientated Marketing Mix Concept

As a simultaneous analysis of all marketing variables in the same context is not usually possible, the marketing mix models, like McCarthy's four P's and Lipson and Darling's subcomponent model, have been developed. Different submixes are thought to be planned separately, and, finally, blended into a total marketing mix. Only the product mix must, in some way, be already shaped, before detailed pricing, distribution, and communication planning can take place.

This is a way of planning an efficient marketing mix for physical goods, and the models are developed for goods marketing. No matter how sophisticated such models are, they take for granted that it is possible to plan submixes, which afterwards can be co-ordinated into one total mix. This is possible, if there is a tangible product involved. Then there is something to develop, to price, to distribute, and to communicate about. That is, in goods marketing there is a tangible core around which the offering can be developed in a manner reflected by the traditional marketing mix models. In service marketing there is no such tangible core. It simply is not possible to plan separate submixes, which can be blended into one total marketing mix. Therefore, the traditional marketing mix concept developed for goods marketing is likely to fail in service marketing planning. This may be the main reason why service firms are less marketing-orientated than other companies.

Planning the Service Offering

The Accessibility of Services

Only direct distribution was earlier mentioned to be possible for service firms, because of the close production/consumption interaction. It may seem so when viewing the matter strictly in the goods sense of the distribution concept. I do believe, however, that a more innovative approach to distribution of services is called for. It seems to me as if the traditional concept ought not to be applied to service marketing at all. Instead of being a useful means of competition it becomes an unnecessary burden to the marketer.

In my opinion *the accessibility of a service* is a much more promising concept for service firms. Resources influencing accessibility are, for example, human resources, machines, offices, buildings, and other physical things as well as extra services. These resources can be managed by the marketer, and they are all aimed at making the service quickly and conveniently accessible to the consumers.

The difference between the concept of distribution channels and the concept of physical distribution does not seem meaningful in the context of services. For example, a guide may be considered part of the channel of distribution for inclusive tours. Without him much experience and many views and facts, which are part of the tours, would not be accessible to the consumers. At the same time he also distributes this part of the service; that is, he performs physical distribution.

Applying the traditional concept it may be difficult to view a person like the guide as a part of the channel of distribution, and he certainly is not performing any physical distribution, because there is nothing tangible to distribute. In terms of accessibility, the guide is, however, a manageable resource making it possible for the customers to consume the service.

I believe that the concept of accessibility can improve the understanding of service marketing in at least two ways. First, it stresses all parts of the service offering, which the consumers may recognise as the service. The service itself is intangible, but the resources—both human and non-human—influencing the accessibility transform the service into a concrete offering, which is accessible to the consumers and can be evaluated by them in comparison with competing offerings. These resources can therefore be labelled *bearers of the service*, because they bring out the service to the market.

Such elements of the service offering are, for instance, the location of a bank, the interior of a bank office or travel agency office, means of transportation and their condition, the interior and exterior of a restaurant, the waiters, ticket-collectors on buses and trains, bank clerks and cashiers, barbers, cheques, pass-books, tickets, computer and telecommunication networks, etc. These elements are indeed of many kinds but they all have two essential features in common: they promote the accessibility of the services, and they can be managed and used as a means of competition by the marketer.

Secondly, I believe that by applying the accessibility concept, service marketing has a chance of breaking free from the burden of the traditional distribution concept[13]. Direct distribution will then by no means be the only way of making the service accessible to the consumers. Insurance vending machines and franchise arrangements used by hotel and catering enterprises are examples of an innovative development of the resources influencing the accessibility[14].

The Human Resources

The consumers of a service will almost always see and meet some representative of the service firm sometimes during the purchasing and/or consumption process. Nearly all employees, irrespective of their place in the organisation, will, on the other hand, at least occasionally get in touch with the customers. Therefore, the manner in which the bank manager, the bank clerk, the travel agency representative, the telephone receptionist, the tour guide, the barber, or the waiter treats the customers, what he says, and how he behaves are very critical to the view of the service which the consumers get. *Almost every single person in a service firm is, therefore, acting as a salesman and is engaged in the personal market communication efforts of the company.*

The human resources of a service firm are also part of the accessibility system of a service, and this fact makes the personnel even more vital to the company and its marketing planning. Thus, *the administration of the human resources must be considered an important means of competition in service marketing.* Marketing training—especially concerning communication and selling—is a much greater task and involves many more people in service industries than in goods industries. For a company producing and marketing physical goods it is satisfactory if the marketing staff is properly trained and the salesmen know how to sell. In a service company almost every employee belongs to the 'marketing department'. This is a fact that must be recognised, e.g., when engaging employees and planning personnel training programmes. And this goes for the financial manager of a bank as well as for the waiter of a restaurant and the telephone receptionist of an airline company.

As so many people in service firms are engaged in marketing tasks, their behaviour influences the success of the company to a great extent. Therefore, it is important to be aware of the *internal marketing task of service firms*, i.e., a service must first be successfully marketed to the personnel, so that the employees accept the service offering and thoroughly engage in performing their marketing duties. Otherwise the service may easily turn out to be a failure in relation to its ultimate target markets.

The importance of the administration of the personnel and of the internal marketing process to the success of service companies is not, I believe, quite recognised today. Frequently the employees have not been engaged to perform any marketing tasks but merely to produce the service. Therefore, it will not be an easy task for a service firm to manage its human resources in a more marketing-orientated manner. First the attitude of the personnel must be changed so that the employees accept that they are not only producers of a service, but, simultaneously, are also engaged in selling the very same service.

The personal market communication and selling tasks performed by the personnel are bearers of the service as well as the resources influencing the accessibility, because the performance of the representatives of the firm is also an element of the service offering, which brings out the intangible service to the market and can be considered by the consumers instead of the service itself.

Auxiliary Services

The accessibility of a service may be influenced by offering extra services. For instance, the bank clerk may fill out forms and supermarkets may offer large parking areas in order to help the customers. But, furthermore, services can be offered as separate means of competition. Such auxiliaries are, for example, hotel booking and inclusive tours arrangements offered by airline companies and coffee offered by barbers' shops.

Sometimes a service may be an extra service influencing the accessibility for one consumer and an auxiliary service for another. Someone may choose to go by train instead of by bus, because he can have his lunch in the restaurant of the train, whereas someone else may take the train just because he enjoys the excellent meals served. But he does not actually have to eat anything.

An auxiliary service is not a bearer of the service, because it does not bring out the service to the market. But it is promoting the service, and it is certainly considered part of the service offering by the consumers.

Intra-Corporate Elements of the Service

In the marketing planning process service firms cannot separate the different kinds of marketing mix variables, as frequently is done in marketing of physical goods. In particular, the personal market communication as part of the administration of human resources, and the resources influencing the accessibility are extremely close to each other and to the intangible service itself.

As a matter of fact, the personal communication and the accessibility of services may be viewed as parts of the service offered to the target markets, i.e., as parts of the 'product' of service industries. They fulfil the function as bearers of the service, which bring out the intangible service to the markets as a concrete service offering, i.e., as a product. Moreover, the auxiliary services offered are from the consumers' point-of-view also part of the service offering. They are, too, shaping the service which the customers evaluate and eventually perhaps buy.

The bearers of the service and the auxiliary services are *intra-corporate elements of the service*, because the marketer can maintain full control over them. Figure 1 shows how the bearers and the auxiliary services are linked together and to the core of the offering, i.e., to the intangible idea of the service.

The figure illustrates how integrated the planning of marketing variables must be in service marketing. Product development is in fact quite another task than one usually thinks about, when applying the product development concept to service marketing in the goods-orientated sense of the concept.

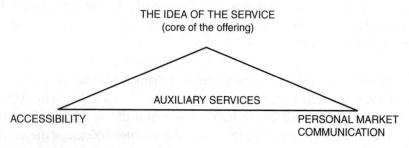

Figure 1   Intra-corporate Elements of the Service

Companies in service industries have to recognise that product development involves many more activities than one traditionally believes it does. *Development of the resources influencing the accessibility, the administration of human resources, and the development of auxiliary services are parts of the product development process*[15]. By accepting such a view service companies can, I believe, achieve considerable improvements in their marketing performance.

The Consumers as Active Participants in Marketing

Usually the consumers are only considered to have needs which are unknown to them or relatively badly satisfied by existing products, and they either buy the product offered to them or do not buy it. They take part in the product development process only in a *passive* manner by having unsatisfied needs. They are not considered as actively shaping the product. Consumer tests and test marketing may be used, but these are actually rather passive ways in which the consumers can influence the product. Only the competitors on the market are thought of as actively influencing the performance of marketing.

When marketing services the situation of the marketer is, however, somewhat different. The traditional view of the consumers' role in the marketplace is an unnecessary restriction on the development of marketing. While this view may express the situation of a goods marketer, service companies have to make other considerations as far as the behaviour of the consumers is concerned.

The consumers are actively taking part in shaping the service offering, i.e., in product development[16]. This is due to the production/consumption interaction, which is characteristic of the service industries, and to the fact that several consumers and/or potential consumers simultaneously are on the same spot either consuming, purchasing, or planning to purchase the service. The consumers influence both the accessibility of a service and the communication about the service, and their influence can be either desirable or undesirable.

A consumer may, for instance, cause queues in a bank, thus causing the quality of the bank's services to deteriorate, or he may be part of the atmosphere in a music hall, thus improving the quality of the concert. He may also be telling potential consumers of, for instance, the restaurant of a hotel, that he, by experience, knows that it is a dull place, thus changing the communication about the restaurant in an unfavourable manner. He may on the other hand enthusiastically encourage others to visit the hotel restaurant, thus making a desirable impact on the communication.

Companies in service industries should, therefore, consider the consumers, not only the competitors, to be elements in the market actively influencing marketing planning. From the consumers' point-of-view, the other consumers, who simultaneously are making their purchasing decision and/or consuming the service, are part of the service itself. The service marketer has to recognise this fact, and include also this active role of the consumers in his marketing planning.

Moreover, the consumer himself can be considered part of the service he buys and consumes. His expectations and acting certainly influence the behaviour of the human representatives of the service firm. Thus, the quality of the service varies according to the behaviour of the consumer. The attitude of the consumers towards the service and towards the organisation producing and marketing the service must from the very beginning be kept favourable, and if the consumer happens to become disappointed, immediate action is called for.

Such activities are also important means of competition in the service industries. And the consumers of a service can be considered *extra-corporate elements of the service*. In Figure 2 these elements have been added to the intra-corporate dimensions of services.

The continuous line in the figure connecting the idea of the service, the accessibility, the personal market communication, and the auxiliary services with each other indicates that these elements of the service can be directly controlled and

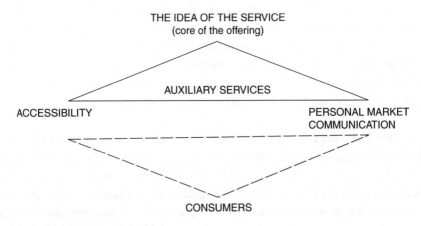

Figure 2 An Extensive View of the Service

managed by the marketer. The dotted line connecting the consumers with the two bearers of the service shows that the consumers may influence both of them, but that the behaviour of the consumers only indirectly can be controlled by the marketer. But the line also stresses the point that the behaviour of the consumer is still, in some way, manageable.

The marketer can in advance anticipate possible patterns of behaviour of the consumers in order to be able to eliminate undesirable effects on both the accessibility and the communication[17]. And he should also be prepared to take advantage of favourable consumer influence, which is improving the quality of the service.

Some Empirical Support

The Study

In order to test the hypothetical view of the service offering put forward in this article, I have during the winter 1976/77 made twelve case studies of marketing planning procedures of successful companies in several service industries in Sweden and in Finland. The information was gathered by means of a two-stage interviewing procedure. First a questionnaire was mailed to the firms, and, in the second stage, the answers were supplemented by personal interviews with the persons responsible for the marketing planning.

My case studies reveal an amazingly uniform picture of the problems of the service firms, and, moreover, of the planning behaviour and the marketing variables applied by the firms. Every company, *irrespective of industry*, seems to have similar problems, mainly those of the intangibility of the services and of developing a concrete offering out of the intangible service. The tools used were also very similar, although varying terms were used.

I am not going to account for all case studies in this article. I will just present two cases, here labelled *inclusive tours marketing* and *barber's shop marketing*. Adding more cases to these would not give any new empirical evidence.

The Case of Inclusive Tours Marketing

A company offering inclusive tours for holidaymakers is operating around an intangible idea of, for example, recreation, change of milieu, experiences, excitement, and adventures. 'We sell a week of power. The consumer purchases a position where he can order others to serve him, where he is the employer, not the employee.'

In order to transform the intangible service into concrete offerings varying kinds of means are used. These means usually also make the service accessible to the consumers, but some of them are mere auxiliary services. The traditional ticket has been replaced by a travel certificate, which is issued and printed out by a computer, at the time when the tour is ordered. The computer facilitates quick and detailed booking information with a minimum of mistakes, thus giving the consumers an impression of exactness and security. 'People are not sure of what service they actually will get. In this way we give them, in advance, a concrete written specification of which services they have bought.' The travel certificate serves as an allround ticket, thus not only in a tangible manner symbolising the service, but also minimising the amount of papers and forms usually needed and, therefore, making the service more conveniently and easily accessible to the consumers.

The hotel, the airline company, and the type of aircraft used, as well as various kinds of auxiliary services, such as meals included in the tour and trips arranged on destination, are also part of the service which the company offers. Because of these resources the inclusive tours become accessible to the consumers. They are thus shaping the service, which the consumers get.

The human resources of the company are considered vitally important to the marketing performance. For example, the manager, the people behind the desk in the booking offices, and the guides are essential to the accessibility. The employees are carefully selected and trained. The performance of the personnel is considered to a great extent to shape the service which is offered. The guides are especially vital, 'because it is the guide who sells the next tour'. As long as the tour lasts the guides are in contact with the consumers, and they are more or less the last contact which the consumers have with the service and the company. If something goes wrong, it is the guides who, as representatives of the firm, have to be capable of reshaping the service so that quality is maintained and the consumers will remain satisfied.

The employees of the firm are performing market communication and selling tasks, and the better they know the destination of a tour, the better they sell. Clearly, the administration of the human resources of the company and the training of the personnel are important to marketing.

The consumers are considered part of the service offering. 'Our image keeps drinkers away, which makes the tours more comfortable to the other consumers.' The consumers also sometimes take part in the communication about the services. One single person may get all the others to complain of something without really having any reason. 'But there can be a person, who gets everybody on an auxiliary trip by enthusiastically telling them that he was on that trip last time and it was marvellous.'

The corporate image is considered important to marketing, because consumers buy the company as well as a certain tour. A favourable and attractive image is vital to the accessibility. If the image is unfavourable, the consumers may not even be interested in recognising other means of competition used by the firm.

To sum up, one can in this case notice the importance of the bearers of the intangible service to marketing. The resources influencing the accessibility and the personal market communication and selling by the personnel, as well as the auxiliary services offered, are marketing variables shaping the service offerings. Furthermore, the consumers are actively influencing the services and taking part in the communication about it.

The Case of Barber's Shop Marketing

A barber's shop offers intangible services concerning personal care, relaxation, etc. In order to transform the intangible services to concrete offerings various means are used.

It is important that the shop is located near people, on busy streets. The interior and exterior of the shop are also vital to the success of the firm. The windows of the shop are not covered, so that the people passing-by can easily see what is going on inside the shop. This is a way of making the services of the barber's shop more concrete. 'We wish to create an atmosphere which pleases the customers. Our customers shall enjoy their stay with us.' Colours and music are important to the milieu and used in order to achieve the right atmosphere.

The people working in the shop and their capability of doing a good job according to the taste and wishes of the customers are perhaps the most important part of the accessibility of the services. They have to be well-trained, but, moreover, their appearance is also considered vital. They are uniformly dressed, and the uniforms are now and then changed.

The behaviour of the personnel is important, too: not only how they do the job, but also what they are talking about and how they are doing it. The human resources are part of the service which the consumers get, and the administration of these resources is important to the success of the barber's shop. 'If our employees are satisfied with their job and enjoy the place, they will do a better job, and then our customers will enjoy our services even more.'

Auxiliary services are offered to some extent. Coffee is served and magazines are available. To minimise the waiting time, the shop actively tries to get its customers to book time in advance. This diminishes the risks of getting irritated customers and of lost business because of queues in the shop.

As a summary, one can notice the extreme importance of the bearers of the intangible barber services. The location, the way in which the shop is planned, the employees and their behaviour as producers and salesmen of the services are all parts of the services, which the consumers buy. Moreover, auxiliary services are offered, and the behaviour of the consumers is to some extent managed by the barber's shop.

Conclusions

The concepts and models for marketing mix planning of today do not seem applicable to companies in service industries. The case studies, both those presented here and the other studies, too, point out how much more integrated the planning of the marketing variables must be in comparison to the traditional marketing mix models. The 'product' of service firms is extremely complicated, and, therefore, the product development process involves elements normally not considered when discussing the topic.

The bearers of the service, i.e., the resources influencing the accessibility of the service and the personal market communication are integrated parts of the service as well as possible auxiliary services. This fact makes the planning of these intra-corporate elements of the service offering parts of product development. Furthermore, the service is also shaped by the consumers, thus actively, as an extra-corporate element of the service, having an impact on the marketing planning.

The corporate image seems to be very important to service firms, because the consumers almost always get in touch with the very company offering the service.

The image is thus part of the accessibility and one of the very first things the consumers may think about. A favourable image may be vital for the firm's attempts to attract customers, whereas an undesirable image may keep people from even being interested in noticing other means of competition.

Marketing variables, which do not seem to be part of the service, have not been considered in this article. However, I believe that they can be grouped into two main categories labelled *pricing* and *non-interactive market communication*, which mainly consists of advertising, publicity, and other possible means of communication where there is no production/consumption interaction between representatives of the service company and the consumers.

A lot of research has still to be done; e.g., a consumer study, the purpose of which will be to find out whether the consumers really evaluate and purchase the same service offerings as indicated by the hypothetical view of the elements of the service put forward in this article and supported by the present case studies.

References

[1] George, W.R. and Barksdale, H.C., 'Marketing Activities in the Service Industries', *Journal of Marketing*, October 1974, p. 65; Bessom, R.M. and Jackson, D.W., Jr., 'Service Retailing: A Strategic Marketing Approach', *Journal of Retailing*, Summer 1975, p. 84; and Holloway, R.J. and Hancock, R.S., *Marketing in a Changing Environment*, New York, John Wiley & Sons, 1973, pp. 55–6: 'Marketing has not yet become an important function for most service institutions... Perhaps we will see the service industries become more marketing-conscious in the decade ahead.'
[2] Back, R. (ed.), *Erfagruppverksamheten* 1975, Report from Marknadstekniskt Centrum, Stockholm, Sweden, 1976.
[3] Levitt, T., 'Product-line approach to service', *Harvard Business Review*, September-October 1972, p. 43.
[4] Wilson, A., *Professional services and the market place*, Report from Marknadstekniskt Centrum, No. 4, Stockholm, Sweden, 1975, p. 5.
[5] There are some efforts to create new concepts, though: for example, the suggestion of a concept of marketing intermediaries in the context of services by Donnelly, J.H., Jr., 'Marketing Intermediaries in Channels of Distribution for Services', *Journal of Marketing*, January 1976, p. 57.
[6] Rathmell, J.M., 'What is Meant by Services?', *Journal of Marketing*, October 1966, pp. 33–4.
[7] Levitt, T., *Marketing for Business Growth*, New York, McGraw-Hill, 1974, p. 8.
[8] Levitt, T., 'Product-line approach to service', *op. cit.*, pp. 41–2.
[9] Judd, R.C., 'The Case for Redefining Services', *Journal of Marketing*, January 1964, p. 59. This definition makes it possible to distinguish between three main categories of services: 'The right to possess and use a product (Rented Goods Services); or 2. the customer creation of, repair, or improvement of a product (Owned Goods Services); or 3. no product element but rather an experience or what might be termed experimental possession (Non-Goods Services).' (*ibid.*, p. 59). Marketing of services should only be

concerned with services of the first and third category. Owned Goods Services are normally, but not necessarily always, means of competition when marketing goods.

[10] Wyckham, R.G., Fitzroy, P.T. and Mandy, G.D., 'Marketing of Services: An Evaluation of the Theory', *European Journal of Marketing*, No. 1, 1975, p. 61.

[11] Stanton, W.J., *Fundamentals of Marketing*, Tokyo, McGraw-Hill Kogakusha, 1975, p. 551.

[12] George and Barksdale, *op. cit.*, p. 67.

[13] Donnelly, J.H., Jr., *op. cit.* Intermediaries replacing the goods-orientated distribution concept suggested by Donnelly are any extra-corporate entity between the producer and the consumers which makes the service available and/or more convenient for the consumers. This certainly is a contribution to service marketing, but he does not, however, include intra-corporate resources with the same purpose, which, in my opinion, is too restricting when expanding the distribution concept in order to help service firms.

[14] A very important part of the service firm is the corporate image. Consumers of physical goods seldom have to see or meet the producing company. Normally they deal with wholesalers and retailers. But the consumers of services nearly always get in touch with the service producing firm. This makes the firm part of the accessibility of the service. Therefore, the corporate image of the service firm may be of vital importance to marketing. If the consumers do not consider the image favourable and attractive, they will perhaps not even be interested in noticing the other means of competition of the company.

[15] In some cases personal market communication can be viewed solely in a communication context and not as part of the service. The performance of a professional salesman, who is only thought of as a salesman by the customers, and not as part of the accessibility system, may be planned separately in the same context as advertising and other means of impersonal communication. However, in marketing to consumer markets personal communication is rarely just communicating about the service offering; it is almost always also shaping the service itself.

[16] See Eiglier, P. and Langeard, E., *Principes de politique marketing pour les enterprises de services*, L'Institute d'Administration des Enterprises, Université d'Aix-Marseille, December 1976, who make this interesting suggestion.

[17] For instance, the *demarketing* concept suggested by Kotler, P. and Levy, S.J., ('Demarketing, yes, demarketing', *Harvard Business Review*, November-December 1971) could be applied in this context.

3

An Applied Service Marketing Theory

Introduction

Both academicians and practitioners have been surprisingly uninterested in the marketing problems of service businesses. As Bessom observed in 1973: 'It is ironic that service businesses, which are necessarily in the most direct contact with consumers, seem to be the last kind of firm to adopt a consumer-oriented marketing concept'[1]. One reasonable explanation of this state of affairs may be the fact that the manufacturing sector of Western economies, starting back in the 19th century with the industrial revolution in England, until the last decades has counted for most of the economic development. This sector of business has been the interesting one, and therefore, to an overwhelming extent, has drawn the attention of academicians and practitioners from other sectors of the economy[2].

Today theories of service marketing have been proposed, and there is now an on-going development of the area. One could say that service marketing now stands at the same point as industrial marketing did some ten years ago.

The first comprehensive service marketing theory or frame of reference was probably the one published by Rathmell in 1974[3]. He tried to use traditional concepts and models from consumer marketing theory in service marketing. His own conclusion was, however, that 'definitions, classifications, data, and concepts

Grönroos, C. An Applied Service Marketing Theory. *European Journal of Marketing*, 1982; **16**(7): 30–41. Reproduced by permission of Emerald Group Publishing Limited.

are lacking, noncomparable, or unreal from a marketing perspective. Moreover, as one attempts to integrate marketing terms, concepts, and practices with firms, institutions, and professions having their own traditions, customs, and practices which are quite foreign to conventional marketing (and much older), the linkage appears awkward and even improper.'[4] Rathmell's findings and reports on the lack of marketing-orientation of service firms[5] point out the need for development of service marketing theory, if service businesses are to be supported in their market-orientation and marketing-orientation efforts.

The development of general theories or frameworks for service marketing seems to have followed two quite different paths. According to one approach, the services offered by service companies ought to be changed in a more product-like manner, so that existing marketing theories could be applied[6]. The other approach starts from a notion that services are different in comparison with physical products and holds that marketing concepts and models have to be developed in a more service-like direction[7].

My own view, based on a substantial amount of empirical research in northern Europe, is that although there are similarities between services and physical products, services do have some basic characteristics which make them fundamentally different from a marketing point of view. It seems inappropriate to try to change the services—for example, to make them more tangible and more impersonal—just in order to be able to apply conventional marketing knowledge. Although service development certainly is a fruitful means of making a service business more profitable, there must be alternative ways to go for the service firm. Developing service offerings in a more product-like direction is only one strategy. There are certainly occasions where service firms will be better off if they apply another strategy, where the offering perhaps is moved even further away from the product-like direction. Therefore, it is my opinion that service marketing could be developed in such a manner that it is geared to the basic characteristics of services and to the marketing situation of service firms, thus making it possible to apply marketing strategies, which involve either product-like development of offerings and product-like marketing activities or some other, maybe more 'service-like' development[8].

In line with my view of service marketing development, the purpose of this article is to put forward a service marketing theory or frame of reference which is based on the basic characteristics of services and on the service firm's customer relation and marketing situation. Thus, conventional consumer goods marketing theory and concepts are not the starting point of this theory development, but they are, of course, used whenever appropriate. Only the service firm's means of competition are considered, whereas other areas of marketing—such as market segmentation and market analysis—are omitted.

The findings reported in this article are based on both theoretical and empirical research. This service marketing theory is the result of an on-going research project, which started in 1976. Because of the limited space, the empirical material is not presented in this context. In English some of it has been published elsewhere[9].

Characteristics of Services and the Nature of Service Marketing

There is a range of characteristics of services, some of which are more important to some service industries and some to other service industries[10]. However, there seem to be at least *three basic characteristics*: the service itself is *physically intangible*, it is an *activity* rather than a thing, and *production and consumption are*, at least to some extent, *simultaneous activities*.

Although there may be a lot of documents, physical equipment, machines or tools connected with the service, the service itself is physically intangible. This goes for a bank's deposit box services as well as for a full-service restaurant's offerings. Like many physical products services are also mentally intangible[11]. Moreover, the service happens, the service-rendering firm does something for the customer. This holds even for situations where there are no human representatives of the firm involved; then the firm uses physical or technical resources and the co-operation of the customer instead, in order to be able to do something for its customers. This activity—for example, a bank service, a restaurant service, or an airline trip—is produced, at least partly, often to a great extent, in the presence of the consumer, with his co-operation, and moreover, while he simultaneously consumes the service.

These basic characteristics of services make the marketing situation and the customer relation of service firms fundamentally different from that of a consumer goods company. The customers of the latter kind of business normally see only the product itself and the marketing mix activities—place, price and promotion—of the firm and of the distribution channels. One could say that the consumers' opinion of the product is based mainly on the traditional marketing mix activities of the firm.

The consumer of a service firm faces an entirely different situation. For a consumer goods company, production and consumption have no contact with each other, and thus no influence on one another. The service consumer, however, enters the production process of the service firm. He can be influenced by the production resources and the production process. Because the service itself is both physically and mentally intangible and is difficult to evaluate as such, he certainly will be influenced by what happens in the simultaneous consumption and production process, and moreover, he will, by his behaviour, have an impact on the production process itself.

Figure 1 illustrates a fundamental difference between the nature of service marketing and that of consumer goods marketing. The *objective of marketing* should be to manage all resources that influence the market's preferences towards products and services on the market. For a consumer goods company these resources are more or less those managed by a marketing department as a bridge between production and consumption. This is indicated by the left part of the figure. The right part of the figure demonstrates how the preferences of a service consumer are influenced. There are separate marketing activities, for example, advertising and other non-interactive means of promotion, in service marketing, too. These are, however, only part of the company's *total marketing function* because the consumer's opinion of the service firm and its services and his future buying behaviour are also determined by what happens in the *buyer-seller interactions* of the simultaneous production and consumption. Therefore, managing these interactions is also part of the total marketing function.

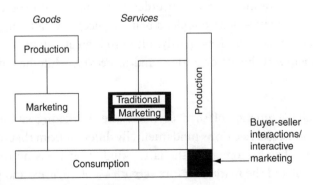

Figure 1   The Relationship between Production, Marketing and Consumption

Source: The illustration is developed from a figure in John Rathmell, *Marketing in the Service Sector*, Winthrop Publishers, Cambridge, Mass., 1974, p. 7.

Thus, the service company has two marketing functions, which are quite different from each other in nature: the *traditional marketing function* and the *interactive marketing function*, where the latter function is concerned with what happens in the interface between production and consumption in Figure 1, i.e., in the buyer-seller interactions.

The Quality of a Service

Because the consumer of a service can and will evaluate a vast amount of different resources and activities in connection with the production resources and the production process when forming his opinion of the service, the quality of a service will be complicated in nature. Figure 2 illustrates a model of service quality. According to this model the total quality of a service is a function of three different components: corporate image, technical quality, and functional quality.

Of course, it is important to the consumer that the service is technically acceptable, i.e., it has *technical quality*. This means that the use of a safe deposit box in a bank, spending a night at a restaurant, having a haircut, etc., must lead to a correct result: the bonds and equities are safe, the consumer has had a good meal, has been able to dance or listen to good music, the style of hairdressing is acceptable. On the other hand, it is also important how the technical quality is transferred to the consumer. The service must have *functional quality*. How the safe deposit service is rendered, what happens during a night at the restaurant, how and in what milieu the haircut is done can be as important to the consumer's opinion as the more technical quality; in many cases the functional quality may be the more important one.

Because of the intangible nature of services, *corporate image* is also vital to the service firm. As one writer observes, 'because a service customer will, in part, judge the quality and nature of the service he is to purchase on the basis of outward

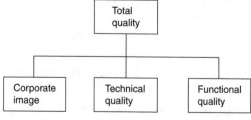

Figure 2 A Model of Service Quality

appearance, the service business must not only be good, it must look good'[12]. If the image is unattractive, the customers may not even expose themselves to the marketing and operational activities of the firm, which, therefore, never will be allowed to prove its high technical and functional quality. Moreover, an outstanding image will be an excuse for minor problems in the other quality components, whereas a bad image easily may lead to definite and negative reaction to accidental troubles with the technical quality or with the functional quality.

When planning the buyer-seller interaction, i.e., the interactive marketing function of the service firm, it is important to recognise all quality components. Otherwise the resources may easily be developed only in order to guarantee good technical quality. This may lead to production-oriented operations and dissatisfied customers. Frequently, it is relatively easy to develop good technical quality, which means that no unique selling proposition can be based on this quality aspect. However, the way of transferring the undifferentiated technical quality may be difficult to duplicate. In such situations, an outstanding functional quality may be a successful means of differentiating the service offering.

Resources in the Buyer-Seller Interactions

The objective of the interactive marketing function is to manage the resources involved in the buyer-seller interactions. The critical resources involved, and the consumer relation of service firms, are excellently illustrated by Eiglier and Langeard[13]. As can be seen from Figure 3, they divide the service company into two parts: one part which is invisible to the customer, and another part which is visible to him. The invisible part consists of the internal organisational system of the firm, the purpose of which is at least twofold: to give physical and management support to the people working in contact with the customers.

The right side of Figure 3 illustrates the resources which are critical to the firm's customer relation. There are three main categories of resources: the physical environment where the service is consumed; the contact personnel, i.e., the employees or other representatives of the firm which are in contact with the customers; and the consumers who take part in the production process.

Traditionally, service industries are very personnel intensive, and this goes for most service businesses even today. As Sasser and Arbeit put it, 'At McDonalds', the technology provides a supportive environment—but to the customer the service is sold, produced and delivered by the service employee. Even if the hamburger is succulent, if the employee is surly, the customer will probably not return. The same is true whether the service is rendered by a consultant, a medical technician, or a kennel keeper.'[14] The quality, service-mindedness, and customer sensitivity of the *contact personnel* is of vital importance to the opinion of the service firm and its services which its consumers form[15]. Consider, for instance, the impact on the service caused by a bank teller, a restaurant waiter, a tour guide, a business consultant or a bus driver.

The other resource category, *the physical environment*, consists of, for example, the exterior and interior of a restaurant, the computer systems of a bank, the air-crafts of an airline company, the documents used by an insurance company, the tools and equipment used by a plumber or electrician. An overall name for these different kinds of resources is the service firm's *physical/technical resources*. The customer experiences such resources either when he comes to the service company to buy and consume a service or when the service employee comes to him to deliver the service.

The third resource category consists of the *consumers*. They do not passively consume the service, but they take part in the production process in an active manner, thus influencing the process. Moreover, consumers may also influence each other.

The service, as it is perceived by the consumer, is the outcome of the various interactions between the resources indicated by Eiglier and Langeard's model of the customer relation of a service business. These interactions, the buyer-seller interactions, are:

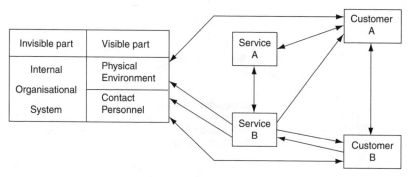

Figure 3   A Model of the Service Firm's Customer Relation

Source: Pierre Eiglier and Eric Langeard, *Principes de politique marketing pour les enterprises de services*, L'Institut d'Administration des Enterprises, Université d'Aix-Marseille, December 1976, p. 11.

- consumer versus the physical/technical resources;
- consumer versus the contact personnel; and
- consumer versus consumers.

However, if the interactive marketing function is to be successful and managed in a market-oriented manner, there must be a clear conception of the needs or wants of the target groups of consumers. The buyer-seller interactions and the resources involved in them cannot be developed without a customer-oriented statement of the company's *service concepts or service ideas*. Only if the company explicitly knows what kinds of needs it could attempt to satisfy, can the resources be planned and used in a truly customer-oriented manner. Otherwise the buyer-seller inter-actions easily become operations-oriented instead of being customer-oriented. Thus, the resources in the model by Eiglier and Langeard need a planning agent, which determines how the physical/technical resources, the contact personnel, the consumers, and their various interactions should be developed in order to become customer-oriented, and thus successfully and profitably used. This is illustrated by Figure 4, where the service concept is the planning agent. Moreover, as indicated by the figure, one should consider the impact of the resources on image and technical quality as well as on functional quality.

One should observe, however, that a customer-oriented interactive marketing may or may not involve contact personnel. In some cases, for some target groups of consumers no human resources are involved, but only physical/technical resources are needed in order to turn the service concept into a concrete and successful service offering. That is why, for example, automatic teller machines

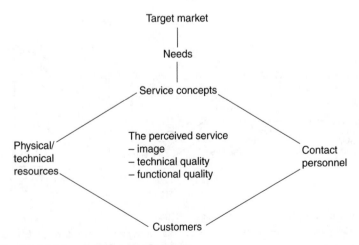

Figure 4 Planning the Interactive Marketing Resources

and self-service restaurants also are successful, whereas other segments look for other, more contact personnel intensive services. In all cases there are buyer-seller interactions involving a range of resources, and the management of these resources and interactions does have an impact on the consumers' preferences and future buying behaviour, which often may be of vital importance to the firm's success on the market.

A Service Marketing Model

Figure 4, derived from Eiglier and Langeard's model of the service firm's customer relation resources, illustrated the planning tools, which a service firm can use in order to develop customer-oriented services, and thus, a successful interactive marketing function. When using these tools, i.e., planning the resources in the buyer/seller interactions, five variables seem to be important: the service concept, the accessibility of the service, the interactive personnel/customer communication, auxiliary services, and consumer influence[16]. These variables are the means of competition related to the service firm's interactive marketing function. In Figure 5, the central part of the figure shows these interactive marketing variables. These are also the components of the service offering, which the consumer gets and evaluates. In Figure 1 they are the marketing activities related to the interface between production and consumption.

As was indicated by the traditional marketing function box in Figure 1, more traditional marketing activities can be applied by the service firm, too. In the

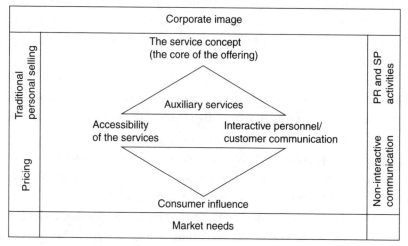

Figure 5 A Service Marketing Model

service marketing model these variables are labelled traditional personal selling, non-interactive communication, PR and SP activities, and pricing. In this context these elements of the model will not be commented upon in any detail. Instead the means of competition of the interactive marketing function will be discussed.

The *service concept* is the core of the service offering, and it must be derived from the needs or wants of a specified target group of consumers. A company will usually have a *general* service concept: for example, offering solutions to people's temporary transportation problems as one Swedish car hire company stated it. Moreover, it should have *specific* service concepts, which are the cores of specific services, e.g., offering candlelight dinners or oriental food may be specific service concepts for restaurants.

The service concept is the core of the service offering, or the product of the service firm, but it is intangible as such. By developing the other four elements of the interactive marketing function this intangible core is turned to a concrete service offering. First of all the *accessibility* of the service has to be considered. The service should be made accessible to the target customers in an attractive and convenient manner, so that they will be satisfied with the way in which they can *both buy and consume* the service. For example, external resources like travel agencies and internal resources like computerised booking systems are purchase-oriented accessibility resources, which can be applied in order to make a hotel's services accessible. These services must, however, also be made accessible during the consumption process, because production and consumption are simultaneous activities. The hotel's internal resources, both the employees and physical/technical resources like the hotel building itself, the rooms, registration forms, etc., are also accessibility resources, which must be considered in the interactive marketing of the hotel's services.

The distribution concept of consumer goods marketing cannot successfully be applied to service marketing, because distribution is too limited a concept. The objective of distribution activities is to make physical goods accessible to the market during the purchasing process, whereas only the product itself can guarantee good accessibility during the consumption process. Distribution is a useful management concept in consumer goods marketing, but in service marketing the wider concept of accessibility is needed. Otherwise the important task of making services truly accessible during consumption is not thought of as a marketing problem[17].

Obviously, both the contact personnel and the physical/technical resources can be developed in order to improve the accessibility of services. Moreover, the consumers should also be considered. Consumers may, for instance, cause queues in a bank, thus causing the functional quality of the bank's services to deteriorate, or they may be part of the atmosphere in a music hall, thus improving the quality of the concert.

Clearly, the accessibility of a service has an impact on all the quality aspects of services, i.e., image, technical quality, and functional quality.

The interactive customer/personnel communication concept is an important means of planning the interactive marketing function, because the customers will in most cases see and meet some representatives of the service firm in the buyer/seller interactions. Nearly all employees will, on the other hand, sometimes get in touch with the customers. Therefore, the manner in which the bank manager, the teller, the travel agency representative, air stewardess, the telephone receptionist, the consultant or the waiter treat the customers, what they say and how they behave are critical to the view of the service which the customers get. The contact personnel of a service firm are, therefore, acting as salesmen and are engaged in the personal market communication efforts of the company.

There is, however, a distinction between this customer/personnel communication and the personal selling efforts by professional salesmen. The latter group of employees are marketing professionals, usually managed by the marketing manager, and their main goal is to create sales. The employees engaged in the customer/personnel communication, on the other hand, are also part of the production system, and usually consider themselves production resources rather than marketing resources. Moreover, what is most important is that they are immediately responsible for the customers' satisfaction during consumption and have, therefore, an immense impact on future buying behaviour.

It is obvious that all quality aspects are influenced by the communication activities of the contact personnel. However, their impact on the functional quality seems to be the most critical one to success in a competitive market situation.

The core service can be made more attractive to the customers by *auxiliary services*. These are services used as means of competition. Such auxiliaries are, for example, hotel booking and inclusive tours arrangements offered by airline companies, or TV sets in hotel rooms and a sauna department in the hotel. These services are not necessarily needed in order to turn the core service into a concrete offering, but they may be the 'extra' which makes the service outstanding in comparison with the services of competitors. The auxiliary services easily become an integral part of the service offering in the minds of the consumers, and there-fore, one should be extremely careful in removing such 'extras', for example in order to cut costs. The result may be disastrous.

The *consumer influence* on the service offering and on the interactive marketing function is twofold. The consumer himself takes part in the production process and, consequently, has an impact on what he gets in return. On the other hand, the other customers simultaneously buying or consuming a service also influence the service offering. Queues and, for example, pleasant or unattractive company during a cruise may make the service quality either increase or decrease. The accessibility of the service is affected. Moreover, consumers may also have a desirable or undesirable impact on the customer/personnel communication. A consumer may, for example, tell potential consumers of a restaurant of a hotel that he, by experience, knows that it is a dull place, thus changing the communication about the restaurant in an unfavourable manner.

From the consumers' point-of-view, the other consumers who simultaneously are making their purchase decision and/or consuming the service are part of the service itself. The service marketer has to recognise this fact, and include also the role of the consumers in his interactive marketing planning. One should note that the consumer influence has an impact on the company's image as well as on technical quality and functional quality.

A Dynamic Aspect of Service Marketing—The Three Stage Model

Marketing is, of course, a dynamic process, where the marketer should not only be interested in getting customers, i.e., in sales, but also in keeping the customers, i.e., in resales and enduring customer contacts. This means that marketing activi-ties must be performed throughout the process where the service firm is in contact with its consumers. Marketing must not stop when sales have been created. Table 1 illustrates a dynamic view of services marketing labelled the *Three Stage Model*[18].

The model holds that, in order to satisfy the needs of its target market, the service firm will have to consider three stages in the customer's opinion of the need-satisfying capabilities of the service offering. These are *interest* in the service

Table 1 The Three Stage Model

Stage	Objective of marketing	Marketing function
Internal stage	To get a customer-conscious and sales-minded personnel	The internal marketing function
Initial stage	To create interest in the firm and its services	The traditional marketing function
Purchasing process	To turn the general interest into sales	The traditional and the interactive marketing function
Consumption process	To create resales and enduring customer contacts	The interactive marketing function

firm and its offerings, *purchase* of a service, and *repeat purchase* of the same or similar services, respectively. A recognition of these three stages has substantial marketing consequences. At each of the stages the *objective* of marketing and the *nature* of marketing (the responsible marketing function) will be different.

At the *initial stage* the objective of marketing is to *create interest* in the company and its services. This is best achieved by the traditional marketing function. Advertising, sales promotion and public relations activities, and personal selling especially as far as industrial services are concerned[19], are useful means of competition.

At the second stage, the *purchasing process, the general interest should be turned into sales*. Here again the marketing activities mentioned above can be used, but also interactive marketing can be applied whenever the customer gets in contact with the firm's production resources before he has made his final decision.

During the *consumption process, resales and enduring customer contacts should be guaranteed*. At this stage the traditional marketing activities have little or no chance to influence the preferences of the customer towards the service. Here the interactive marketing function is responsible for success or failure, i.e., decisions concerning services concepts, accessibility of the services, interactive customer/personnel communication, auxiliary services, and consumer influence are of vital importance, if customers are not to be lost at this final stage.

In Table 1, there is also a pre-stage, the *internal stage*, which is concerned with the internal situation of the service company. Because the employees, and especially the contact personnel, frequently are of such importance to the interactive marketing, it is essential that *the personnel are customer-conscious and sales-minded*. As one writer puts it: '. . . to have satisfied customers, the firm must also have satisfied employees'[20]. The contact personnel are the first market of the service firm[21], and if the firm cannot make them customer-conscious and sell its services, auxiliary services and campaigns to them, it will probably not succeed in its ultimate markets either. Consequently, there is a third marketing function, which must not be forgotten, i.e., the *internal marketing function*, which especially in personnel intensive service businesses is a prerequisite for a successfully implemented interactive marketing.

Concluding Remarks

According to the service marketing theory which is presented in this article the traditional marketing activities of consumer goods marketing theory can only be applied to part of a service firm's total marketing function. Instead, another kind of marketing effort, the interactive marketing activity, can be of vital importance. The company must continuously demonstrate its capability of handling the buyer/seller interactions throughout the whole purchasing and consumption process. If it fails to do that, it will probably lose customers, whereas a competitor that successfully manages its interactive marketing function will get a positive reputation and a desirable corporate image followed by satisfied customers and enduring customer contacts.

References

[1] Bessom, R.M., 'Unique Aspects of Marketing Services', *Arizona Business Bulletin*, No. 9, November 1973, p. 14.
[2] Chisnall, P.M., 'Marketing in a service economy', *European Research*, No. 4, July 1977, p. 181.
[3] Rathmell, J.M., *Marketing in the Service Sector*, Cambridge, Mass., Winthrop Publishers, 1974.
[4] Ibid., p. vii.
[5] See, for example, George, W.R. and Barksdale, H.C., 'Marketing Activities in the Service Industries', *Journal of Marketing*, No. 4 (October 1974), p. 65.
[6] See, for example Bonoma, T.V. and Mills, M.K., *Developmental Service Marketing*, working Paper series, Graduate School of Business, University of Pittsburgh, April 1979. See also Levitt, T., 'Product-line approach to service', *Harvard Business Review*, September-October 1972 and 'The industrialization of service', *Harvard Business Review*, September-October 1976.
[7] See, for example, Bessom, R.M., *op. cit.*; Eiglier, P. and Langeard, E., 'Une approche nouvelle du marketing des services', *Revue Francaise de Gestion*, No. 2 (novembre 1975) and *Principes de politique marketing pour les enterprises de services*, Working paper, L'Institut d'Administration des Enterprises, Université d'Aix-Marseille, (décembre 1976); Shostack, G.L., 'Breaking Free from Product

Marketing', *Journal of Marketing*, No. 2 April 1977, and George, W.R., 'The Retailing of Services—A Challenging Future', *Journal of Retailing*, No. 3 Fall 1977. From the area of professional service marketing see, for example, Wilson, A., *The Marketing of Professional Services*, London, McGraw-Hill, 1972 and Gummesson, E., 'Toward a Theory of Professional Service Marketing', *Industrial Marketing Management*, April 1976.

[8] See Grönroos, C., 'A Service-Orientated Approach to Marketing of Services', *European Journal of Marketing*, No. 8, 1978; 'An Applied Theory for Marketing Industrial Services', *Industrial Marketing Management*, No. 1, 1979; 'Designing a Long Range Marketing Strategy for Services', *Long Range Planning*, April 1980; and *Marketing Services: A study of the marketing function of service firms*, Stockholm, Marketing Techniques Center, 1979.

[9] See Grönroos, C., 'A Service-Orientated Approach to Marketing of Services', *op. cit.*; and 'Designing a Long Range Marketing Strategy for Services', *op. cit.*

[10] See, for example, Bessom, R.M., *op. cit.*; Rathmell, J.M., *Marketing in the Service Sector*, *op. cit.*; Shostack, G.L., 'Breaking Free from Product Marketing', *op. cit.*; Sasser, W.E., 'Match Supply and Demand in Service Industries', *Harvard Business Review*, November-December 1976; and Eiglier, P. and Langeard, E., *op. cit.*

[11] See Bateson, J.E.G., *et al.*, *Testing a Conceptual Framework for Consumer Service Marketing*, project description, Marketing Science Institute, August 1978, p. 11.

[12] Bessom, R.M., *op. cit.*, pp. 13–14.

[13] See, for example, Eiglier, P. and Langeard, E., *op. cit.*, p. 11, and Bateson, J.E.G., *et al.*, *op. cit.*, pp. 29–31.

[14] Sasser, W.E. and Arbeit, S.P., 'Selling Jobs in the Service Sector', *Business Horizons*, June 1976, p. 62.

[15] See also Besson, R.M., *op. cit.*, p. 12.

[16] As has been noted earlier in the text, the empirical data in support of these research results are not presented here, because of space limitations.

[17] The only innovative attempt to develop the distribution concept in a service-oriented direction seems to be the marketing intermediary concept suggested by James H. Donnelly, Jr. in his article, 'Marketing Intermediaries in the Channels of Distribution for Services', *Journal of Marketing*, No. 1, January 1976.

[18] See Grönroos, C., 'Designing a Long Range Marketing Strategy for Services', *op. cit.*

[19] See Grönroos, C., 'An Applied Theory for Marketing Industrial Services', *op. cit.*

[20] George, W.R., 'The Retailing of Services—A Challenging Future', *op. cit.*, p. 91.

[21] See Sasser, W.E. and Arbeit, S.P., *op. cit.*, p. 61.

4

A Service Quality Model and its Marketing Implications

The Missing Service Quality Concept

In order to be able to develop service marketing models and service management models one has to have a clear picture of what customers in the marketplace really are looking for and what they are evaluating in the customer relation of service firms. Nevertheless, publications on service marketing—research reports, scientific articles and books—do not include any explicit model of how the quality of a service is perceived and evaluated by consumers[1]. What we need is a model of service quality, i.e., a model which describes how the quality of services is perceived by customers. When we know this, and the components of service quality, we will be able to develop service-oriented concepts and models more successfully.

The term 'service quality' is frequently used by both academicians and practitioners. However, it is never defined in a way which could guide management decisions. Too often the term 'quality' is used as if it were a variable itself, and not a function of a range of resources and activities. To state that service firms, for instance, will have to develop the quality of their services to be able to compete successfully in the future is meaningless, unless one can: (1) define *how service quality is perceived* by the consumers; and (2) determine *in what way service quality is influenced*.

Grönroos, C. A Service Quality Model and its Marketing Implications. *European Journal of Marketing,* 1984; **18**(4): 36–44. Reproduced by permission of Emerald Group Publishing Limited.

Today we have no service quality concept. Therefore, the purpose of the present report is to develop a service quality model. This model is tested on a sample of service business executives.

Expected Service and Perceived Service

To answer the first question of how service quality is perceived, we may find some guidance in the literature on consumer behaviour. However, theories and models of consumer behaviour and buying behaviour do not explicitly consider services. Still, literature from those areas is of some help to us.

Consumer researchers have not explicitly considered the effects of consumers' perceptions of a product after consumption to any considerable extent[2]. However, several researchers have studied the effect of expectations about product performance on post-consumption evaluations of the product[3]. Among other things, it has been found that higher levels of performance lead to higher evaluations, if expectations are held constant[4] and that conflict arousal, in relation to the consumption of a product, depends on product performance relative to the expectations of the consumer[5].

According to one writer[6] the outcome of a product will be more important to post-consumption evaluations, the higher the degree of the consumer's personal involvement in the consumption process. Higher involvement leads, for instance, to a greater degree of noticing.

Typically, services are products which require high consumer involvement in the consumption process. In the buyer-seller interactions, during the simultaneous parts of production and consumption, the consumer usually will find a lot of resources and activities to notice, and evaluate. As an example we could think of an airline company or a provider of conference services. Hence, the consumer's experience of a service can be expected to influence his post-consumption evaluation of the service quality which he has experienced, i.e., the perceived quality of the service[7].

Consequently, it is reasonable to state that the perceived quality of a given service will be the outcome of an evaluation process, where the consumer compares his expectations with the service he perceives he has received, i.e., he puts the *perceived service* against the *expected service*. The result of this process will be *the perceived quality of the service*.

Hence, the quality of the service is dependent on two variables: expected service and perceived service. Therefore, in a service quality model we need to know the resources and activities, under the control and outside the immediate control of the firms that have an impact on these variables, i.e., an answer to the second question stated in the first section of this article. We shall turn to this question in the following sections.

Promises and Performance

Traditional marketing activities—advertising, field selling, pricing, etc.—can be used in order to give *promises* to target customers[8]. Such promises influence the expectations of the customers, and have an impact on the expected service. Moreover, traditions ('we have always done so') and ideology (religion, political involvement, etc.) may also have an effect on a given customer's expectations. The same goes for word-of-mouth communication.

Furthermore, previous experience with a service also influences the expectations of a customer. The perceived service, on the other hand, is the result of the consumer's perception of the service itself. We shall now turn to the issue of how the service is perceived.

Swan and Combs have suggested that the perceived performance of a product can be divided into two sub-processes; namely, instrumental performance and expressive performance[9]. In empirical tests of these concepts and their impact on consumer satisfaction, made by these two researchers and by others[10], mostly consumer goods have been considered. The tests and the results of them are, however, of considerable theoretical relevance to services, too.

The *instrumental performance* of a product is the technical dimension of the product. In the context of services, it would be the technical result of a service production process: e.g., a passenger has been transported from one place to another, a medical problem has been attended to in a hospital, financial transactions of a firm have been performed. It is, so to speak, what the customer is left with, when the production process is finished. *Expressive performance* is related to 'psychological' level of performance. In a service context, the expressive performance would be related to the buyer-seller interactions, i.e., to the contacts the consumer has with various resources and activities of the service firm, during the service production process when the technical outcome, the instrumental performance, is created. As an example, we may think of an airline passenger's contacts with the employees of the company, physical and technical resources, such as in-checking desks, the plane itself, seats, meals and the passenger's contacts with other passengers. The passenger's interactions with such human and non-human resources during the pre-flight, in-flight, and post-flight production processes will certainly have an effect on his evaluations of the service, and on the service he perceives he has received.

Swan and Combs argue that satisfactory instrumental performance of a product is a prerequisite for consumer satisfaction, but that this is not enough. If the expressive performance of a product is not considered satisfactory, the consumer will still feel unsatisfied, irrespective of the degree of satisfaction caused by the instrumental performance[11].

For example, a bank may manage the affairs of a customer perfectly in a technical sense—the instrumental performance is satisfactory—but if the customer is dissatisfied with the performance of the manager or the teller, or if he does not accept the idea of an automatic teller machine he is supposed to use, he will probably feel unhappy with the service he gets from the bank. Similar examples can easily be found from other areas of the service sector, such as hotels and restaurants, transportation, health care, repair and maintenance, shipping and consultancy.

In a service quality model, the different kinds of product performance ought to be translated into quality terms. In the next section we will develop the quality model.

Technical Quality and Functional Quality

The service is basically immaterial and can be characterised as an activity where production and consumption to a considerable extent take place simultaneously. In the buyer-seller interactions the service is rendered to the consumer. Clearly, what happens in these interactions will have an impact on the perceived service.

The hotel guest will get a room and a bed to sleep in, the consumer of a restaurant's services will get a meal, the train passenger will be transported from one place to another, the client of a business consultant may get a new organisation scheme, a manufacturer may get its goods transported from its inventories to a customer by a transportation firm, a bank customer may be granted a loan, etc. As we have noticed earlier, this mere technical outcome of the production process corresponds to the instrumental performance of the service. And clearly, this technical outcome of the process, i.e., *what* the consumer receives as a result of his interactions with a service firm, is important to him and to his evaluation of the quality of the service. This can be called the *technical quality* dimension. Frequently, it can be measured by the consumer in a rather objective manner, as any technical dimension of a product.

However, as the service is produced in interaction with the consumers, this technical quality dimension will not count for the total quality that the consumer perceives he gets. Obviously, he will also be influenced by the way in which the technical quality is transferred to him functionally.

The accessibility of a teller machine, a restaurant or a business consultant, the appearance and behaviour of waiters, bank tellers, travel agency representatives, bus drivers, cabin attendants, business consultants, plumbers, how these service firm employees perform, what they say and how they say it do also have an impact on the customer's view of the service. Furthermore, the more a consumer accepts self-service activities or other production-related routines, which he is expected to perform, the better he will, probably, consider the service. Moreover, the other customers simultaneously consuming the same or similar services may influence the way in which a given customer will perceive a service. Other customers may cause queues, disturb the customer, or they may, on the other hand, have a favourable impact on the atmosphere of the buyer-seller interactions.

In summary, the consumer is not only interested in what he receives as an outcome of the production process, but in the process itself. *How* he gets the technical outcome—or technical quality—functionally, is also important to him and to his view of the service he has received. This quality dimension can be called *functional quality*. Functional quality corresponds to the expressive performance of a service. Hence, we have two quality dimensions, which are quite different in nature: technical quality which answers the question of *what* the customer gets, and functional quality which, on the other hand, answers the question of *how* he gets it. Obviously, the functional quality dimension cannot be evaluated as objectively as the technical dimension. As a matter of fact, the functional dimension is perceived in a very subjective way.

The perceived service is the result of a consumer's view of a bundle of service dimensions, some of which are technical and some of which are functional in nature. When this perceived service is compared with the expected service, we get the perceived service quality. This is schematically illustrated in Figure 1.

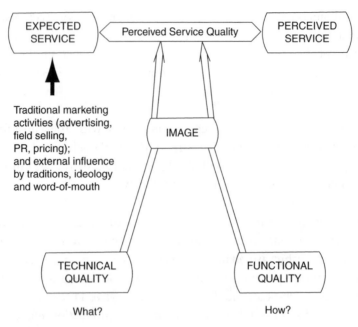

Figure 1 The Service Quality Model

However, the figure includes a third quality dimension, the corporate image, which in some cases can be viewed as a third variable in the quality model. We shall turn to image as a quality dimension in the next section.

Image as a Quality Dimension

Usually, a service firm cannot hide behind brand names or distributors. In most cases the consumers will be able to see the firm and its resources during buyer-seller interaction. Therefore, *corporate image*, or sometimes local image of an office or another organisational unit, is of utmost importance to most service firms[12]. The expectations of the consumers are influenced by their view of the company, i.e., by the image.

The corporate image is the result of how the consumers perceive the firm. The most important part of a firm, which its customers see and perceive, is its services. Therefore, the corporate image can be expected to be built up mainly by the technical quality and the functional quality of its services. Of course, there are other factors, which also may influence the image, but they are normally less important. One may choose between two types of such factors: external factors, such as tradition, ideology and word-of-mouth, and on the other hand, traditional marketing activities, such as advertising, pricing and public relations.

When a service firm wants to inform new target markets about its image, traditional marketing activities like image advertising can be the most effective means of doing so. Moreover, if customers in an existing market, for some reason or another, have an image of the firm which does not correspond with reality, traditional marketing activities can again be expected to be an effective way of communicating the real image to the market. In our opinion, however, advertising campaigns, or other traditional marketing activities, should not be launched, if the picture of the firm that is given the customers does not reflect an existing technical quality and functional quality. All traditional marketing efforts have an impact on the expectations of the customer, and an advertising campaign which gives the impression that the technical and/or the functional quality of the service are better than they really are, will result in an increased expected service level. If the perceived service remains on the same level as before, the gap between the expected service and the perceived service will grow, which may lead to conflict arousal. The firm will get disappointed customers. Finally, disappointed customers may cause the image to deteriorate.

However, the image may be a quality dimension. If a consumer believes that he goes to a good restaurant and the meal, for instance, is not perfect, or the behaviour of the waiter is irritating, he may still find the perceived service satisfactory. His positive image of the restaurant makes him find excuses for his negative experiences. Obviously, if he is disappointed many times, his image of the restaurant will deteriorate. In a corresponding manner, a negative image may easily increase perceived problems with service quality. Moreover, the bad image will probably become even more unfavourable.

Some Empirical Evidence Concerning the Service Quality Model

Tests in the instrumental performance and expressive performance of products indicate that the first kind of performance is a necessary, but not sufficient, condition for satisfaction[13]. Swan and Combs also argue that a satisfied consumer will be more likely to mention expressive attributes, rather than instrumental attributes, as a reason for his satisfaction.

As far as services are concerned, these observations would suggest that functional quality is more important to the perceived service than the technical quality, at least as long as the latter quality dimension is on a satisfactory level. Informal case studies, which we have done as pilot studies, lead us to the same conclusion.

This is especially important to such service industries, where the mere technical quality is very similar among firms in the marketplace, and is difficult to differentiate. As we know, this is the case for a very large number of services.

The hypothesis stated above was tested on a sample consisting of Swedish service firm executives in 1981. A random sample was drawn from a population consisting of persons participating in a series of service marketing seminars, and a questionnaire was mailed to the respondents on average six months after the seminar. The respondents represent top management as well as marketing and other business functions, mainly internal training and personnel. Moreover, a wide range of service industries are included in the sample: e.g., banks, insurance companies, hotels, restaurants, shipping, airline companies, cleaning and maintenance, car rental companies, travel agencies, engineering consultants, architects, business consultants, advertising agencies, and a range of institutions from the public sector.

The items concerning service quality and corporate image are one part of the total questionnaire only. Approximately 60 per cent of the questionnaires were returned. This equals 219 respondents. As most service industries are very personnel intensive, and are likely to stay so in the relevant future, the performance of the employees involved in the buyer-seller interactions—the contact personnel—was used in order to operationalise the functional quality dimension. The terms contact personnel, technical quality and functional quality were familiar to the respondents.

The items used, as well as the results, are illustrated in Table 1. The answers were given on Likert-type scales with five points ranging from 'agree strongly' (5) to 'disagree strongly' (1). The scales were analysed separately, and the results are given separately. In the table the results for all respondents are given. The picture did not change when the data were broken down according to the background variables used, such as industry, size, position of the respondent, and type of customers.

As we may see from Table 1, a very large proportion of the respondents agree strongly or partly with the five first items. The buyer-seller interaction, where the

Table 1 Items and Results Concerning Service Quality and Corporate Image

Item	(1) Proportion agreeing strongly/partly(%)	(2) n	(3) No answer
In most cases the everyday contact with customers (the buyer-seller interaction) is a more important part of marketing than traditional marketing activities, such as advertising, mass communication, etc.	94.1	218	1
The corporate image is more the result of the customer's contacts with the company (the buyer-seller interaction) than the result of traditional marketing activities	88.8	216	3
Traditional marketing activities are of marginal importance only to the view of the corporate image of the customers *the firm has today*	74.0	218	1
Word-of-mouth communication has a more substantial impact on *potential customers* than traditional marketing activities	83.5	216	3
The contact personnel's way of handling the contacts with the customers, if it is customer-oriented and service-minded, will compensate for *temporary problems* with the technical quality of the service	91.3	219	0
The contact personnel's way of handling the contacts with the customers, if it is customer-oriented and service-minded, will compensate for an overall *lower technical quality level*	37.9	217	2

Comments: The proportions in column 1 are significantly larger than 50 per cent on any significance level, except for the last item. The frequency distribution is U-shaped for this item. Consequently, no statistical tests have been applied on the total data material.

functional quality emerges, is considered a more important part of marketing than traditional marketing activities. This stresses the view that the quality-generating process, and especially the buyer-seller interaction, is of utmost importance to service marketing. We have, in other contexts, defined the management of the buyer-seller interaction as the *interactive marketing function*[14] of service firms as a complement to the traditional marketing function.

Items 2 through 4 indicate that traditional marketing activities are considered marginally important to corporate image, whereas the buyer-seller interaction and word-of-mouth is considered more effective. The fifth item indicates that functional quality is considered very important; in fact so important that a high level of functional quality (contact personnel performance) may compensate for temporary problems with the technical quality. One may also notice that more than one-third of the respondents agree strongly or partly with the sixth item, which says that good contact personnel performance may even compensate for an overall lower technical quality level.

Conclusions and Marketing Implications

We may conclude that the functional quality, in fact, seems to be a very important dimension of the perceived service. In some cases it is more important than the technical quality dimension. Successful service management may, therefore, mean that attention is paid to improving the functional quality of a firm's services. Managing the buyer-seller interaction, and thus creating good functional quality, may be a powerful marketing function (interactive marketing), more important than traditional marketing activities.

The importance of traditional marketing activities to corporate image should not be over-estimated. The image is mainly the result of the perceived service. Moreover, the importance of word-of-mouth ought to be remembered.

Managing the perceived service quality means that the firm has to match the expected service and the perceived service to each other so that consumer satisfaction is achieved. In order to keep the gap between the expected service and perceived service as small as possible, two things seem to be critical to the service firm:

(1) The promises about how the service will perform given by traditional marketing activities, and communicated by word-of-mouth, must not be unrealistic when compared to the service the customers eventually will perceive.
(2) Managers have to understand how the technical quality and the functional quality of a service is influenced, and how these quality dimensions are perceived by the customers.

The first consideration has implications for advertising and other traditional marketing efforts. By such activities a view of the service which is not based on reality should not be given to the customers. Moreover, for the firm's present customers such activities are probably far less effective than the impact of the customers perceptions of the service. As potential customers are concerned, traditional marketing is more powerful.

The second consideration brings us back to the service quality model, illustrated in Figure 1. Management has to understand the importance of the functional quality, and how the two quality dimensions can be developed. The technical quality dimension is obviously a result of the know-how which the firm has. This means good technical solutions, technical abilities of the employees, etc. By appropriate use of machines and computer-based systems the technical quality may be improved.

However, as we have seen this is not enough. To ensure that the consumers are satisfied an acceptable functional quality is demanded. The contact personnel are often of vital importance to functional quality. Moreover, customer-oriented physical resources and technical resources, as well as the accessibility of the firm's services, the consumer orientation of self-service systems, and the firm's ability to maintain a continuous contact with its customers are examples of ways of influencing the functional quality dimension.

In conclusion, one should notice that the quality dimensions are interrelated. An acceptable technical quality can be thought of as a prerequisite for a successful functional quality. On the other hand, it seems as if temporary problems with the technical quality may be excused, if the functional quality is good enough. Finally, the importance of the image should be recognised.

Of course, much more research is needed, especially research on the consumers' view of service quality.

References

[1] See, for example, publications by Wilson, Rathmell, Levitt, Eiglier and Langeard, Berry, Bateson, Gummesson, George, Thomas, Lovelock, Grönroos and others.
[2] Bettman, J.R., *An Information Processing Theory of Consumer Choice*, Reading, Mass., Addison-Wesley, 1979, p. 275.
[3] See, for example, Lewin, K. *et al.*, 'Level of Aspiration', in Hunt, J.M. (ed), *Personality and Behaviour Disorders*, Vol. 1, New York, Ronalds, 1944; Cardozo, R.N., 'An Experimental Study of Consumer Effort, Expectation and Satisfaction', *Journal of Marketing Research*, August, 1965; Cohen, J. and Goldberg, M.E., 'The Effects of Brand Familiarity and Performance upon Post-Decision Product Evaluation', Paper presented at the American Marketing Association's Workshop on Experimental

Research in Consumer Behaviour, Ohio State University, 1969; Olshavsky, R.W., and Miller, J.A., 'Consumer Expectations, Product Performance and Perceived Product Quality', *Journal of Marketing Research*, February, 1972; Anderson, R.E., 'Consumer Dissatisfaction: The Effect of Disconfirmed Expectancy on Perceived Product Performance', *Journal of Marketing Research*, February, 1973; and Oliver, R.L., 'Effect of Expectation and Disconfirmation on Post-exposure Product Evaluations: An Alternative Interpretation', *Journal of Applied Psychology*, August, 1977.

[4] See Oliver, R.L., *op. cit.*, 1977.

[5] Hansen, F., *Consumer Choice Behaviour: A Cognitive Theory*, New York, The Free Press, 1972, p. 179.

[6] Bettman, J.R., *op. cit.*, p. 272.

[7] In the area of industrial services, Johnston and Bonoma have found that firms which successfully have rendered or currently render a service, often are the only one solicited when a repeat purchase is to be made. See Johnston, W.J. and Bonoma, T.V., 'Purchase Process for Capital Equipment and Services', *Industrial Marketing Management*, No. 4, 1981, p. 261.

[8] Calonius, H., 'Behövs begreppet löfte?', *Marknadsvetande*, No. 1, 1980 and Calonius, H., 'On the Promise Concept', unpublished working paper, Swedish School of Economics, 1983.

[9] Swan, J.E. and Combs, L.J., 'Product Performance and Consumer Satisfaction: A New Concept', *Journal of Marketing*, April, 1976, p. 26.

[10] See Maddox, R.N., 'Two-factor Theory and Consumer Satisfaction: Replication and Extension', *Journal of Consumer Research*, June, 1981.

[11] Swan, J.E. and Combs, L.J., *op. cit.*, p. 26.

[12] Bessom, R.M., 'Unique Aspects of Marketing of Services', *Arizona Business Bulletin*, November, 1973, p. 78, and Bessom, R.M. and Jackson, D.W. Jr., 'Service Retailing: A Strategic Marketing Approach', *Journal of Retailing*, Summer, 1975, p. 78.

[13] Swan, J.E. and Combs, L.J., *op. cit.*, pp. 27 and 32.

[14] See Grönroos, C., 'A Service-oriented Approach to Marketing of Services', *European Journal of Marketing*, Vol. 12 No. 8, 1978, and Grönroos, C., 'Strategic Management and Marketing in the Service Sector', Helsingfors, Finland, Swedish School of Economics, 1982, p. 136ff.

5

Marketing Services: The Case of a Missing Product

Introduction

In the service marketing literature, services are frequently described by charac-teristics such as intangibility, heterogeneity, inseparability of consumption from production and the impossibility to keep services in stock. Many of these, for example the first two, are not specific for services, and others, for example the last two, follow from the most important characteristic of services, i.e. the process nature of services. Physical goods are preproduced in a factory, whereas services are produced in a process in which consumers interact with the production resources of the service firm. Some part of the service may be prepared before the customers enter the process, but for service quality perception the crucial part of the service process[1] takes place in interaction with customers and in their presence. What the customer consumes in a service context is, therefore, fundamentally different from what is the focus of consumption in the context of physical goods.

Discussing solutions to customer problems

The purpose of the present article is to discuss solutions to customer problems – and at the same time the objects of marketing – in a service context and the implications for service marketing that follow from the characteristic of service consumption. The analysis is based on the research tradition of the Nordic School

Grönroos, C. Marketing Services: The Case of a Missing Product. *Journal of Business & Industrial Marketing*, 1998; **13**(4–5): 322–338. Reproduced by permission of Emerald Group Publishing Limited.

of marketing thought (see Grönroos and Gummesson, 1985), which has been recognized as one of three major research streams in service marketing (Berry and Parasuraman, 1993).

Process and outcome consumption

A central part of service marketing is based on the fact that the consumption of a service is *process consumption* rather than *outcome consumption*, where the consumer or user perceives the production process as part of the service consumption, not just the outcome of that process as in traditional marketing of physical goods. When consuming a physical product customers make use of the product itself, i.e. they consume the outcome of the production process. In contrast, when consuming services customers perceive the process of producing the service to a larger or smaller degree, but always to a critical extent, moreover taking part in the process. The consumption process leads to an outcome for the customer, which is the result of the service process. Thus, the consumption of the service process is a critical part of the service experience. As service quality research demonstrates, perception of the process is important for the perception of the total quality of a service, even though a satisfactory outcome is necessary and a prerequisite for good perceived quality. In many situations the service firm cannot differentiate its outcomes from those of its competitors. In some situations the customers take the quality of the outcome for granted, but in other situations it is difficult for the customer to evaluate the quality of the outcome of the service process. However, in all situations customers take part in the production process and sometimes more, sometimes less actively interact with the employees, physical resources and production system of the service organization. Because of this inseparability of the service process and the consumption of a service, the process can be characterized as an open process. Hence, regardless of how the customer perceives the outcome of a service process, service consumption is basically process consumption.

Thus service consumption and production have interfaces that are always critical to the customers' perception of the service and consequently to their long-term purchasing behavior. In the service marketing literature, the management of these interfaces is called interactive marketing (Grönroos, 1982, 1990). If a service firm wants to keep its customers, interactive marketing, i.e. the marketing effect of the simultaneous service production and consumption processes, must be positive. Hence, for the long-term success of a service firm the customer orientation of the service process is crucial. If the process fails from the customers' point of view, no traditional external marketing efforts, and frequently not even a good outcome of the service process, will make them stay in the long run. Only a low price may save the situation, at least for a while.

Traditional product marketing

In traditional product marketing, the physical goods, that is the products that are the outcomes of the production process, are the key variable around which the other marketing activities revolve. According to the 4P model, there has to be a preproduced product that can be priced, communicated about, and distributed to the consumers. However, when there is no such product, marketing becomes different, because there is no ready-made, preproduced object of marketing and consumption. There is only a process that cannot begin until the consumer or user enters the process.

In the following sections we will first discuss the nature of traditional marketing of physical goods, i.e. product marketing which is traditionally based on outcome consumption. Next we will explore how the nature of marketing changes when outcome consumption is replaced by process consumption as is the case with services. As a means of illustrating the nature of marketing we use the marketing triangle. This way of illustrating the field of marketing is adapted from Philip Kotler (1991), who uses it to illustrate the holistic concept of marketing suggested by the Nordic School approach to services marketing and management.

A closed process

Outcome consumption and the nature of product marketing

A product in the traditional sense, is the result of how various resources, such as people, technologies, raw materials, knowledge and information, have been managed in a factory so that a number of features that customers in target markets are looking for are incorporated into it. The production process can be characterized as a closed process, where the customer takes no direct part. Thus, a product evolves as a more or less preproduced package of resources and features that is ready to be exchanged. The task of marketing (including sales) is to find out what product features the customers are interested in and to give promises about such features to a segment of potential customers through external marketing activities such as sales and advertising campaigns. If the product includes features that the customers want, it will almost by itself fulfil the promises that have been

Figure 1 The product-oriented perspective: outcome consumption and marketing
Source: Adapted from Grönroos (1997, p. 414)

given to the customers. This marketing situation is illustrated in the product marketing triangle in Figure 1.

Three key parties of marketing

In Figure 1 the three key parties of marketing in a physical good or product context are shown. These are the firm, represented by a marketing and/or sales department, the market, and the product. Normally, marketing (including sales) is the responsibility of a department (or departments) of specialists or full-time marketers (and salespeople). Customers are viewed in terms of markets of more or less anonymous individuals. The market offering is a preproduced physical product. Along the sides of the triangle three key functions of marketing are displayed, viz. to give promises, to fulfil promises, and to enable promises. Calonius (1988) has suggested that the promise concept, and marketing's role in giving and fulfilling promises should be given a central position in marketing models. Recently Bitner (1995) added the expression 'enabling promises' in the context of internal marketing. Promises are normally given through mass marketing and in business-to-business contexts also through sales. Promises are fulfilled through a number of product features and enabled through the process of continuous product development based on market research performed by full-time marketers and on technological capabilities of the firm. Marketing is very much directed toward giving promises through external marketing campaigns. The value that customers are looking for is guaranteed by appropriate product features, and the existence of a product with the appropriate features will make sure that promises given are also kept. 'The idea of marketing as a sequence of activities giving and fulfilling promises is not expressed explicitly in the . . . [product] marketing literature, probably because it is taken for granted that the products are developed with such features that any promises which external marketing and sales have given are kept' (Grönroos, 1996, p. 9).

Process consumption

The view of marketing illustrated in the product marketing triangle of Figure 1 is based on the notion of outcome consumption. Customers consume a product as a preproduced package of features that does not change during the consumption process. Different customers may perceive the product in different ways, but the product is the same. However, the situation changes when this type of outcome consumption is replaced by process consumption, as is the case with services. Next we will examine how the nature of marketing changes when we move to process consumption.

Process consumption and the nature of service marketing

For a service firm the scope and content of marketing become more compli-cated. The notion of a preproduced product with features that customers are looking for is too limited to be useful in a service context. Also, in the context of business-to-business marketing the traditional product construct is too restrictive, as has been demonstrated, for example, in the network approach to marketing in business relationships (cf. Håkansson and Snehota, 1995; Mattsson, 1997) and in the relationship marketing approach (cf. Grönroos, 1996; Sheth and Parvatiyar, 1995). Even in the early 1980s Levitt (1983) argued for an extended product concept. However, in the present article we focus on service contexts only, either the marketing of service firms or service organizations of manufacturing firms. In another context we have analyzed the need to expand the product construct in a relationship marketing context (Grönroos, 1997).

Adjusting resources

In many cases it is not known at the beginning of the service process what the customer wants and expects in detail, and consequently what resources should be used and to what extent and in what configuration they should be used. For example, the service requirements of a machine that has been delivered to a customer may vary, the need to provide training of the customer's personnel and the need to handle claims may vary. Thus the firm has to adjust its resources and its ways of using its resources accordingly.

In Figure 2 (the service marketing triangle), marketing in a service context is illustrated in the same way as product marketing was in Figure 1. As can be seen, most elements in the figure are different.

The most important change from the product marketing situation is the fact that the product is missing. In the case of process consumption, no preproduced bundle of features that constitutes a product can be present. Only preparations for a service process can be made beforehand and partly prepared services can exist. In many service contexts, such as fast-food restaurants or car rental services, also physical product elements with specific features are present as integral parts of the service process. These product elements are sometimes, as in the case of car rental, preproduced, and sometimes, as in the case of the hamburger in a fast-food operation, they are partly preproduced, partly made to order. However, such physical products have no meaning as such, unless they fit the service process. They become one type of resource among many other types that have to be integrated into a functioning service process. A bundle of different types of resources creates value for the customers when these resources are used in their presence and in interaction with them. Even if service firms try to create products out of the resources available, they do not come up with more than a more or less standardised plan that guides the ways of using existing resources in the simultaneous service production and service consumption processes. 'They (service firms) only have a set of resources and, in the best case scenario, a well-planned way of using these resources as soon as the customer enters the arena'

Figure 2 The service-oriented perspective: process consumption and marketing
Source: Adapted from Grönroos (1997, p. 415)

(Grönroos, 1996, p. 10). Customer-perceived value follows from a successful and customer-oriented management of resources relative to customer sacrifice, not from a preproduced bundle of features.

Treated individually

The firm may still have a centralised marketing and sales staff, the full-time marketers, but they do not represent all the marketers and salespeople of the firm. In most cases the service firm has direct contacts with its customers, and information about each and every customer can be obtained on an individual basis. Moreover, in many cases customers, organizational customers and individual consumers and households alike, like to be treated much more individually than before. In principle, no customer must remain anonymous to the firm if this can be justified from an economic or practical standpoint (cf. Peppers and Rogers, 1993) or if the customer does not want to stay anonymous (cf. Grönroos, 1997).

In Figure 2 the resources of a firm are divided into five groups: personnel, technology, knowledge and information, customer's time and the customer. Many of the people representing the firm create value for customers in various service processes, such as deliveries, customer training, claims handling, service and maintenance, etc. and some of them are directly engaged in sales and cross-sales activities. Thus, they are involved in marketing as part-time marketers, to use an expression coined by Gummesson (1991). He observes that in industrial markets and in service businesses, the part-time marketers typically outnumber the full-time marketers of the marketing and sales departments several times over. Furthermore, he concludes that 'marketing and sales departments (the full-time marketers) are not able to handle more than a limited portion of the marketing as their staff cannot be at the right place at the right time with the right customer contacts' (Gummesson, 1990, p. 13).

Technological resources

In addition to the part-time marketers, other types of resources influence the quality and value perceived by the customer and hence are important from a marketing perspective as well. Technologies, the knowledge that employees have and that is embedded in technical solutions, and the firm's way of managing the customer's time are such resources. Physical product elements in the service process can, for example, be viewed as technological resources. Moreover, the customers themselves as individual consumers or as users representing organizations often become a value-generating resource. The impact of customers on the final development or design of a technical solution or on the timeliness of a service activity may be critical to the value perceived by them.

In summary, from the customers' point of view, in process consumption the solutions to their problems are formed by a set of resources needed to create a good customer-perceived service quality and value. In addition, the firm must have competencies to acquire and/or develop the resources needed and to manage and implement the service process in a way that creates value for each customer. Thus, a governing system is needed for the integration of the various types of resources and for the management of the service process.

Promises given by sales and external marketing are fulfilled through the use of the various types of resources. In order to prepare an appropriate set of resources continuous product development in its traditional form is not enough, because the service process encompasses a large part of the activities of the service firm. Instead internal marketing and a continuous development of the competencies and of the resource structure of the firm are needed.

Customer-perceived value

The conclusion of the discussion so far is that service firms, or service organizations of manufacturing firms, do not have products (understood as preproduced bundles of resources and features); they only have processes to offer their customers. Of course, these processes lead to an outcome that is also important for the customer. However, as the outcome of, for example, a management consultancy assignment or an elevator maintenance process cannot exist without the process, and because from the customers' perspective the process is an open process, it is fruitful to view the outcome as a part of the process. Both the process and its outcome have an impact on the perception of the quality of a service and consequently on customer-perceived value. In contrast, in the case of preproduced physical products, it is only the outcome of the process of production that counts for the customers.

In search of the missing product: the perceived service quality concept

Within the Nordic School research tradition, attempts to conceptualize the phenomenon of the missing product of service firms were made as early as the late 1970s (e.g. Gummesson, 1977) and in the early 1980s (e.g. Grönroos, 1982).

The characteristics of the service process – for example, its heterogeneity and the inseparability of production from consumption – made it difficult to conceptualize easily the service process and its outcome as a solution to customer problems and as marketing objects. Instead, studying the quality of the service as perceived by the users offered a possible way of understanding the marketing situation. Hence, the question 'How is the quality of a solution to problems or needs perceived by consumers or users of services?' was addressed. By taking such a consumer-oriented approach, the conceptualization of the service process could be achieved and the missing product of service firms be replaced by a genuinely service-based, and moreover, customer-oriented construct.

Basic perceived service quality

Based on some previously suggested aspects of the quality of services (Gummesson, 1977) and on perspectives from cognitive psychology (cf. Bettman, 1979), the concept of perceived service quality was developed as a solution to the problem of the missing product of service firms (Grönroos, 1982, 1984). In Figure 3 the basic perceived service quality model is illustrated. The original perceived service quality model from 1982 is (a), and the extended model where the quality dimensions and the disconfirmation notion of the model are put into their marketing context, is illustrated in (b). The extended model includes the same phenomena as the 'giving promises' and 'keeping promises' sides of the service marketing triangle in Figure 2.

The disconfirmation concept was introduced because it seemed theoretically obvious that quality perception is a function of what the customer expects of the process as well as of what in fact is experienced. In the model, customers' perceptions of the process are divided into two dimensions, the process dimension or how the service process functions and the output dimension or what the process leads to as a result of the process. In the perceived service quality model (Grönroos, 1982, 1984), these two quality dimensions were called functional quality (how the service process functions) and technical quality (what the service process leads to for the customer in a 'technical' sense). Image, on a company and/or local level was introduced in the model as a filter that influences the quality perception either favorably, neutrally or unfavorably depending on whether the customer considers the service firm good, neutral or bad. As the image changes over time depending on the quality perceptions of a given user of a service, the image component adds a dynamic aspect to the model, which in other respects is static (cf. Grönroos, 1993).

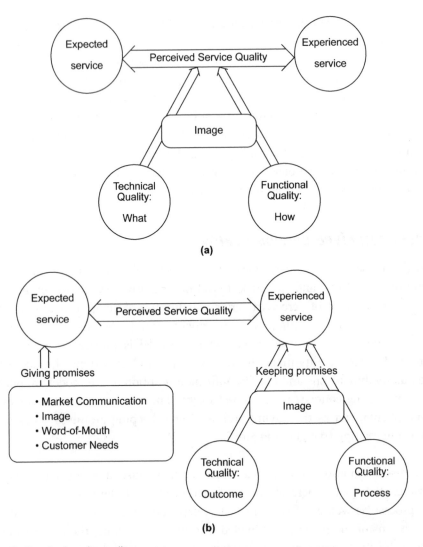

Figure 3 Perceived service quality
Source: Adapted from Grönroos (1983, p. 28; 1990, p. 47)

An abductive research process

The perceived service quality model emerged in what now would be called an abductive research process (see Coffey and Atkinson, 1996, pp. 155–6), that is in a process where theoretical deduction and a qualitative case study in the context of industrial services supported each other. In a major quantitative study in the service sector (Grönroos, 1982), where among other service marketing elements perceived service quality was empirically studied, the 'how' and 'what' dimensions of the model as well as the image component were clearly supported.

This study also indicated that the perception of the process (functional quality, how) frequently seemed to be at least as important to the total perception of the quality of a service as the outcome (technical quality, what). Subsequently these findings have been supported by a number of studies about service quality in business-to-business markets as well as in consumer markets (e.g. Brown and Swartz, 1989; Chandon *et al.*, 1997; Crosby *et al.*, 1990; Lapierre, 1996; Lehtinen and Lehtinen, 1991; Palmer, 1997; Price *et al.*, 1995). Of course, the importance of the process dimension does not contradict the position of the outcome dimension as a prerequisite for good service quality.

A theoretical construct

The perceived service quality model was never intended to be an operational model of service quality. It was developed and introduced as a theoretical construct to help academics and practitioners understand the nature of the missing product of service firms, i.e. to understand the service process itself as the solution to customer problems – the object of marketing – in order to develop a consistent service marketing model and well-functioning marketing programs in service firms. How good the quality of the service was perceived to be by customers was expected to be measured using customer satisfaction approaches.

However, the introduction of the perceived service quality model created an interest in measuring service quality instead of only measuring customer satisfaction as traditionally was done. The best measurement instrument is the SERVQUAL model developed by Berry, Parasuraman and Zeithaml (Parasuraman *et al.*, 1988, 1994). When operationalizing the perceived service quality model it has become evident that the expectation construct is complicated and difficult to measure in a valid way. For example, customers' expectations after the service process may be different from their expectations before the process (cf. Boulding *et al.*, 1989; Gardial *et al.*, 1994; Grönroos, 1993). Furthermore, expectations that change during the service consumption process may also affect how the service is perceived. Based on their empirical findings, Boulding *et al.* (1989) note that 'a person's expectations color the way he or she perceives reality' (p. 11). They suggest two types of expectations: predictive 'will' expectations and normative 'should' expectations, and finally observe that 'though we suggest conceptually, and demonstrate empirically, that customers update their expectations and perceptions, interesting aspects of this process have not been investigated' (p. 25). Recent research by Johnson and Matthews (1997) suggests that customers' experiences influence the formation of 'will' expectations but not of 'should' expectations.

More than one comparison standard may be used

Tse and Wilton (1988) propose that more than one comparison standard may be used by customers. In a study in the service sector of how several comparison standards function in a disconfirmation approach Liljander (1995) showed that the best approximation of perceived service quality is achieved by omitting the expectation variable and other comparison standards altogether and only measuring the service experience. This is in line with the observations of Teas (1993) and Cronin and Taylor (1994). Theoretically the disconfirmation concept still seems to make sense for the understanding of how service quality is perceived (Grönroos, 1993; see also Cronin and Taylor, 1994). However, even the theoretical value of the disconfirmation concept has been questioned in a recently published study of the validity of the perceived service quality construct (Persson and Lindquist, 1997).

Here and now perception

As the original perceived service quality model was intended to be a replacement of the preproduced product that is missing in service contexts, it is obvious that this quality construct relates to one single service process and one single service experience. Hence, it is not a long-term quality perception. It is the quality perception here and now. From this follows clearly that the perceived service quality construct cannot be a synonym of customer satisfaction. In addition to the perception of a service, satisfaction with a service is also at least dependent on the sacrifice incurred by a customer for this service. Because the perceived service quality construct has often been interpreted as something else and more than the perception of quality of a given service process here and now (with the outcome of the process as an integral part of it), there has been substantial confusion about the relationship between perceived quality and satisfaction in the service marketing and service quality literature. Sometimes service quality is considered to influence customer satisfaction (e.g. Parasuraman et al., 1985), sometimes again service quality is considered a long-term concept, whereas customer satisfaction is described as something that is perceived on the basis of a specific service encounter (cf. Cronin and Taylor, 1994 citing research conducted by Parasuraman et al. reported in Parasuraman et al. 1988). Teas (1993) argues that service quality comes before customer satisfaction and suggests two service quality concepts, a transaction-specific quality concept that influences customer satisfaction and a relational quality concept that is a long-term concept. Spreng and Mackoy (1996) draw the following conclusion: 'There seems to be great deal of similarity between these two concepts (service quality and customer satisfaction), yet researchers are usually careful to state that these are different constructs' (p. 201). (For a further discussion of the relationship between service quality and customer satisfaction see, for example, Oliver, 1993.)

Perceived quality comes first

However, if the perceived service quality construct had been understood as a construct that replaces the missing product in a service marketing context, this rather confusing debate could have been avoided. Perceived service quality comes first, then satisfaction with quality (and the value of this given quality). From this also follows that perceived service quality can be viewed as a concept for the understanding of how to develop services, whereas customer satisfaction is a concept for the evaluation of how successfully these services are fulfilling the needs and desires of customers.

Managing the missing product

In order to create good perceived quality of a service, the firm must manage the service process as well as all resources needed in that process. As previously was observed, this process is an open process, where the customer not only sees and experiences how the process functions but also takes part in it and interacts with the resources that the firm directly controls. In Figure 2 these resources were systematized as personnel, technology, knowledge, the customer's time as well as the customer. A system has to be developed so that these resources are used in a way that leads to good perceived quality. As early as the 1970s Eiglier and Langeard in France developed a structure for the understanding of these resources and of the system for managing them (Eiglier and Langeard, 1976; see also Eiglier and Langeard, 1981). In Figure 4 a service process model based on the

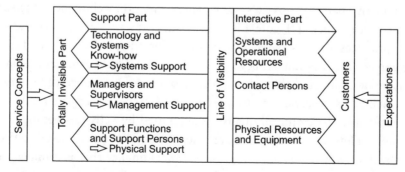

Figure 4 The service system
Source: Adapted from Grönroos (1990, p. 208)

earlier work by the two French researchers as well as by Lehtinen in Finland (Lehtinen, 1983) is developed (cf. Grönroos, 1990).

Contact persons

In the service process model the resources that are interacting in the company/customer interface, the interactive part of the system, are contact persons with certain knowledge about how to perform their tasks and how to interact with the customers, with systems and operational resources as well as physical resources and equipment. The customers themselves are also important resources in the service process. They should know how to perform in the system, and they have a given amount of time at their disposal which they expect the firm to make effective use of. The service process and its functional and technical quality impact depend on how this service system functions. If it functions well, the equivalent of the physical product in a service context is good. The four parts of the interactive system, including the customer as one part, have an impact on each other. For example, the systems and the physical resources used have a direct influence on the quality perception of customers, as have the attitudes and behaviors of the contact personnel. The contact persons' style of performance must match the style of consumption of the customers (Lehtinen, 1983). If the customers feel comfortable with the systems, the resources and the personnel, these resources are probably service oriented and will produce a good perceived quality. On the other hand, systems and physical resources, as well as customers, may have a negative impact on the employees, who thus easily create a negative quality perception.

Support part

The interactive part of a service system cannot function well without the support of a back office, which in Figure 4 is called a support part. This part of the service system produces various types of support to the interactive system. From the user's perspective it is hidden beyond a line of visibility. Customers seldom see what is going on behind this line, and they often do not realize the importance to the quality of a service of the part of the service process that takes place there. Especially the technical quality is supported by activities behind the line of visibility. However, there is also an interaction between the back office and the interactive process. Too often good technical quality that is founded on the support process of the back office is destroyed by bad functional quality created in the interactive process in front of the line of visibility.

As is illustrated in Figure 4, the perceived service quality is dependent on systems support, management support and physical support from the support system. For example, the service provider has to know how to develop and use a comprehensive customer database in order to be able to create such a support system (systems support), managers and supervisors must support and encourage the contact personnel to perform well (management support), and information systems and people running such systems must produce accurate and timely input for the interactive system (physical support).

Behind the support part a totally invisible part of the service system exists. This part has no direct or indirect impact on the perceived quality of the service process and its outcome. Frequently, there are surprisingly few parts of a service firm that are truly invisible in this respect.

Sometimes the service process becomes even more complicated, for example when a service firm uses the support of an outside partner or subcontractor to perform some parts of the support system or the interactive system. This of course makes it more complicated to manage the service system and the resulting perceived service quality, because all resources are not under the immediate control of the service firm.

Good service quality

A case illustration: elevator repair and maintenance

As an illustration of how the missing product of a service organization was replaced by a quality-generating service system so that good service quality was created, the study of a case of elevator repair and maintenance services will be presented. The case company is the largest repair and maintenance provider on the Scandinavian market. Its business had, however, been unprofitable for some time and it was losing more service contracts annually than it managed to replace.

Diagnosing the problem

To find out the reason for the loss of customers, a large-scale survey among the firm's customers was conducted. The questionnaire was based on the assumption that the case company offered a product that more or less could be described as the result of repair and maintenance activities. This quantitative study indicated that the product of the firm was of low quality and that the price of this product was high. This result led to a substantial amount of consternation among top management of the firm and the marketing and sales group, because they knew that the firm as the largest service provider on the market had by far the best trained service technicians, the best possible tools and equipment for taking care of any repair and maintenance job, and the widest possible assortment of spare parts. No other company could handle an equally large number of repair and maintenance problems. Everybody in the firm considered it to have the best product on the market, and hence they could not understand that the quality of the repair and maintenance services was considered low by customers. High price was easier to understand, because being a large company it had high overhead costs and had to maintain a high price level.

A second qualitative study was initiated

Because top management had difficulties in accepting the results of the study, a second, qualitative study was initiated. One hundred former customers, representing mostly business markets such as office buildings and institutions but also markets such as residential buildings, were interviewed in an unstructured fashion. The main interview question could be phrased as 'What went wrong?'. In spite of some variations in the results, the average lost customer expressed the following opinion:

> We realize that you have the best capabilities on the market to repair and maintain elevators, and in most cases you do a good job in this respect. However, we do not feel comfortable with the way you are doing the job. We cannot trust your service technicians to start doing the repair or maintenance task according to what has been promised, and quite often you do not give exact promises about when the job will start. Although some of your people are attentive and show an interest in our concerns regarding the elevator and its problems, most of them could not care less about us and the need of information that we sometimes have. Sometimes we do not even recognize them as your employees. Quite often the service technician just leaves an unfinished job and we do not know for what reason or when he will be back to finish the job. Because we cannot always trust your way of doing the job and because it, therefore, is complicated for us to be your customers, we think that the quality of your services is low and that we, therefore, pay too much for it.

The implications of the second study were quite obvious. Top management and the marketing and sales group thought that the company had products, the results of repair and maintenance, whereas the customers considered the company to be offering processes. Furthermore, although the customers recognized that the processes have to include a successful outcome, their concerns regarding the repair and maintenance services were associated with the process and with problems occurring in the process.

Technical and functional quality

Understanding the service and the quality of the service

It was understood that the object of the elevator repair and maintenance business was the service process, and that it really was the case of a missing product. It was realized that the solution to the customers' problems consisted of the outcome as well as the process itself. The outcome has to be of an acceptable quality, but when this is the case it becomes transparent in the minds of the customers and the process itself becomes the issue. Both the outcome and the process have to be carefully planned and well implemented, if the repair and maintenance service is to be considered good. The service has to lead to both good quality of the outcome (technical quality; what) and good quality of the process (functional quality; how), where the former is perceived by the customers as a prerequisite and where in the final analysis it is the quality of the process that counts.

The technologies and knowledge required to create a good outcome of the repair and maintenance processes already existed. However, the systems as well as the attitudes and skills of the employees necessary for implementing the process well were lacking. Hence, a new service system was developed and subsequently implemented. In the rest of this section the changes in the interactive and the support parts of the service system and their impact on the service process are presented and discussed.

Service technicians

Systems and operational resources

Previously the supervisor of a regional or local service group (covering a smaller city or part of a bigger city) every morning allocated the repair and maintenance objects to the service technicians available every morning, without considering the previous history of the various customers or whether a given service technician had any previous experience of the customers and elevators that were assigned to him. In this way no relationship between the two parties, a given customer and a given service technician could develop, and moreover, the service technicians did not develop a knowledge of and responsibility for any of the customers. After the second study this was changed, so that every service technician was given long-term responsibility for the same customers. A back-up system to be used in case the regular technician fell ill was also developed.

A specific systems knowledge

In order for the company to change the operational system, a specific systems knowledge had to be developed. This was not an easy process because of the history of how to organize the workflow in the company. However, by developing the new understanding of how the operational systems should function, a systems support was created that enabled the service technicians to get a far better knowledge of the history of the elevators they were responsible for as well as to feel more responsible for the customers they had been assigned to.

Favorable impact on operational system used

Physical resources and equipment

Moreover, previously the service technicians had had a limited stock of spare parts and a limited assortment of tools in their vans. In case they needed something else, they had to leave the job and get the missing spare part or tool from a central depot. This was one of the reasons why customers once in a while were left wondering where the service technician had gone and why he left the job unfinished. Now a decision to invest in new and bigger vans and to keep more spare parts and tools in stock was taken. (A decision to renew the car park had already been taken, but instead of purchasing the vans that originally had been planned the company bought bigger vans.) This made it possible for the service technicians to finish almost all jobs without interruptions. Hence, this decision did not only improve the usefulness of the physical resources used in the service process, it also had a favorable impact on the operational systems used in the process.

By changing the technology used, the company created an additional systems support that made it possible for the service technicians to perform in a more customer-oriented fashion.

Contact persons

It was quite obvious that the service technicians were preoccupied with the outcome of the repair and maintenance tasks, whereas they were much less concerned with the way they were doing their jobs and with their interactions with people representing the customers. Furthermore, the operational systems and the management support from supervisors had been outcome oriented and had not encouraged an interest in the process itself. As a result of the study an internal marketing process was initiated, where the objective was to focus the interest of service technicians as well as their supervisors and upper-level managers on the quality perceptions of the customers and especially on the importance of the functional quality perception of the process. The reasons for the changes in systems and equipment were explained. By this internal marketing process the management wanted to achieve a change in the attitudes of all categories of employees toward the customers and toward their jobs, so that a more customer-oriented performance in the service process would be achieved.

Process perspective

Traditionally the focus of supervisors and managers had been on the outcome of the service process – a product orientation – whereas the understanding of how to support and manage the process of repair and maintenance from a quality perspective had been neglected. The use of elevator repair and maintenance had been thought of as solely outcome consumption, but as the extended study demonstrated, in reality it was a case of process consumption. Now a process perspective was taken, supported by the internal marketing process. Hence, management support by supervisors and upper-level managers was created.

In the back office a support function responsible for information about customers already existed. Through more customer-oriented market research, more accurate physical support in the form of better customer information was achieved.

Positive results

Customers

The new service system was intended to make it easier for the customer to interact with the service technicians. Customers would feel that their viewpoints are recognized and that they more effortlessly get answers to questions that they may have. Also, the customers' time could be expected to be used more effectively, because unnecessary stops in the repair and maintenance jobs could be avoided in the future.

The results of the development of the service system were positive. The customer defection rate went down, while the company managed to maintain its premium price level. The business turned profitable.

Conclusions

From the case presented in the previous section as well as from the analysis of the particular characteristics of the object of marketing in a service firm the following conclusions can be drawn:

(1) Service firms do not have products in the form of preproduced solutions to customers' problems; they have processes as solutions to such problems.

(2) From a customer's perspective the process has two dimensions, viz. the process itself and the outcome for the customer that it leads to.

(3) The process as the object of marketing (instead of a product as the object of marketing) can be analyzed in terms of its quality implications, viz. the functional quality perception (how well the process functions) and the technical quality perception (what outcome for the customer the process results in). In addition, the image of the service provider has an impact on the overall quality perception.

(4) As successful marketing of physical goods requires that the object of marketing (the product) is good enough, successful marketing of services requires that the process is good enough. Thus, even if it may lead to a good outcome, an inferior process (poor interactive marketing) jeopardizes the long-term success of service marketing.

(5) Although the development of products with certain product features to be produced in a factory can be done in a product development department, the development of the processes of service firms is much more complicated. It requires decisions and actions in a number of departments: internal marketing as well as investments in people, tools and equipment and the development of all parts of the interactive and support parts of the service

system (including investment in the serviscape, to use a term introduced in Bitner, 1992).

Understanding the services

As the discussion has shown, understanding the services requires a different logic than understanding physical goods. Important reasons for this are the fact that the consumption of services can be characterized as process consumption, whereas the consumption of physical goods can be understood as outcome consumption, as well as the observation that services are processes, not preproduced products. However, from a marketing point of view it is in many cases no longer meaningful to keep up a strict borderline between goods and services. Most firms offer both goods and services, and increasingly often they do so in a long-term relationship with their customers. The concept of relationship marketing is especially relevant for situations where firms offer their customers solutions that include the provision of both goods and services (cf. Christopher *et al.*, 1992; Grönroos, 1996; Gummesson, 1995; Sheth and Parvatiyar, 1995).

However, one of the key observations in relationship marketing is that regardless of whether its business traditionally is service-oriented or goods-oriented, a firm that adopts a relationship marketing approach has to define itself as a service business (Webster, 1994). In a long-term relationship the customer is looking for service, and the goods that are exchanged in the relationships become a service element among others in a continuous relationship (Grönroos, 1996). For example, in the production of physical goods, such as cars, customers can be drawn into the planning of the goods and the processes of the factory, among other things through the use of the internet and modern design techniques. In such cases the customers' interactions with the production process become part of their consumption process, and the consumption of the physical product becomes partly process consumption. What the firm is offering in a situation like this is a factory-related service element in the solution to customer problems. The physical goods become more and more service oriented, and service marketing and management knowledge are required to manage the business successfully.

Understanding services process

Thus it seems inevitable that understanding services processes is becoming an imperative for all types of businesses, not just for what used to be called service businesses.

Note

1. We use the term *service process* for the process that, in the service marketing and management literature, is frequently called service production process or service delivery process.

References

Berry, L.L. and Parasuraman, A. (1993), 'Building a new academic field – the case of services marketing', *Journal of Retailing*, Vol. 69 No. 1, pp. 13–60.

Bettman, J.R. (1979), *An Information Processing Theory of Consumer Choice*, Addison-Wesley, Reading, MA.

Bitner, M.J. (1992), 'Serviscapes: the impact of physical surroundings on customers and employees', *Journal of Marketing*, Vol. 56, April, pp. 57–71.

Bitner, M.J. (1995), 'Building service relationships: it's all about promises', *Journal of the Academy of Marketing Science*, Vol. 23 No. 4, pp. 246–51.

Boulding, W., Kalra, A., Staelin, R. and Zeithaml, V.A. (1989), 'A dynamic process model of service quality: from expectations to behavioral intentions', *Journal of Marketing Research*, Vol. 30, February, pp. 7–27.

Brown, S.W. and Swartz, T.A. (1989), 'A gap analysis of professional services quality', *Journal of Marketing*, Vol. 54, April, pp. 92–8.

Calonius, H. (1988), 'A buying process model', in Blois, K. and Parkinson, S. (Eds), *Innovative Marketing – A European Perspective, Proceedings of the XVIIth Annual Conference of the European Marketing Academy*, University of Bradford, England.

Chandon, J.-L., Leo, P.-Y. and Philippe, J. (1997), 'Service encounter dimensions – a dyadic perspective. Measuring the dimensions of service encounters as perceived by customers and personnel', *International Journal of Service Industry Management*, Vol. 8 No. 1, pp. 65–86.

Christopher, M., Payne, A. and Ballantyne, D. (1992), *Relationship Marketing. Bringing Quality, Customer Service and Marketing Together*, Butterworth, London.

Coffey, A. and Atkinson, P. (1996), *Making Sense of Qualitative Data. Complementary Research Strategies*, Sage Publications, Thousand Oaks, CA.

Cowell, D. (1985), *The Marketing of Services*, Heinemann, London.

Cronin, J.J. Jr and Taylor, S.A. (1994), 'SERVPERF versus SERVQUAL: reconciling performance-based and perceptions-minus-expectations measurement of service quality', *Journal of Marketing*, Vol. 58, January, pp. 125–31.

Crosby, L.A., Evans, K. and Cowles, D. (1990), 'Relationship quality in personal selling: an interpersonal influence perspective', *Journal of Marketing*, Vol. 54, July, pp. 68–81.

Eiglier, P. and Langeard, E. (1976), *Principes Politiques de Marketing pour les Enterprises de Service*, Working paper, Institute d'Administration des Enterprises, Université d'Aix-Marseille, December.

Eiglier, P. and Langeard, E. (1981), 'A conceptual approach of the service offering', in Larsen, H., Hanne, H. and Søren (Eds), *Proceedings of the Xth EAARM Annual Conference*, Copenhagen School of Economics and Business Administration, May.

Gardial, S.F., Clemons, D., Woodruff, D.W., Schumann, D.W. and Burns, M.J. (1994), 'Comparing consumers' recall of prepurchase and postpurchase product evaluations experiences', *Journal of Consumer Research*, Vol. 20, March, pp. 548–60.

Grönroos, C. (1982), *Strategic Management and Marketing in the Service Sector*, Swedish School of Economics Finland, Helsingfors, published in 1983 in the USA by Marketing Science Institute and in the UK by Studentlitteratur/Chartwell-Bratt.

Grönroos, C. (1984), 'A service quality model and its marketing implications', *European Journal of Marketing*, Vol. 18 No. 4, pp. 36–44.

Grönroos, C. (1990), *Service Management and Marketing. Managing the Moments of Truth in Service Competition*, Lexington Books, Lexington, MA.

Grönroos, C. (1993), 'Toward a third phase in service quality research', in Swartz, T.A., Bowen, D.A. and Brown, S.W. (Eds), *Advances in Services Marketing and Management Vol. 2*, JAI Press, Greenwich, CT, pp. 49–64.

Grönroos, C. (1996), 'The relationship marketing logic', *Asia-Australia Marketing Journal*, Vol. 4 No. 1, pp. 7–18.

Grönroos, C. (1997), 'Value-driven relational marketing: from products to resources and competencies', *Journal of Marketing Management*, Vol. 13 No. 5, pp. 407–19.

Grönroos, C. and Gummesson, E. (1985), 'The Nordic School of Service Marketing', in Grönroos, C. and Gummesson, E. (Eds), *Service Marketing – Nordic School Perspectives*, Stockholm University, Sweden, pp. 6–11.

Gummesson, E. (1977), *Marknadsföring och inköp av konsulttjänster* (Marketing and Purchasing of Professional Services), Akademilitteratur, Stockholm, Sweden.

Gummesson, E. (1990), *The Part-Time Marketer*, Center for Service Research, Karlstad, Sweden.

Gummesson, E. (1991), 'Marketing revisited: the crucial role of the part-time marketers', *European Journal of Marketing*, Vol. 25 No. 2, pp. 60–7.

Gummesson, E. (1995), *Relationsmarknadsföring. Från 4 P till 30 R (Relationship Marketing. From 4P to 30 R)*, Liber-Hermods, Stockholm, Sweden.

Håkansson, H. and Snehota, I. (1995), *Developing Relationships in Business Networks*, Routledge, London.

Johnson, C. and Mathews, B.P. (1997), 'The influence of experience on service expectations', *International Journal of Service Industry Management*, Vol. 8 No. 4, pp. 290–305.

Kotler, P. (1991), *Marketing Management. Analysis, Planning, and Control*, 7th edition, Prentice-Hall, Englewood Cliffs, NJ.

Lapierre, J. (1996), 'Service quality: the construct, its dimensionality and measurement', in Swartz, T.A., Bowen, D.E. and Brown, S.W. (Eds), *Advances in Services Marketing and Management Vol. 5*, JAI Press, Greenwich, CT, pp. 45–70.

Lehtinen, J.R. (1983), *Asiakasohjautuva palveluyritys (Customer-driven Service Firm)*, Weilin+Göös, Espoo, Finland.

Lehtinen, U. and Lehtinen, J.R. (1991), 'Two approaches to service quality dimensions', *The Service Industry Journal*, Vol. 11 No. 3, pp. 287–303.

Levitt, T. (1983), 'After the sale is over', *Harvard Business Review*, Vol. 61, September-October, pp. 87–93.

Liljander, V. (1995), *Comparison Standards in Perceived Service Quality*, Diss., Research report A:63, CERS Center for Relationship Marketing and Service Management, Swedish School of Economics Finland, Helsingfors.

Mattsson, L-G. (1997), '"Relationship marketing" and the "market-as-networks approach": a comparison analysis of two evolving streams of research', *Journal of Marketing Management*, Vol. 13 No. 5, pp. 447–61.

Oliver, R.L. (1993), 'A conceptual model of service quality and service satisfaction: compatible goals, different concepts', in Swartz, T.A., Bowen, D.A. and Brown, S.W. (Eds), *Advances in Services Marketing and Management Vol. 2*, JAI Press, Greenwich, CT.

Palmer, E. (1997), *Aspects of Professional Service Quality: A Focus on Customer Satisfaction including Relationship Impacts*, diss., The University of Auckland, New Zealand.

Parasuraman, A., Zeithaml, V.A. and Berry, L.L. (1985), 'A conceptual model of service quality and its implications for further research', *Journal of Marketing*, Vol. 49, Fall, pp. 41–50.

Parasuraman, A., Zeithaml, V.A. and Berry, L.L. (1988), 'SERVQUAL: a multiple-item scale for measuring consumer perceptions of service quality', *Journal of Retailing*, Vol. 64 No. 1, pp. 12–37.

Parasuraman, A., Zeithaml, V.A. and Berry, L.L. (1994), 'Reassessment of expectations as a comparison standard in measuring service quality: implications for future research', *Journal of Marketing*, Vol. 58, January, pp. 111–24.

Peppers, D. and Rogers, M. (1993), *One-to-One Future: Building Relationships One Customer at a Time*, Currency/Doubleday, New York, NY.

Persson, J.E. and Lindquist, H. (1997), *Kundupplevd kvalitet i tjänsteverksamheter. En analys och kritik av den företagsekonomiska dialogen (Customer Perceived Quality in Services. Analysis and Criticism of the Dialogue in Business Research)*, Lund University, Sweden.

Price, L.L., Arnould, E.J. and Tierney, P. (1995), 'Going to extremes: managing service encounters and assessing provider performance', *Journal of Marketing*, Vol. 59, April, pp. 83–97.

Sheth, J.N. and Parvatiyar, A. (1995), 'The evolution of relationship marketing', *International Business Review*, Vol. 4 No. 4, pp. 397–418.

Spreng, R.A. and Mackoy, R.D. (1996), 'An empirical examination of a model of perceived service quality and satisfaction', *Journal of Retailing*, Vol. 72 No. 2, pp. 201–14.

Teas, R.K. (1993), 'Expectations, performance evaluation, and consumers' perception of quality', *Journal of Marketing*, Vol. 57, October, pp. 18–34.

Tse, D.K. and Wilton, P.C. (1988), 'Models of consumer satisfaction formation: an extension', *Journal of Marketing Research*, Vol. 25, May, pp. 204–12.

Webster, F.E. Jr (1994), 'Executing the new marketing concept', *Marketing Management*, Vol. 3 No. 1, pp. 9–18.

Part Two
Articles on Relationship Marketing

6

Relationship Approach to Marketing in Service Contexts: The Marketing and Organizational Behavior Interface

A relationship approach to marketing is described. Marketing in a service context, i.e., concerning both service firms and service operations of manufacturers, is considered especially. The traditional view of marketing as a function for specialists planning and executing a marketing mix may not be altogether true when services are concerned. Instead, marketing can be considered as revolving around relationships, some of which are like single transactions, narrow in scope and not involving much or any social relationship (e.g., marketing soap or breakfast cereals). Other relationships, on the other hand, are broader in scope and may involve even substantial social contacts and be continuous and enduring in nature (e.g., marketing financial or hospitality services). The nature of a relationship marketing strategy is explored. Two interfaces between marketing and organizational behavior, both as business functions and as academic disciplines, which follow from this approach to marketing are discussed, viz., the need for a

Reprinted from the *Journal of Business Research*, vol. **20**(1), Grönroos, C. Relationship Approach to Marketing in Service Contexts: The Marketing and Organizational Behavior Interface, Copyright © 1990, pp. 3–11, with permission from Elsevier.

service culture, and internal marketing. These areas represent a major challenge for marketing and organizational behavior, practitioners and academic alike, to remove traditional borderlines and work together.

Introduction

The purpose of this article is to describe the nature and contents of the marketing function in a service organization and how this function is related to other business functions and academic disciplines, especially to personnel and organizational behavior. The approach is that of what internationally has been called the *Nordic School of Services*, originating in Scandinavia/Northern Europe (see, e.g., Grönroos, 1983; and Grönroos and Gummesson, 1985). The expression *service contexts* implies all types of service activities, irrespective of whether they occur in so-called service firms or in public institutions, not-for-profit organizations, or manufacturers of goods.

The Traditional Role of Marketing

Traditionally, marketing is viewed as an intermediate function, where the specialists of the marketing department are the only persons who have an impact on the customers' views of the firm and on their buying behavior. Employees in other departments are neither recruited nor trained to think marketing, nor are they supervised so that they would feel any marketing responsibilities. In this approach, the core of marketing is the marketing mix. In many consumer packaged goods situations, this conceptualization of marketing functions sufficiently well. If the product is a preproduced item with no needs for service or other contacts between the firm and its customers, marketing specialists are clearly capable of taking care of the customer relationships. Good market research, packaging, promotion, pricing, and distribution decisions by the marketing specialists lead to good results.

As a general framework, the 4 P's of the marketing mix (introduced by McCarthy [1960] based on Borden's [e.g., 1965] and Culliton's [1948] notions of the marketer as a 'mixer of ingredients'), in spite of its pedagogical virtues, is far too simplistic and may easily misguide both academics and practitioners; and it has never been empirically tested (compare Cowell, 1984, Grönroos, 1989; Kent, 1986). Particularly in services marketing, and also in industrial marketing, the marketing mix approach frequently does not cover all resources and activities that appear in the customer relationships at various stages of the customer relationship life cycle (see Grönroos, in press, 1983, 1989; Grönroos and Gummesson, 1986, Gummesson, 1987a,b, as well as Hakansson, 1982; Hakansson and Snehota, 1976, Kent, 1986, Webster, 1982). Especially during the consumption process, there is a range of contacts between the service firm and its customer, which are outside the traditional marketing function as defined by the P's of the marketing mix (compare Rathmell, 1974). Managing and operating these contacts (e.g., with bank and hotel facilities, automatic teller machines, waiters, air stewardesses, telephone receptionists and bus drivers, R&D people, design engineers, maintenance people, etc.) are the responsibilities of operations and other nonmarketing departments only. However, these buyer–seller interactions or interfaces, or the service encounter, have an immense impact on the future buying behavior of the customers as well as on word of mouth, and, therefore, they should be considered marketing resources and activities. The marketing function is spread throughout the entire organization (Gummesson, 1987a), and the customers take an active part in the production process.

A Relationship Approach to the Buyer–Seller Interface

Far too often, customers are seen in terms of numbers. When someone stops being a customer, there are new potential customers to take the empty place. Customers, individuals, and organizations alike are numbers only. In reality, this is, of course, not true. Every single customer forms a customer relationship with the seller that is broad or narrow in scope, continuous or discrete, short or lasting in nature, which the firm has to develop and maintain. Customer relationships are not just there; they have to be earned. According to an alternative approach to defining marketing, this function is considered to revolve around customer relationships, where the objectives of the parties involved are met through various kinds of exchanges, which take place in order to establish and maintain such relationships.

Especially long-term relationships with customers are important (Gummesson, 1987b). In services, as in general, short-term relationships, where the customers come and go, are normally more expensive to develop. The marketing budget needed to create an interest in the firm's offerings and make potential customers accept the firm's promises are often very high. As Berry (1983) observes, 'clearly, marketing to protect the customer base is becoming exceedingly important to a variety of service industries' (p. 25). This holds true for industrial marketing as well (see Hakansson, 1982, Jackson, 1985). This is not to say that new customers who perhaps make one purchase only would not be desirable, but it means, however, that the emphasis should be on developing and maintaining enduring, long-term customer relationships. Berry (1983) introduced the concept of relationship marketing, as opposed to transaction marketing, to describe such a long-term approach to marketing strategy (see also Crosby *et al.*, 1988; Gummesson, 1987b, Rosenberg and Czepiel, 1984). If close and long-term relationships can be achieved, the possibility is high that this will lead to continuing exchanges, requiring lower marketing costs per customer.

A Relationship Definition of Marketing

The marketing concept as the basic philosophy guiding marketing in practice still holds. The marketing mix approach to transferring this concept to marketing in practice is, however, considered too simplistic and too narrow in scope to be more than partly useful in most service situations. In conclusion to this discussion we formulate a relationship definition of marketing (Grönroos, in press, 1989, also compare Gummesson 1987a,b; Berry, 1983). This definition states that

> Marketing is to establish, maintain, enhance and commercialize customer relationships (often but not necessarily always long term relationships) so that the objectives of the parties involved are met. This is done by a mutual exchange and fulfillment of promises

Furthermore, this definition can be accompanied by the following supplement. The resources of the seller—personnel, technology and systems—have to be used in such a manner that the customer's trust in the resources involved and, thus, in the firm itself is maintained and strengthened. The various resources the customer encounters in the relation may be of any kind and part of any business function. However, these resources and activities cannot be totally predetermined and explicitly categorized in a general definition.

The concept of promises as an integral part of marketing vocabulary has been stressed by the Finnish researcher Calonious (1986, 1988). In establishing and maintaining customer relationships, the seller gives a set of promises concerning, e.g., goods, services or systems of goods and services, financial solutions, materials administration, transfer of information, social contacts, and a range of future commitments. On the other hand, the buyer gives another set of promises concerning his commitments in the relationship. Then, the promises have to be kept on both sides, if the relationship is expected to be maintained and enhanced for the mutual benefits of the parties involved.

Long-term customer relationships mean that the objective of marketing is mainly to go for enduring relationships with the customers. Of course, in some situations, short-term sales—what sometimes is called transaction marketing—may be profitable (see, e.g., Jackson, 1985). However, generally speaking, the long-term scope is vital to profitable marketing. Thus, commercializing the customer relationships means that the cost–benefit ratio of transactions of goods, services, or systems of goods and services is positive at least in the long run.

Establishing, maintaining and enhancing customer relationships, respectively, implies that the marketing situation is different depending on how far the customer relationships have developed. From the service provider's point of view, 1) establishing a relationship involves giving promises, 2) maintaining a relationship is based on fulfillment of promises, and, finally, 3) enhancing a relationship means that a new set of promises are given with the fulfillment of earlier promises as a prerequisite.

This relationship definition of marketing does not say that the traditional elements of the marketing mix, such as advertising, personal selling, pricing, and conceptualizing of the product, are less important than earlier. However, it demonstrates that so much else may be of importance to marketing than the means of competition of the marketing mix. It is based on how to develop and execute good marketing performance, rather than just on what decisions to make to do marketing.

Implications of the Relationship Approach to Marketing

A distinct difference exists between handling the moments of truth (to use an expression introduced in the service management literature by Normann, 1984) of the buyer–seller interactions as a marketing task and executing traditional marketing activities, such as advertising, personal selling, and sales promotion. Normally, the latter are planned and implemented by marketing and sales specialists. On the other hand, the former tasks are implemented by persons who are specialists in other fields. Moreover, how the moments of truth are carried out is frequently planned and managed by nonmarketing managers and supervisors. To put it bluntly, the moments of truth with their tremendous marketing impacts are frequently both managed and executed by people who neither are aware of their marketing responsibilities nor are interested in customers and marketing.

The employees involved in marketing as nonspecialists have been called 'part-time marketers' by Gummesson (1981, 1987a; compare also Grönroos, 1988). They are, of course, specialists in their areas, and they are supposed to remain so. At the same time, however, they will have to learn to perform their tasks in a marketinglike manner so that the customers will want to return, and the customer relationships are strengthened. Hence, they, and their bosses as well, will have to learn to think in terms of marketing and customer impact.

The marketing aspect of the moments of truth is related to interactive processes, and, therefore, this part of marketing is called the Interactive Marketing Function (see, e.g., Grönroos, 1980, 1983). The impact of the 'part-time marketers' as well as the customer orientation of systems, technology, and physical resources is paramount to the success of interactive marketing. Hence, the interactive marketing function recognizes that every component—human as well as other—in producing a service, every production resource used and every stage in the service production and delivery process, should be the concern of marketing as well, and not considered operations or personnel problems only. The marketing consequences of every resource and activity involved in interactive marketing situations have to be acknowledged in the planning process, so that the production resources and operations support and enhance the organization's attempts to develop and maintain relationships with its customers.

As Gummesson (in press) observes, 'there is extreme interdependence between the traditional departments of a service firm—production, delivery, personnel, administration, finance, etc—and marketing'. For example, marketing, personnel, operations, and technological development have to go hand in hand. These functions are linked together by the common objective of providing customers with good service. As Schneider and Rentsch (1987) formulate it, service has to become an 'organizational imperative.' Here, we shall only focus upon one interrelationship between business functions, the one between marketing and personnel/organizational behavior. Because the marketing impact of the 'part-time marketers' is crucial, efforts have to be made to secure service orientation and marketing-oriented attitudes and corresponding skills among the personnel. Next, we are going to discuss, very briefly, two important and interrelated aspects of human resources development that emerge from a service-oriented and relationship-oriented approach to marketing.

The Need for a Service Culture

In a service context a strong and well-established corporate culture, which enhances an appreciation for good service and customer orientation, is extremely important (e.g., Bowen and Schneider, 1988, George and Grönroos, in press, Grönroos, in press, Schneider, 1986). This follows from the nature of services. Normally, service production cannot be standardized as completely as an assembly line, because of the human impact on the buyer–seller interface. Customers and their behavior cannot be standardized and totally predetermined. The situations vary, and, therefore, a distinct service-oriented culture is needed that tells employees how to respond to new, unforeseen and even awkward situations (Schneider, 1986). The culture has a vital impact on how service-oriented its employees are and, thus, how well they act as 'part-time marketers' (Bowen and Schneider, 1988).

Internal projects or activities, such as service or marketing training programs, probably have no significant impact on the thinking and behavior of, e.g., employees of firms where goods-oriented standards are regarded highly. Moreover, Schneider and Bowen (1985) have found that when employees identify with the norms and values of an organization, they are less inclined to quit, and, furthermore, customers seem to be more satisfied with the service. In addition to this, 'when employee turnover is minimized, service values and norms are more transmitted to newcomers and successive generations of service employees' (Bowen and Schneider, 1988, p. 63).

Developing a service culture is clearly a means of creating and enhancing good interactive marketing performance needed for implementing a relationship marketing strategy. The corporate culture issue is closely linked to another personnel-related issue that has emerged from the research into services marketing. This is internal marketing.

The Need for Internal Marketing

During the past 10 years or so, the concept of internal marketing has emerged first in the literature on services marketing (see, e.g., Berry, 1981; Compton et al., 1987, George et al., 1987, George and Grönroos, in press; Grönroos, 1978, 1981, 1985, see also Eiglier and Langeard, 1976), and then was adopted by the service management literature (see, e.g., Carlzon, 1987, Normann, 1984), and also found to be valuable in industrial marketing (Grönroos and Gummesson, 1985).

Heskett (1987) recently touches upon this phenomenon as well observing that 'high-performing service companies have gained their status in large measure by turning the strategic service vision inward' (pp. 120–121). An increasing number of firms have recognized the need for internal marketing programs. Maybe the most spectacular internal marketing process is the one implemented by Scandinavian Airline System (SAS) (Carlzon, 1987). Today, internal marketing is considered a prerequisite for successful external marketing (see, e.g., Compton et al., 1987; Grönroos, 1985).

First of all, internal marketing is a management philosophy. Management should create, continuously encourage, and enhance an understanding of and an appreciation for the roles of the employees in the organization. Employees should have holistic views of their jobs. This is illustrated by an anecdote told by Jan Carlzon, president and CEO of SAS, about two stone cutters who were chipping square blocks out of granite. 'A visitor to the quarry asked what they were doing. The first stone cutter, looking rather sour, grumbled, "I'm cutting this damned stone into a block". The second, who looked pleased with his work, replied proudly, "I'm on this team that's building a cathedral."' (Carlzon, 1987, p. 135) (It is interesting to notice that in slightly different words, this anecdote is also told by Michail Gorbatjov in his book on the perestroika in the Soviet Union [Gorbatjov, 1987]).

The focus of internal marketing is on how to get and retain customer-conscious employees. It is also a means of developing and maintaining a service culture, although internal marketing alone is not sufficient (see George and Grönroos, in press, Grönroos, 1989). Goods and services as well as specific external marketing campaigns, new technology, and new systems of functioning have to be marketed to employees before these goods and services are marketed externally. Every organization has an internal market of employees, which first has to be successfully taken care of. Unless this is done properly, the success of the organization's operations on its ultimate, external markets will be jeopardized. To put it in the words of Heskett (1987), 'Effective service requires people who understand the idea' (p. 124).

Conclusions

Joint Challenges for Marketing and Organizational Behavior

Clearly, the tasks of developing and maintaining a service culture and of internal marketing offer an important interface between marketing and organizational behavior. Hence, they also offer an arena where marketing practitioners and academics on one hand, and personnel and human resources development people and academics from the field of organizational behavior on the other hand, are challenged to work together.

This, of course, requires that among other things, the traditional borderlines that far too often have become insurmountable walls between marketing and personnel as business functions and as academic disciplines are challenged and, if necessary, torn down.

References

Berry, Leonard L, Relationship Marketing, in *Emerging Perspectives on Services Marketing* L L Berry et al., eds, American Marketing Association, Chicago, 1983, pp. 25–28.

Berry, Leonard L, The Employee as Customer, *Journal of Retail Banking* 3 (March 1981) 33–40.

Borden, Neil H, The Concept of the Marketing Mix, in *Science in Marketing* G Schwartz, ed, Wiley, New York, 1965.

Bowen, David E, and Schneider, Benjamin, Services Marketing and Management Implications for Organizational Behavior, in *Research in Organizational Behavior* B Stow and L L Cummings, eds, JAI Press, Greenwich, CT, Vol 10, 1988.

Calonius, Henrik, A Buying Process Model, in *Innovative Marketing—A European perspective* K Blois and S Parkinson, eds, Proceedings from the XVII Annual Conference of the European Marketing Academy, University of Bradford, England, 1988.

Calonius, Henrik, A Market Behaviour Framework, in *Contemporary Research in Marketing* K Moller and M Paltschik, eds, Proceedings from the XV Annual Conference of the European Marketing Academy, Helsinki, Finland, 1986.

Carlzon, Jan, *Moments of Truth*, Ballinger, New York, 1987.

Compton, Fran, George, William R, Grönroos, Christian, and Karvinen, Matti, Internal Marketing, in *The Service Challenge Integrating for Competitive Advantage* J A Czepiel et al., eds, American Marketing Association, Chicago, 1987, pp. 7–12.

Cowell, Donald, *The Marketing of Services*, Heineman, London, 1984.

Crosby, Lawrence A, Evans, Ken R, and Cowles, Deborah, *Relationship Quality in Service Selling An Interpersonal Influence Perspective*, Working Paper No 5, First Interstate Center for Services Marketing, Arizona State University, 1988.

Culliton, John W, *The Management of Marketing Costs*, The Andover Press, Andover, MA, 1948.

Deshpande, R, and Webster, Jr, Frederick E, *Organizational Culture and Marketing Defining the Research Agenda* Report No 87–106 Marketing Science Institute, Cambridge, MA, 1987.

Eiglier, Pierre, and Langeard, Eric, *Principles Politique Marketing pour les Enterprises des Service*, Working Paper, Institut d'Administration des Enterprises, Aix-en-Provence, France, 1976.

George, William, R, Internal Communications Programs as a Mechanism for Doing Internal Marketing, in *Creativity in Services Marketing* V Venkatesan et al., eds, American Marketing Association, Chicago, 1986, pp. 83–84.

George, William R, Internal Marketing for Retailers The Junior Executive Employee, in *Developments in Marketing Science* J D Lindqvist, ed, Academy of Marketing Science, 1984, Vol VII, pp. 322–325.

George, William R, and Grönroos, Christian, Developing Customer-Conscious Employees at Every Level: Internal Marketing, in *Handbook of Services Marketing* C A Congram and M L Friedman, eds, AMACON, in press.

Gorbatjov, Mikhail, *Perestroika—New Thinking for our Country and the World*, Harper & Row, New York, 1987.

Grönroos, Christian, Defining Marketing. A Market-Oriented Approach, *European Journal of Marketing* 23 (1989) 52–60.

Grönroos, Christian, New Competition of the Service Economy. The Five Rules of Service, *International Journal of Operations & Production Management* 8 (1988) 9–19.

Grönroos, Christian, Internal Marketing—Theory and Practice, in *Services Marketing in a Changing Environment* T M Bloch et al., ed, American Marketing Association, Chicago, 1985, pp. 41–47.

Grönroos, Christian, *Strategic Management and Marketing in the Service Sector*, Marketing Science Institute, Cambridge, MA, 1983.

Grönroos, Christian, Internal Marketing—An Integral Part of Marketing Theory, in *Marketing of Services* J H Donnelly and W R George, eds, American Marketing Association, Chicago, 1981, pp. 236–238.

Grönroos, Christian, Designing a Long Range Marketing Strategy for Services, *Long Range Planning* 13 (April 1980) 36–42.

Grönroos, Christian, A Service-Oriented Approach to Marketing of Services, *European Journal of Marketing* 12 (1978) 588–601.

Grönroos, Christian, *Service Management and Marketing Managing the Moments of Truth in Service Competition* Lexington, MA D C Heath Lexington Books, in press.

Grönroos, Christian, and Gummesson, Evert, Service Orientation in Industrial Marketing, in *Creativity in Services Marketing What's New, What Works, What's Developing*, American Marketing Association, Chicago, 1986, pp. 23–26.

Grönroos, Christian, and Gummesson, Evert, eds *Service Marketing—Nordic School Perspectives*, Stockholm University, Sweden, 1985.

Gummesson, Evert, The New Marketing—Developing Long-Term Interactive Relationships, *Long Range Planning* 20 (1987a) 10–20.

Gummesson, Evert, *Marketing—A Long Term Interactive Relationship Contribution to a New Marketing Theory*, Marketing Technique Center, Stockholm, Sweden, 1987b.

Gummesson, Evert, Marketing Cost Concept in Service Firms, *Industrial Marketing Management* 10 (1981) 175–182.

Gummesson, Evert, Organizing for Marketing and Marketing Organizations, in *Handbook on Services Marketing* C A Congram and M L Friedman, eds, Amacon, New York, in press.

Hakansson, Hakan, ed *International Marketing and Purchasing of Industrial Goods*, Wiley, New York, 1982.

Hakansson, Hakan, and Snehota, Ivan, *Marknadsplanering Ett satt att skapa nya problem?* (Marketing Planning A Way of Creating New Problems?), Studentlitteratur, Malmo, Sweden, 1976.

Heskett, James L, Lessons in the Service Sector, *Harvard Business Review* 65 (March–April 1987) 118–126.

Jackson, Barbara B, Build Customer Relationships That Last, *Harvard Business Review* 63 (November–December 1985) 120–128.

Kent, Ray A, Faith in Four Ps: An Alternative, *Journal of Marketing Management* 2 (1986) 145–154.

Kotler, Philip, *Marketing Management, Analysis, Planning, and Control* Prentice-Hall, Englewood Cliffs, NJ, 1984.

Levitt, Theodore, After the Sale is Over, *Harvard Business Review* 61 (September–October 1983) 87–93.

McCarthy, E Jerome, *Basic Marketing*, Irwin, Homewood, IL, 1960.

Normann, Richard, *Service Management*, Wiley, New York, 1984.

Rathmell, John R, *Marketing in the Service Sector*, Winthrop, Cambridge, MA, 1974.

Rosenberg, Larry J, and Czepiel, John A, A Marketing Approach for Customer Retention, *The Journal of Consumer Marketing* 1 (1984) 45–51.

Schneider, Benjamin, Notes on Climate and Culture, in *Creativity in Services Marketing, What's New, What Works, What's Developing* F Venkatesan et al., eds, American Marketing Association, Chicago, IL, 1986, pp. 63–67.

Schneider, Benjamin, and Bowen, David E, Employee and Customer Perceptions of Service in Banks. Replication and Extension, *Journal of Applied Psychology* 70 (1985) 423–433.

Schneider, Benjamin, and Rentsch, J, The Management of Climate and Culture A Futures Perspective, in *Futures of Organizations* J Hage, ed, D C Health Lexington Books, Lexington, MA, 1987.

Webster, Jr, Fredrick E, Management Science in Industrial Marketing, *Journal of Marketing* 1 (January 1978) 21–27.

7

Quo Vadis, Marketing? Toward a Relationship Marketing Paradigm

The marketing mix and its 4Ps have remained the marketing paradigm for decades. In the article it is argued that the foundation for this paradigm is weak and that it has had negative effects on marketing research and practice. Contemporary research into services marketing and industrial marketing demonstrates that a new approach to marketing is required. This new approach is based on building and management of relationships. A paradigm shift in marketing is under way. The thoughts and actions of marketing academics and practitioners should not be constrained by a paradigm from the 1950s and 1960s.

Introduction

The first true analytical contribution to marketing was probably made by Joel Dean (e.g. 1951), an economist. However, marketing the way most textbooks treat it today was introduced around 1960. The concept of the *marketing mix* and the four P's of marketing—product, price, place and promotion—entered the marketing textbooks at that time (McCarthy 1960). Quickly they also became the unchallenged basic *theory of marketing* so totally overpowering previous models and approaches, such as, for example, the organic *functionalist* approach advocated by Wroe Alderson (1950 and 1957) as well as other systems-oriented approaches (e.g. Fisk 1967 and Fisk and Dixon 1967) and the *institutional approach* (e.g. Duddy and Revzan 1947) that these are hardly remembered even

Grönroos, C. Quo Vadis, Marketing? Toward a Relationship Marketing Paradigm. *Journal of Marketing Management*, 1994; **10**(5): 347–360. Reproduced by permission of Westburn Publishers.

with a footnote in most textbooks of today. The American Marketing Association, in its most recent definition states that 'marketing is the process of planning and executing the *conception, pricing, promotion* and *distribution* of ideas, goods and services to create exchange and satisfy individual and organizational objectives' (emphasis added) AMA Board 1985).

For decades the four P's of the marketing mix became an indisputable paradigm in academic research, the validity of which was taken for granted (Kent 1986; Grönroos 1989 and 1990a). For most marketing researchers in large parts of the academic world it seems to remain the marketing truth even today. Kent (1986) refers to the four P's of the marketing mix as 'the holy quadruple . . . of the marketing faith . . . written in tablets of stone' (p. 146). As he argues, the mnemonic of the four P's, by offering a seductive sense of simplicity to students, teachers and practitioners of marketing, has become an article of faith" (p. 145). For an academic researcher looking for tenure and promotion, to question it has been to stick out his or her neck too far. And prospective authors of textbooks, who suggest another organization than the four P solution for their books, are quickly corrected by most publishers. As a result, empirical studies of what the key marketing variables are, and how they are perceived and used by marketing managers have been neglected. Moreover, structure has been vastly favoured over process considerations (Kent 1986).

In marketing education, teaching students how to use a toolbox has become the totally dominating task instead of discussing the meaning and consequences of the marketing concept and the process nature of market relationships. Marketing in practice has to a large extent been turned into managing this toolbox instead of truly exploring the nature of the firm's market relationships and genuinely taking care of the real needs and desires of customers.

What is the History of the Marketing Mix?

A paradigm like this has to be well founded by theoretical deduction and empirical research; otherwise much of marketing research is based on a loose foundation and the results of it questionable. Let us look at the history of the marketing mix paradigm and the four P's.

The marketing mix developed from a notion of the marketer as a 'mixer of ingredients', which was an expression originally used by James Culliton (1948) in a study of marketing costs in 1947 and 1948. The marketer plans various means of competitions and blends them into a 'marketing mix', so that a profit function is optimized, or rather satisfied. The 'marketing mix' concept was introduced by Neil Borden in the 1950s (e.g. Borden 1964), and the mix of different means of competitions was soon labelled the four P's (McCarthy 1960).*

The marketing mix is actually a list of categories of marketing variables, and to begin with, this way of defining or describing a phenomenon can never be considered a very valid one. A list never includes all relevant elements, it does not fit every situation, and it becomes obsolete. And indeed, marketing academics every now and then offer additional P's to the list, once they have found the standard 'tablet of faith' too limited. Kotler (1986) has, in the context of *megamarketing*, added *public relations* and *politics*, thus expanding the list to six P's. In service marketing, Booms and Bitner (1982) have suggested three additional P's, *people, physical evidence* and *process*. Judd (1987) among others, has argued for just one new P, *people*.† Advocators of the marketing mix paradigm sometimes have suggested that *service* should be added to the list of P's (e.g. Lambert and Harrington 1989 and Collier 1991).‡ It is, by the way, interesting to notice that after the four P's were definitely canonized sometime in the early 1970s new items to the list are almost exclusively put in the form of P's.§

It is also noteworthy that Borden's original marketing mix included 12 elements, and that this list was not intended to be a definition at all. Borden considered it guidelines only, which the marketer probably would have to reconsider in any given situation. In line with the 'mixer of ingredients' metaphor he also implied

---

*McCarthy was not, however, the first person to organize marketing variables in a four P-like structure. The first marketing textbook organized in this way was published by Harry Hansen (1956), where he used the following six categories: product policy, distribution channel, advertising, personal selling, pricing and sales programs (see Shugan, forthcoming).

† As a matter of fact, even in the homeland of the marketing mix there has been at least some debate about this paradigm. However, the basic way of handling the problem has always been to use the same clinical approach, i.e. to simplify the market relationship by developing a list of decision making variables. No real innovativeness and challenge of the foundation of the paradigm have been presented. In the 1960s and early 1970s, categories which did not begin with the letter P were suggested; e.g. Staudt and Taylor 1965, Lipson and Darling 1971 and Kelly and Lazer 1973 (three categories each), whereas the letter P almost always has been present in lists of categories put forward in the 1980s and 1990s; e.g. Traynor 1985 (five categories), Johnson 1986 (12), Keely 1987 (four C's), Berry 1990, Mason and Mayer 1990 (six), Collier 1991 (seven) and LeDoux 1991 (five).

‡This would be disastrous, because it would isolate customer service as a marketing variable from the rest of the organization, just as has happened with the four P marketing mix variables. It would effectively counteract all attempts to make customer service a responsibility of everyone and not of a separate department only.

§In spite of all the additional categories of marketing variables that have been offered by various authors, there is only one textbook that is thoroughly based on anything else than the four P's: Donald Cowell's (1984) book on the marketing of services which is organized around the seven P framework.

that the marketer would blend the various ingredients or variables of the mix into an integrated marketing program. This is a fact that advocators of the four P's (or five, six, seven or more P's) and of today's marketing mix approach seem to have totally forgotten.

In fact, the four P's represent a significant oversimplification of Borden's original concept. McCarthy either misunderstood the meaning of Borden's marketing mix when he reformulated the original list in the shape of the rigid mnemonic of the four P's where no blending of the P's is explicitly included; or his followers misinterpreted McCarthy's intentions. In many marketing textbooks organized around the marketing mix, such as Philip Kotler's well-known *Marketing Management* (e.g. 1991), the blending aspect and the need for integration of the four P's are discussed, even in depth, but such discussions are always limited due to the fact that the model does not explicitly include an integrative dimension.

The original idea of a list of a large number of marketing mix ingredients that have to be reconsidered in every given situation was probably shortened for pedagogical reasons and because a more limited number of marketing variables seemed to fit typical situations observed by the initiators of the short list of four standardized P's. These typical situations can be described as involving consumer packaged goods in a North American environment with huge mass markets, a highly competitive distribution system and very commercial mass media. However, in other markets the infrastructure is to varying degrees different and the products are only partly consumer packaged goods. Nevertheless the four P's of the marketing mix have become *the universal marketing theory* and an almost totally dominating *paradigm* for most academics, and they have had a tremendous impact on the practice of marketing as well. Is there any justification for this? Let us first look at the paradigm itself.

The Nature of the Marketing Mix

As has previously been said, the marketing mix is a list of variables, and we have already pointed out the shortcomings of such a way of defining a phenomenon. Moreover, any marketing paradigm should be well set to fulfil the *marketing concept*, i.e. the notion that the firm is best off by designing and directing its activities according to the needs and desires of customers in chosen target markets. How well is the marketing mix fit to do that?

One can easily argue that the four P's of the marketing mix are badly fit to fulfil the requirements of the marketing concept. As Dixon and Blois (1983) put it, '... indeed it would not be unfair to suggest that far from being concerned with a customer's interests (i.e. somebody *for whom* something is done) the views implicit in the four P approach is that the customer is somebody to *whom* something is done!' (emphasis added) (p. 4). To use a marketing metaphor, the marketing mix and its 4 P's constitute a *production-oriented* definition of marketing, and not a market-oriented or customer-oriented one (see Grönroos 1989 and 1990a). Moreover, although McCarthy (1960) recognizes the interactive nature of the P's, the model itself does not explicitly include any interactive elements. Furthermore, it does not indicate the nature and scope of such interactions.

The marketing mix makes marketing seem so easy to handle and organize. Marketing is separated from other activities of the firm and delegated to specialists who take care of the analysis, planning and implementation of various marketing tasks, such as market analysis, marketing planning, advertising, sales promotion, sales, pricing, distribution and product packaging. Marketing departments are created to take responsibility for the marketing function of the firm, sometimes together with outside specialists on, for example, market analysis and advertising. Both in the marketing literature and in everyday marketing vocabulary the expression *marketing department*, an organizational unit, is used as a synonym for *marketing function*, which is the process of taking care of the fulfilment of customer needs and desires. As a consequence, the rest of the organization is alienated from marketing, and the marketers are isolated from design, production, deliveries, technical service, complaints handling, and other activities of the firm.

In conclusion, the problems with the marketing mix paradigm are not the number or conceptualization of the decision variables, the P's, as the American Marketing Association as well as the authors of most publications criticising the marketing mix paradigm argue. Rather, the problem is of theoretical nature. The four P's and the whole marketing mix paradigm are, theoretically, based on a loose foundation, which in a recent *Journal of Marketing* article was demonstrated by van Watershoot and Van den Bulte (1992; see also Van den Bulte 1991 and Kent 1986). Many marketing-related phenomena are not included (Möller 1992), and as Johan Arndt (1980 and 1985) has concluded, marketing research remains narrow in scope and even myopic, and methodological issues become more important than substance matters. 'Research in marketing gives the impression of being based on a conceptually sterile and unimaginative positivism. . . . The consequence . . . is that most of the resources are directed toward less significant issues, overexplaining what we already know, and toward supporting and legitimizing the status quo.' (Arndt 1980, p. 399) Unfortunately, far too little has changed in mainstream marketing research since this was written over a decade ago.

The usefulness of the four P's as a general marketing theory for practical purposes is, to say the least, highly questionable. Originally, although they were largely based on empirical induction, they were probably developed under the influence of microeconomic theory and especially the theory of monopolistic competition of the 1930s (e.g. Chamberlin 1933), in order to add more realism to that theory. However, very soon the connection to microeconomic theory was cut off and subsequently totally forgotten. Theoretically, the marketing mix became just a list of P's without roots.

Marketing Variables in Economic Theory and in Parameter Theory

A closer analysis of the nature of the marketing mix shows that it is not a remarkable leap forward from microeconomic theory as developed 60 years ago. As Dixon and Blois (1983) observe, when discussing the work of Chamberlin (1933) and Joan Robinson (1933), '. . . thus Joan Robinson's . . . writing discusses the subdivision of market and the firm's response through the use of the price elements of the four P's. At the same time Chamberlin . . . recognizes that all aspects of the product, location, communication, as well as price may be altered with subsequent effects on demand' (p. 5). Chamberlin's basic decision variables were price, product and promotion, although in his theory of monopolistic competition, price was treated as the main variable. In this same tradition, for example, researchers such as Brems (1951) and Abbott (1955) added new decision variables to the traditional price variables of economic price theory. However, as Mickwitz (1959) observes, instead of price they '. . . have put quality in the centre of their systems' (p. 9). This is an interesting fact to observe today when quality again has become a key issue in business practice and research. For example, Abbott, who uses the term 'quality competition', has an astonishingly modern view of quality: 'The term "quality" will be used . . . in its broadest sense, to include all the qualitative elements in the competitive exchange process—*materials, design, services provided, location* and so forth' (Abbott 1955, p. 4) (emphasis added). The two other decision variables in his system were price and advertising (including sales promotion).

Later, but well before the four P's were formulated as the ultimate marketing wisdom for decades, Gösta Mickwitz (1959) and others (e.g. Kjaer-Hansen 1945 and Rasmussen 1955), representing a research approach for which Mickwitz (1966) coined the label 'Copenhagen School', discussed an expanded view along the same lines, which they labelled *parameter theory*. This theoretical approach, especially as it is presented by Gösta Mickwitz was, in fact, theoretically more developed and more realistic than the four P's of today's mainstream marketing literature. As Mickwitz (1959) observes, 'when empirically based works on marketing mechanisms show that the enterprise uses a number of different parameters markedly distinct from each other, a theory of the behaviour of the enterprise in the market will be very unrealistic if it is content to deal only with . . . (a few) . . . of them. We have therefore tried throughout to pay attention to the presence of a number of different methods which firms employ in order to increase their sales' (p. 237). The interactive nature of the marketing variables was explicitly recognized and accounted for in parameter theory by means of varying market elasticities of the parameters over the product life cycle.

The concept 'parameter theory' further developed by Mickwitz was originally suggested by Arne Rasmussen (1955). However, the foundation for it was laid much earlier by Frisch (1933), who in 1933 introduced the idea of *action parameters*, although he did not in detail discuss more parameters than price and quality. In 1939, von Stackelberg expanded the number of parameters into a larger system (von Stackelberg 1939). He did not, however, go into any details in his analysis. Although it had its shortcomings, parameter theory was a step forward towards managerial realism, and it also had a theoretical base due to its background in microeconomic theory.

In conclusion, when analysing the firm's use of marketing variables, it is not unfair to say that as the parameter theory of the 1950s was a definite leap forward from the expanded price theory in the form of, for example, Chamberlin's theory of monopolistic competition of the 1930s, the introduction of the four P's of the marketing mix with their simplistic view of reality can be characterized as a step back to the level of, in a sense equally simplistic, microeconomic theory of the 1930s.

Contemporary Theories of Marketing

In most marketing textbooks the marketing mix paradigm and its four P's are still considered *the* theory of marketing. And indeed, this is the case in much of the academic research into marketing, especially in North America but also to a considerable extent in other parts of the world as well. However, since the 1960s, alternative theories of marketing have been developed. As Möller (1992) observes in a recent overview of research traditions in marketing, 'from the functional view of marketing "mix" management our focus has extended to the strategic role of marketing, aspects of service marketing, political dimensions of channel management, interactions in industrial networks; to mention just a few evolving trends' (p. 197). Some of these theories have been based on studies of the market relationships of firms in specific types of industries. In this section the emerging theories and models of the *interaction/network approach to industrial marketing* and the *marketing of services* will be discussed. In the final section the *relationship marketing* concept will be described.

The *interaction/network* approach to industrial marketing originated in Sweden at Uppsala University during the 1960s (see, for example, Blankenburg and Holm 1990) and has since spread to a large number of European countries. Between the parties in a network various interactions take place, where exchanges and adaptations to each other occur. A flow of goods and information as well as financial and social exchanges takes place in the network. (See, for example, Håkansson 1982, Johanson and Mattsson 1985 and Kock 1991.) In such a network the role and forms of marketing are not very clear. All exchanges, all sorts of interactions have an impact on the position of the parties in the network. The interactions are not necessarily initiated by the seller—the marketer according to the marketing mix paradigm—and they may continue over a long period of time, for example, for several years.

The seller, who at the same time may be the buyer in a reciprocal setting, may of course employ marketing specialists, such as sales representatives, market communication people and market analysts but in addition to them a large number of persons in functions which according to the marketing mix paradigm are non-marketing, such as research and development, design, deliveries, customer training, invoicing and credit management, have a decisive impact on the marketing success of the 'seller' in the network. Gummesson (1987) has coined the term *part-time marketers* for such employees of a firm. He observes that in industrial markets and in service businesses, the part-time marketers typically outnumber several times the full-time marketers, i.e. the marketing specialists of the marketing and sales departments. Furthermore, he concludes that 'marketing and sales departments (the full-time marketers) are not able to handle more than a limited portion of the marketing *as its staff cannot be at the right place at the right time with the right customer contacts*' (Gummesson

1990, p. 13). Hence, the part-time marketers do not only outnumber the full-time marketers, the specialists; often they are the only marketers around.

In the early 1970s the *marketing of services* started to emerge as a separate area of marketing with concepts and models of its own geared to typical characteristics of services. In Scandinavia and Finland the *Nordic School of Services* more than research into this field elsewhere looked at the marketing of services as something that cannot be separated from overall management (see Grönroos and Gummesson 1985). In North America research into service marketing has to a much greater extent remained within the boundaries of the marketing mix paradigm, although it has produced some creative results (e.g. Berry 1983, Berry and Parasuraman 1991). Grönroos brought quality back into a marketing context by introducing the *perceived service quality* concept in 1982 (Grönroos 1982), and he introduced the concept of the *interactive marketing function* (Grönroos 1979 and 1982) to cover the marketing impact on the customer during the consumption process, where the consumer of a service typically interacts with systems, physical resources and employees of the service provider. In France, Langeard and Eiglier (e.g. 1987) developed the *servuction* concept for this system of interactions. These interactions occur between the customer and employees who normally are not considered marketing people, neither by themselves nor by their managers, and who do not belong to a marketing or sales department. Nevertheless, they are part-time marketers. In many situations long-lasting relationships between service providers and their customers may develop. Again, the marketing success of a firm is only partly determined by the 'full-time marketers'. In fact, the 'part-time marketers' of a service provider may often have a much more important impact on the future purchasing decisions of a customer than, for example, professional sales people or advertising campaigns (e.g. Gummesson 1987 and Grönroos 1990a).

The New Approaches and the Marketing Mix

The interaction and network approach of industrial marketing and modern service marketing approaches, especially the one by the Nordic School, clearly views marketing as an interactive process in a social context where *relationship building* and *management* is a vital cornerstone. They are in some respects clearly related to the systems-based approaches to marketing of the 1950s (compare, for example, Alderson 1957). The marketing mix paradigm and its four P's, on the other hand, is a much more clinical approach, which makes the seller the active part and the buyer and consumer passive. No personalized relationship with the producer and marketer of a product is supposed to exist, other than with professional sales representatives in some cases.

Obviously, this later view of marketing does not fit the reality of industrial marketing and the marketing of services very well. Moreover, the organizational approach inherent in the marketing mix paradigm that puts marketing in the hands of marketing specialists in a marketing department is not very useful either (see, for example, Piercy 1985, and Grönroos 1982 and 1990a). The psychological effect on the rest of the organization of a separate marketing department is, in the long run, often devastating to the development of a customer orientation or market orientation in a firm. A *marketing orientation* with, for example, high-budget advertising campaigns may be developed, but this does not necessarily have much to do with true *market orientation* and a real appreciation for the needs and desires of the customers. The existence or introduction of such a depart-ment may be a trigger that makes everybody else lose whatever little interest in the customers they may have had (Grönroos 1982). The marketing department approach to organizing the marketing function has isolated marketing from other business functions and vice versa. Therefore, it has made it difficult, often even impossible, to turn marketing into the 'integrative function' that would provide other departments with the market-related input needed in order to make the organization truly market-oriented and reach a stage of 'coordinated marketing' (compare Kotler 1991, pp. 19–24).

The development of innovative theories, models and concepts of industrial marketing (interaction/network approach) and service marketing has clearly demonstrated that the marketing mix paradigm and its four P's finally have reached the end of the road as *the universal* marketing theory. Marketing research can, again, make a similar leap forward as the development of parameter theory out of the price-dominated microeconomic theory was in the 1950s. Parameter theory with its theoretical analysis of market elasticities was at least to a consid-erable degree market oriented,[1] whereas from a theoretical point of view the marketing mix paradigm and the four P's turned the clock back.

From a management point of view the four P's, undoubtedly, may have been helpful. The use of various means of competition became more organized. However, the four P's were never applicable to all markets and to all types

---

[1] Gösta Mickwitz (1982) has even made an attempt to analyse an international marketing issue in the same tradition.

of marketing situations. The development of alternative marketing theories discussed above demonstrate that even from a management perspective, the marketing mix and its four P's became a problem. Their pedagogic elegance and deceiving sense of simplicity made practical marketing management look all too clinical and straight-forward even for actors in the consumer packaged goods field where they were originally intended to be used.

Consumer goods amounts to a considerable business, and there the four P's could still fulfil a function. However, many of the customer relationships of manufacturers of consumer goods are industrial-type relationships with wholesalers and retailers, and the retailers of consumer goods more and more consider themselves service providers. In such situations the four P's have less to offer even in the consumer goods field. Moreover, as far as the marketing of consumer goods from the manufacturer to the ultimate consumers is concerned, there is a growing debate whether one can continue to apply marketing in the traditional mass marketing way. Regis McKenna (1991), a respected marketing consultant and writer, concludes in a discussion about the decline in North America of advertising, the flagship of traditional marketing, that 'the underlying reasons behind... (this decline)... is advertising's dirty little secret: it serves no useful purpose. In today's market, advertising simply misses the fundamental point of marketing—adaptability, flexibility, and responsiveness' (p. 13). Undoubtedly, this is to take it a little bit to the extreme, but the point is well taken. An interest in turning anonymous masses of potential and existing customers into interactive relationships with well-defined customers is becoming increasingly important. However, the grip of the marketing mix paradigm as the 'marketing faith' is in many parts of the world so strong among academics working in the field of consumer goods marketing that this discussion seems to go on mostly between marketing practitioners (see, for example, Rapp and Collins 1990, McKenna 1991 and Clancy and Shulman 1991). In some standard marketing textbooks, though, one can already see some signs of these new concepts and approaches (e.g. Kotler 1991).

The Future: The Relationship Marketing Concept

The concept *relationship marketing* has emerged within the fields of service marketing and industrial marketing (e.g. Berry 1982, Jackson 1985a, Grönroos 1989 and 1990b, Grönroos 1991, and Gummesson 1987 and 1990). To a considerable extent both these approaches to marketing are based on establishing and maintaining relationships between sellers and buyers and other parties on the marketplace. Grönroos (1990a) defines relationship marketing in the following way: 'Marketing is to establish, maintain, and enhance . . . relationships with customers and other partners, at a profit, so that the objectives of the parties involved are met. This is achieved by a mutual exchange and fulfilment of promises' (p. 138). Such relationships are usually but not necessarily always long term.

An integral element of the relationship marketing approach is the *promise concept*, which has been strongly emphasized by Henrik Calonius (e.g. 1988). According to him the responsibilities of marketing do not only, or predominantly, including giving promises and thus persuading customers as passive counterparts on the marketplace to act in a given way. Fulfilling promises that have been given is equally important as a means of achieving customer satisfaction, retention of the customer base, and long-term profitability (compare also Reichheld and Sasser 1990). He also stresses the fact that promises are mutually given and fulfilled.

Relationship marketing is still in its infancy as a marketing concept. Its importance is recognized to a growing extent, however. Philip Kotler (1992) concludes in a recent article that 'companies must move from a short-term *transaction-oriented* goal to a long-term *relationship-building* goal' (p. 1). So far, there seems to be only two books for textbook purposes that are based on this emerging paradigm (Christopher *et al.*, 1992 in English and Blomqvist *et al.*, 1993 in Swedish). However, relationship marketing is clearly the underlying approach in several books on service marketing (e.g. Grönroos 1990a and Berry and Parasuraman 1991) and industrial marketing (e.g. Håkansson 1982, Jackson 1985b and Vavra 1992). In a growing number of articles relationship issues are addressed (e.g. Jackson 1985a, Gummesson 1987, Sonnenberg 1988, Grönroos 1989 and 1990b, Copulinsky and Wolf 1990 and Czepiel 1990) and conferences on relationship marketing are being arranged. The importance of relationship building is advancing even into books from the world of consumer goods marketing (see, for example, Rapp and Collins 1990). In the future, this marketing approach most certainly will be a focal point of marketing research, thus positioning itself as a leading marketing paradigm. However, remembering the damaging long-term effects of the marketing mix, hopefully it will not establish itself as the only one.

Some Final Observations

Why has the marketing mix paradigm and the four P model become such a straightjacket for marketers? The main reason for this is probably the pedagogical virtues of the four P's that makes teaching marketing so easy and straightforward. The simplicity of the model seduces teachers to toolbox thinking instead of constantly reminding them of the fact that marketing is a social process with far more facets than that. As a consequence of this researchers and marketing managers are also constrained by the simplistic nature of the four P's. The victims are marketing theory and customers.

The marketing mix paradigm served a function at one time in the development of marketing theory. However, when it established itself as the universal truth in marketing, it started to cause more harm than good. Most damaging is the fact that marketing and the marketers have become so isolated in the organization. Both from an organizational point of view and from a psychological standpoint the marketing department is off side. Relationship marketing requires the support of people in other departments and business functions to be effective and successful. Today, this is very difficult to achieve.

Furthermore, the marketing specialists organized in a marketing department may get alienated from the customers. Managing the marketing mix means relying on mass marketing. Customers become numbers for the marketing specialists, whose actions, therefore, are typically based on surface information obtained from market research reports and market share statistics. Frequently such 'full-time marketers' act without ever really having encountered a real customer.

The marketing department concept is obsolete and has to be replaced by some other way of organizing the marketing function, so that the organization shall have a chance to become market oriented. A traditional marketing department will always, in the final analysis, stay in the way of spreading market orientation and an interest in the customer throughout the organization (compare Piercy 1985, and Grönroos 1982 and 1990a).

Finally, the marketing mix paradigm and the four P's have alienated people in the rest of an organization from marketing and from the 'full-time marketers', and vice versa. The term marketing has become a burden for the marketing function. Managers as well as their subordinates in other departments and functions do not want to take part in the marketing function. But according to the relationship marketing approach and contemporary models of industrial marketing and service marketing they do undoubtedly belong to this function. The use of the marketing mix paradigm and the four P's has made it very difficult for the marketing function to earn credibility. Some firms have solved this problem not only by downscaling or altogether terminating their marketing departments but also by banning the use of the term marketing for the marketing function (compare Grönroos 1982). Perhaps we even need this kind of semantics.

In the final analysis, what we are experiencing today with the growing awareness of the relationship marketing approach is a return to the 'natural' systems-oriented way of managing customer relationships that existed before marketing became a far too clinical decision making discipline, and an overorganized and isolated function. But even if the marketing mix is dying as a dominating marketing paradigm and the four P model needs to be replaced, this does not mean that the P's themselves would be less valuable than before as marketing variables. For example, advertising, pricing and product branding will still be needed, but along with a host of other activities and resources. However, what marketing deserves is new approaches, new paradigms, which are more market oriented and where the customer indeed is the focal point as suggested by the marketing concept. After all, we experience the enormous change and complexity of the 1990s. Our thoughts and actions should not be constrained by a paradigm from the 1950s and 1960s.

References

Abbott, L. (1955), *Quality and Competition*, New York, NY, Columbia University Press.
Alderson (1950), 'Survival and Adjustment in Organized Behavior Systems'. In: *Theory of Marketing*, (Eds) Cox, R. and Alderson, W. (Homewood, IL), Irwin, pp. 65–88.
Alderson, W. (1957), *Marketing Behavior and Executive Action*. Homewood, IL, Irwin.
AMA Board Approves New Marketing Definition. *Marketing News*, 1 March 1985.
Arndt, J. (1980), 'Perspectives for a Theory in Marketing', *Journal of Business Research*, Vol. 9, No. 3, pp. 389–402.
Arndt, J. (1985), 'On Making Marketing Science More Scientific: Role of Orientations, Paradigms, Metaphors, and Puzzle Solving', *Journal of Marketing*, Vol. 49, Summer, pp. 11–23.
Berry, D. (1990), 'Marketing Mix for the 90's Adds an S and 2 C's to the 4 P's', *Marketing News*, 24 December p. 10.
Berry, L.L. (1983), 'Relationship Marketing'. In *Emerging Perspectives of Services Marketing*. (Eds) Berry, L.L., Shostack, G.L. and Upah, G.D. Chicago, IL, American Marketing Association, pp. 25–28.
Berry, L.L. and Parasuraman, A. (1991), *Marketing Services. Competing Through Quality*. Lexington, MA, Free Press/Lexington Books.
Blankenburg, D. and Holm, U. (1990), 'Centrala steg i utvecklingen av nätverks-synsättet inom Uppsalaskolan'. In: *Uppsalaskolan och dess rötter* (*The Uppsala school and its roots*), (Eds) Gunnarsson, E. and Wallerstedt, E., Uppsala University, Sweden.
Blomqvist, R., Dahl, J. and Haeger, T. (1993), *Relationsmarknadsföring. Strategi och metod för servicekonkurren.* (*Relationship marketing. Strategy and methods for service competition*). Göteborg, Sweden, IHM Förlag.

Booms, B.H. and Bitner, M.J. (1982), 'Marketing Strategies and Organization Structures for Service Firms'. In: *Marketing of Services*, (Eds) Donnelly, J.H. and George, W.R. (Chicago, IL), American Marketing Association, pp. 47–51.

Borden, N.H. (1964), 'The Concept of the Marketing Mix'. *Journal of Advertising Research*, Vol. 4, June, pp. 2–7.

Brems, H. (1951), *Product Equilibrium under Monopolistic Competition*, Cambridge, MA, Harvard University Press.

Bruner, II, G.C. (1980), 'The Marketing Mix: Time for Reconceptualization', *Journal of Marketing Education*, Vol. 11, Summer, pp. 72–77.

Calonius, H. (1988), 'A Buying Process Model'. In: *Innovative Marketing—A European Perspective*. (Eds) Blois, K. and Parkinson, S. Proceedings from the XVIIth Annual Conference of the European Marketing Academy, University of Bradford, England, pp. 86–103.

Chamberlin, E.H. (1933), *The Theory of Monopolistic Competition*, Cambridge, MA, Harvard University Press.

Christopher, M., Payne, A. and Ballantyne, D. (1992), *Relationship Marketing. Bringing Quality, Customer Service and Marketing Together*, London, Butterworth.

Clancy, K.J. and Shulman, R.S. (1991), *The Marketing Revolution. A Radical Manifesto for Dominating the Marketplace*, New York, NY, Harper Business.

Collier, D.A. (1991), 'New Marketing Mix Stresses Services', *The Journal of Business Strategy*, Vol. 12, March–April, pp. 42–45.

Copulinksly, J.R. and Wolf, M.J. (1990), 'Relationship Marketing: Positioning for the Future', *Journal of Business Strategy*, Vol. 11, July/August, pp. 116–120.

Cowell, D. (1984) *The Marketing of Services*, London, Heinemann.

Culliton, J.W. (1948), *The Management of Marketing Costs*, Boston, MA, Harvard University.

Czepiel, J.A. (1990), 'Managing Relationships with Customers: A Differentiating Philosophy of Marketing'. In: *Service Management Effectiveness*. (Eds) Bowen, D.E. and Chase, R.D. (San Francisco, CA), Jossey-Bass, pp. 299–323.

Dean, J. (1951), *Managerial Economics*, New York, NY, Prentice-Hall.

Dixon, D.F. and Blois, K.J. (1983), *Some Limitations of the 4P's as a Paradigm for Marketing*, Marketing Education Group Annual Conference, Cranfield Institute of Technology, UK, July.

Duddy, E.A. and Revzan, D.A. (1947), *Marketing. An Institutional Approach*, New York, NY, McGraw-Hill.

Fisk, G. (1967), *Marketing Systems*, New York, Harper & Row.

Fisk, G. and Dixon, D.F. (1967), *Theories of Marketing Systems*, New York, Harper & Row.

Frisch, R. (1933), 'Monopole–Polypole—la notion de la force dans l'economie', *Nationalokonomisk Tidsskrift*, Denmark, pp. 241–259.

Grönroos, C. (1979), *Marknadsföring av tjänster. En Studie av marknadsföringsfunktionen i tjänsteföretag* (Marketing of services. A study of the marketing function of service firms). With an English summary (diss.; Swedish School of Economics and Business Administration Finland). Stockholm, Akademilittertur/Marketing Technique Center.

Grönroos, C. (1982), *Strategic Management and Marketing in the Service Sector*, Helsingfors, Finland: Swedish School of Economics and Business Administration (published in 1983 in the U.S. by Marketing Science Institute and in the UK by Studentlittertur/Chartwell-Bratt)

Grönroos, C. (1989), 'Defining Marketing: A Market-Oriented Approach', *European Journal of Marketing*, Vol. 23, No. 1, pp. 52–60.

Grönroos, C. (1990a), *Service Management and Marketing. Managing the Moments of Truth in Service Competition*, Lexington, MA, Free Press/Lexington Books.

Grönroos, C. (1990b), 'Relationship Approach to the Marketing Function in Service Contexts: The Marketing and Organizational Behavior Interface', *Journal of Business Research*, Vol. 20, No. 1, pp. 3–12.

Grönroos, C. (1991), 'The Marketing Strategy Continuum: A Marketing Concept for the 1990's', *Management Decision*, Vol. 29, No. 1, pp. 7–13.

Grönroos, C. and Gummesson, E. (1985), 'The Nordic School of Service Marketing'. In *Service Marketing—Nordic School Perspectives*, (Eds) Grönroos, C. and Gummesson, E., Stockholm University, Sweden, pp. 6–11.

Gummesson, E. (1987), 'The New Marketing—Developing Long-Term Interactive Relationships', *Long Range Planning*, Vol. 20, No. 4, pp. 10–20.

Gummesson, E. (1990), *The Part-Time Marketer*, Karlstad, Sweden, Center for Service Research.

Hansen, H.L. (1956), *Marketing: Text, Cases and Readings*, Homewood, IL, Irwin.

Håkansson, H., (Ed.) (1982), *International Marketing and Purchasing of Industrial Goods*, New York, NY, Wiley.

Jackson, B.B. (1985a), 'Build Customer Relationships That Last', *Harvard Business Review*, Vol. 63, November/December, pp. 120–128.

Jackson, B.B. (1985b), *Winning and Keeping Industrial Customers. The Dynamics of Customer Relationships*, Lexington, MA, Lexington Books.

Johanson, J. and Mattsson, L-G. (1985), 'Marketing Investments and Market Investments in Industrial Networks', *International Journal of Research in Marketing*, No. 4, pp. 185–195.

Johnson, A.A. (1986), 'Adding more P's to the Pod or—12 Essential Elements of Marketing', *Marketing News*, 11 April p. 2.

Judd, V.C. (1987), 'Differentiate with the 5th P: People', *Industrial Marketing Management*, Vol. 16, November, pp. 241–247.

Kelly, E.J. and Lazer, W. (1973), *Managerial Marketing*, Homewood, IL, Irwin.

Kent, R.A. (1986), 'Faith in Four P's: An Alternative', *Journal of Marketing Management*, Vol. 2, No. 2, pp. 145–154.

Keely, A. (1987), 'The "New Marketing" Has Its Own Set of P's', *Marketing News*, Vol. 21, 6 November, pp. 10–11.

Kjaer-Hansen, M. (1945), *Afsaetningsokonomi* (Marketing), Copenhagen, Denmark, Erhvervsokonomisk Forlag.

Kock, S. (1991), *A Strategic Process for Gaining External Resources through Long-Lasting Relationships*, Helsingfors/Vasa, Finland, Swedish School of Economics and Business Administration.

Kotler, P. (1986), 'Megamarketing', *Harvard Business Review*, Vol. 64, March/April, pp. 117–124.

Kotler, P. (1991), *Marketing Management. Analysis, Planning, and Control*, 7th ed, Englewood Cliffs, NJ, Prentice-Hall.

Kotler, P. (1992), 'It's Time for Total Marketing', *Business Week ADVANCE Executive Brief*, Vol. 2.

Lambert, D.D. and Harrington, T.C. (1989), 'Establishing Customer Service Strategies within the Marketing Mix: More Empirical Evidence', *Journal of Business Logistics*, Vol. 10, No. 2, pp. 44–60.

Langeard, E. and Eiglier, P. (1987), *Servuction. Le marketing des Services*, Paris, Wiley.

LeDoux, L. (1991), 'Is Preservation the Fifth "P" or Just Another Microenvironmental Factor?' In: *Challenges of New Decade in Marketing Education*, (Eds) McKinnon, G.F. and Kelley, C.A., Western Marketing Educators' Association, pp. 82–86.

Lipson, H.A. and Darling, J.R. (1971), *Introduction to Marketing: An Administration Approach*, New York, NY, Wiley.

Mason, B. and Mayer, M.L. (1990), *Modern Retailing Theory and Practice*, Homewood, IL, Irwin.

McCarthy, E.J. (1960), *Basic Marketing*, Homewood, IL, Irwin.

McKenna, R. (1991), *Relationship Marketing. Successful Strategies for the Age of the Customer*, Reading, MA, Addison-Wesley.

Mickwitz, G. (1959), *Marketing and Competition*, Helsingfors, Finland, Societas Scientarium Fennica (available for University Microfilms, Ann Arbor, MI).

Mickwitz, G. (1966), 'The Copenhagen School and Scandinavian Theory of Competition and Marketing'. In: *Readings in Danish Theory of Marketing*, (Ed.) Kjaer-Hansen, M., Copenhagen, Denmark, Erhvervsokonomisk Forlag (originally published in Det Danske Marked, May 1964).

Mickwitz, G. (1982), 'Non-linearities in the Marketing Mix of International Trade', *Discussion and working papers*, No. 168, University of Helsinki, Finland.

Möller, K. (1992), 'Research Traditions in Marketing: Theoretical Notes. In: *Economics and Marketing. Essays in Honour of Gösta Mickwitz*, (Eds) Blomqvist, H.C., Grönroos, C. and Lindqvist, L.J. Economy and Society, No. 48, Helsingfors, Finland, Swedish School of Economics and Business Administration.

Piercy, N. (1985), *Marketing Organisation. An Analysis of Information Processing, Power and Politics*, London, George Allen & Unwin.

Rapp, S. and Collins, T. (1990), *The Great Marketing Turnaround*, Englewood Cliffs, NJ, Prentice-Hall.

Rasmussen, A. (1955), *Pristeori eller parameterteori—studier omkring virksomhedens afsaetning* (Price theory or parameter theory—studies of the sales of the firm). Copenhagen, Denmark, Erhvervsokonomisk Forlag.

Reichheld, F.E. and Sasser, Jr, W.E. (1990), Zero Defections: Quality Comes to Service, *Harvard Business Review*, Vol. 68, September/October, pp. 105–111.

Robinson, J. (1933), *The Economics of Imperfect Competition*, London, Macmillan.

Shugan, S. (forthcoming), *Marketing and Managing Services. A Context Specific Approach*, Homewood, IL, Dow Jones-Irwin.

Sonnenberg, F.K. (1988), 'Relationship Management Is More Than Winning and Dining', *Journal of Business Strategy*, Vol. 9, May/June, pp. 60–63.

Stackelberg, H. von (1939), 'Theorie der Vertriebspolitik und der Qualitätsvariation', *Schmollers Jahrbuch*, 63/1.

Staudt, T.A. and Taylor, D.A. (1965), *Marketing. A Managerial Approach*, Homewood, IL, Irwin.

Traynor, K. (1985), 'Research Deserves Status as Marketing's Fifth "P" ', *Marketing News* (special marketing manager's issue), 8 November.

Van den Bulte, C. (1991), 'The Concept of Marketing Mix Revisited: A Case Analysis of Metaphor in Marketing Theory and Management', *Working Paper*, State University of Ghent, Belgium.

Vavra, T.G. (1992), *Aftermarketing. How to Keep Customers for Life Through Relationship Marketing*, Homewood, IL, Business One Irwin.

Waterschoot, W. van and Van den Bulte, C. (1992), 'The 4P Classification of the Marketing Mix Revisited', *Journal of Marketing*, Vol. 56, October, pp. 83–93.

8

Relationship Marketing: Challenges for the Organization

Relationship marketing has been offered as a new marketing paradigm. However, a relationship approach to marketing challenges many fundamental cornerstones of marketing, such as the definition of marketing variables, the marketing department as a useful organizational solution, marketing planning as an effective way of planning marketing resources and activities, and others. If a firm is to take a relationship marketing approach many existing attitudes, behaviors, and structures will have to be rethought. In the present article, such behaviors and structures are challenged and eight 'cornerstone' viewpoints about the implementation of relationship marketing are suggested.

The marketing mix concept was gradually developed after World War II and its 4 P model was introduced around 1960 (McCarthy, 1960). In the industrial society of the post-World War II era, marketing mix management and its trans-actional approach to marketing inevitably was helpful for very many industries in many markets. The rise of marketing mix management coincides with the time when the industrial society was reaching the peak of its life cycle in the Western world.

Reprinted from the *Journal of Business Research*, vol. 46(3). Grönroos, C. Relationship Marketing: Challenges for the Organization. Copyright © 1999, pp. 327–335 with permission from Elsevier.

However, since that time, the market situation has changed, especially in Western economies, among other reasons because of the emergence of the postindustrial society. First, the once dominant mass markets are becoming more and more fragmented. Second, most customers no longer want to remain anonymous and want individual treatment and they are becoming more sophisticated. Third, more and more markets are maturing. Fourth, competition is increasing and becoming global. Fifth, the market offerings have become less standardized, because, in many situations, customers demand it, and new technology makes this possible in a way totally different from the past.

Relationship marketing is an emerging marketing perspective that has been discussed in the marketing literature throughout the 1990s. In marketing practice, relationship marketing is drawing more and more attention. It is suggested that a relationship approach to marketing is a new paradigm that goes back to the roots of the marketing phenomenon (Sheth and Parvatiyar, 1995). This new approach can be seen as an alternative way of looking at the marketing phenomenon as compared to the mass-marketing orientation of marketing mix management, rather than as a tool within the marketing mix.

Relationship marketing as an alternative perspective may require that basic marketing structures are reshaped. The purpose of this article is to discuss how established marketing behaviors and structures may need to be rethought. It is proposed that fundamental cornerstones of marketing need to be challenged. Eight 'cornerstone' viewpoints about relationship marketing are formulated and discussed. These viewpoints are not formulated as formal propositions that can be tested. Rather, they are put forward as thought-provoking suggestions for further theoretical and empirical research. Six of the viewpoints have, however, been tested using data from quantitative and qualitative studies in New Zealand and Canada. According to preliminary results, all except the last (eighth) viewpoint are supported, and, interestingly enough, the two untested viewpoints (fourth and seventh) emerged in the qualitative studies (see Brodie, 1997).

Relationship Marketing—A Marketing Paradigm for the 1990s and Beyond

Transaction-oriented mass marketing based on the management of the 4 Ps of the marketing mix is, no doubt, still a valid marketing approach, especially for marketers of consumer packaged goods. However, from the 1970s, an alternate approach to marketing based on the establishment and management of relationships has emerged in various contexts of marketing research and practice. Elements of this new approach have been especially evident in two streams of research emanating in Scandinavia and Northern Europe and eventually spreading to other parts of the Western world. These streams of research are the Nordic School of Service (Grönroos and Gummesson, 1985; Berry and Parasuraman, 1993), which examines management and marketing from a service perspective, and the IMP Group (Håkansson, 1982; Håkansson and Snehota, 1995), which takes a network and interaction approach to understanding industrial businesses. A common denominator of these two schools of thought is that marketing is more a management issue than a function, and that managing marketing normally must be built upon relationships, not on transactions alone.

Building and managing relationship has become a philosophical cornerstone of both the Nordic School of Service and the IMP Group since the late 1970s. However, 'relationship marketing' as a term was not commonly used until the latter part of the 1980s, although it was first coined in 1983 in the United States by Berry (1983). In the 1990s, the relationship marketing perspective has attracted growing attention in the United States (Kotler, 1992; Webster, 1994; Hunt and Morgan, 1994; Sheth and Parvatiyar, 1995) as well as in Britain and Australia (Christopher, Payne, and Ballantyne, 1992; Brodie, Coviello, Brookes, Richard, and Little, 1997). Although the concepts used in various areas of relationship-oriented marketing differ to some extent, and the viewpoints taken are somewhat different, we can probably conclude that an understanding of services and how to manage and market services is one key to understanding the nature of relationship marketing. Another one is understanding how to manage networks (Håkansson and Snehota, 1995) and partnerships (Hunt and Morgan, 1994), and how to make use of the integrated marketing communications notion is yet another (Schultz, 1996; Stewart, 1996). However, when using a relationship approach, every firm offers services (Webster, 1994). 'When *service competition* is the key to success practically for everybody and the product has to be defined as a service, *every business is a service business*' (Grönroos, 1996, p. 13).

In the literature, there is no agreement on a definition of relationship marketing. Although most definitions have common denominators, there are differences in scope. A comprehensive definition (Grönroos, 1989, 1990, 1997) states that, according to a relationship approach

Marketing is the process of identifying and establishing, maintaining, and enhancing, and when necessary also terminating relationships with customers and other stakeholders, at a profit, so that the objectives of all parties involved are met; and this is done by a mutual exchange and fulfillment of promises. (Grönroos, 1997, p. 407)

Key aspects of such a marketing approach are not only to get customers and create transactions (identifying and establishing), but maintaining and enhancing on-going relationships are also important, and making promises is not the only responsibility of marketing, such promises must also be kept (Calonius, 1988). Profitable business relationships rely on a firm's ability to develop trust in itself and its performance with its customers and other stakeholders, and its ability to establish itself as an attractive business partner (see Halinen, 1994, who discusses the concept of *attraction* in business relationships).

Although they vary in terms of broadness and emphasis, most definitions of relationship marketing in the literature have a similar meaning (Christopher, Payne, and Ballantyne, 1992; Blomqvist, Dahl, and Haeger, 1993; Hunt and Morgan, 1994; Sheth and Parvatiyar, 1994; Gummesson, 1995). For example, Sheth and Parvatiyar (1994) state that relationship marketing is 'the understanding, explanation and management of the on-going collaborative business relationship between suppliers and customers' (p. 2); whereas, Gummesson (1995, p. 16) defines relationship marketing as a marketing approach based on relationships, interactions, and networks.

In more general terms, the Grönroos definition of a relationship-oriented approach to marketing (relationship marketing) can be formulated as a generic definition: *'Marketing is to manage the firm's market relationships'* (Grönroos, 1996, p. 11; emphasis added). This definition includes the fundamental notion of marketing as a phenomenon related to the relationships between a firm and its environment. It points out that marketing includes all necessary efforts required to prepare the organization for activities and to implement those activities needed to manage the interfaces with its environment. Markets are, of course, of several kinds: customers, distributors, suppliers, networks of cooperating partners.

Relationship marketing is not a new phenomenon (Sheth and Parvatiyar, 1995). Rather, it is a return to what can be called the 'roots of trade and commerce', before scientific management principles were intensively used, and before the emergence of the middleman, which broke up the relationship between suppliers and users. Marketing was based on management of relationships. The orientation toward mass production, mass distribution, and mass consumption, which at a period in the history of economic development in the Western world, well served the creation of wealth, made it difficult to maintain this basic nature of marketing. As noted previously in this article, today we have already entered a postindustrial society with a new business environment and new marketing challenges. New management principles are needed. This makes it necessary for marketing to return to its roots.

In none of the definitions of relationship marketing is the concept of *exchange* (Baggozzi, 1975), which for about two decades has been considered a foundation of marketing, explicitly mentioned. Focusing on exchange is considered too narrow a view. A relationship is also a *mindset*; hence, a relationship includes much more than exchanges. If a trusting relationship between two or several parties in the marketplace exists, exchanges should inevitably occur. However, there is so much more to an on-going relationship that also has to be taken care of, if exchanges of offerings for money are to take place. The relationship is a more fundamental unit of study than the exchanges that occur within it. Hence, *the basic concept of marketing is the relationship itself rather than singular exchanges* that occur in the relationship. A relationship can be analyzed on several levels; for example, on relationship, sequence, episode, action, and step levels, as suggested by Holmlund (1996) and further developed by Wrange (1997).

Cornerstones of Marketing Challenged by the Relationship Marketing Perspective

Marketing mix management that continues to dominate mainstream marketing textbooks and large parts of research into marketing includes the following 'cornerstones': the marketing mix itself; the product concept; the marketing department; marketing planning; market segmentation; and market research and market share statistics. None of these, as they are treated in mainstream marketing, can be taken for granted when a relationship marketing approach is taken. They were developed in situations where a transaction-orientation approach served marketing well, and the task of getting customers dominated marketing. When marketing is based on relationships, and keeping customers is considered at least equally important as getting customers, new structures for analyzing, planning, implementing, and monitoring marketing and its effects may be needed. In fact, we argue that major changes in existing structures and behaviors are required. In the sections that follow, these six cornerstones of marketing are analyzed in view of the transition to a relationship marketing philosophy, and relationship-oriented structures are proposed.

Marketing Variables and Resources

The *marketing mix and its 4P model* define the variables that are considered part of marketing. Although the Ps are not obsolete as marketing variables today, often the philosophical foundation of the marketing mix and its Ps do not fit well in the competitive situation that has been emerging in many industries in the Western world. Mass-marketing and transaction orientation, as well as the adversarial approach to customers, do not allow the firm to adjust its market performance to the demands of more and more customers today; for example, enhanced value around the core product, reliable service to accompany the product, a trusting relationship with customers, suppliers, and distributors. As Dixon and Blois (1983) state, '. . . indeed, it would not be unfair to suggest that far from being concerned with a customer's interests (i.e., somebody *for whom* something is done), the view implicit in the 4P approach is that the customer is somebody *to whom* something is done!' (p. 4, emphasis added). Today, with more sophis-ticated customers, maturing markets, and intensifying global competition, this approach to customers will not serve marketers as well as it did. Cooperation, in a competitive environment, rather than an adversarial approach is a better foundation for marketing in today's market climate.

The marketing mix clearly includes such variables as advertising and other means of marketing communications, selling, and pricing that are needed in a relationship-oriented marketing approach. However, the basic tenet that the marketing mix consists of a number of predetermined groups of decision-making areas that together are what should be planned as marketing is challenged. It fits a situation where the customer is anonymous, and the market offering is a fairly simple product, such as many consumer packaged goods. When the firm can iden-tify its customers (or distributors or suppliers), when interactions between these parties and their staff occur, and when it is important to make current customers interested in buying again (Reichheld and Sasser, 1990), marketing impact is created by a large number of people, the *part-time marketers* (Gummesson, 1987), and by other resources in the organization, in addition to the efforts of the full-time marketers in marketing departments. Hence, marketing variables can neither be predetermined, because they vary from case to case, nor separated from activities that, for example, belong to production and operations, deliveries, customer service, or a host of other business processes. We can offer the first viewpoint about how to understand the nature of marketing variables in relationship marketing:

> *Viewpoint 1 :* In relationship marketing, the firm cannot predetermine a set of marketing variables. Instead, depending upon the stage and nature of the relationship with any given existing or potential customer, it must use all resources and activities that make a desired marketing impact by creating value and enhancing satisfaction, regardless of where in the organization they are located.

The Marketed Object

In the marketing literature, the *product concept* has a firm position. The product—a good or a service—is the core around which the rest of marketing revolves. To use the 4P model, the product has to be developed and packaged so that it can be priced, promoted, and distributed. Although the product may be complicated, including not only the technical core but also packaging and such augmenting services as warranties, it is considered more or less prefabricated before the marketing process begins. This view of the phenomenon, which is offered as a solution to customer problems, is transaction oriented. The product must exist, if a transaction is to take place at a given moment. As long as transactions or exchanges are the focus of marketing, a prefabricated product is required. However, when the focus is shifted from singular exchanges to relationships, quite another view of how solutions to customer problems develop emerges.

The technical solution embedded in a product (a physical good or a service) is only the prerequisite for a good solution to a problem. In addition, customers expect, for example, well-handled deliveries, service and maintenance, information, customer-oriented complaints-handling routines, as well as skillful and service-minded employees who demonstrate an interest in the needs and desires of customers and show service-oriented attitudes and behaviors when performing their tasks. Moreover, customers do not want to spend too much time getting their problems resolved.

When solutions to customers' problems are viewed in a relationship perspective, the traditional product becomes transparent. In fact, normally several competitors offer a similar 'product'. What is important is a firm's ability to create a total system of caring for its customers on an on-going basis so the customers are served better by a given supplier or service firm than by its competitors (Levitt, 1969). The customers must be truly *served*. Hence, a total *service offering* that, indeed, serves the customer must be designed. The technical solution, or the 'product', becomes only one resource among many. When the solution to a customer's problem is viewed in this way, two things follow. First, the product does not exist as a prefabricated phenomenon. Second, the solution is developing over time when the firm manages its resources so that an acceptable total offering gradually emerges.

What is needed is a governing system that matches the various resources with the needs and desires of the customer over time. Of course, to some degree a prefabricated technical solution, a 'product', is always needed, but it is only one technology among many used to create the offering over time. The resources that must be managed through a customer-oriented governing system can, for example, be grouped into the following categories: *people, technology, know-how*, and *time* (Grönroos, 1997). Time, of course, refers to how efficiently and effectively the firm manages *the customer's time*. People includes *both personnel and customers*. The customer also becomes a resource, because in an on-going relationship, much of what is emerging is based on customer-driven information, initiatives, and actions. Hence, we can formulate the second viewpoint about the total offering, which in a relationship marketing context replaces the product concept.

> *Viewpoint 2:* In relationship marketing, the firm cannot rely on a prefabricated product. It must develop such resources as personnel, technology, know-how, the customer's time, and the customer itself as a resource, as well as create a governing system that manages these resources during the on-going relationship in such a manner that a satisfactory total service offering emerges over time.

The Organizational Solution

The *marketing department*, including specialists on various subareas of marketing, is the traditional organization solution for managing, planning, and implementing marketing activities. This functionalistic organizational solution is inherent in the marketing mix management approach and follows the general principles of scientific management (Taylor, 1947). Specialists should perform their specialties. However (except for such cases as many consumer packaged goods), marketing is no longer the sole task of marketing specialists. Marketing is spread throughout the organization, and this is true for a growing number of businesses, in service industries, and in the manufacturing sector (Gummesson, 1987; Grönroos, 1990, 1995).

Marketing and marketers have become isolated in organizations over time. As we have observed in another context, 'both from an organizational point of view and from a psychological standpoint *the marketing department is off side*' (Grönroos, 1994, p. 356; emphasis added). The marketing department cannot influence the people in the rest of the organization outside the marketing department to play their roles as *part-time marketers*, to use a term coined by Gummesson (1987). Part-time marketers are those people outside the marketing department (i.e., not marketing specialists), who are specialist in, say, maintenance, deliveries of goods, claims handling, operating telephone exchanges, or just about any type of job, where their attitudes and way of doing their job have an impact on the customer's perception of the firm and of the quality of its market offerings. Hence, they have *dual responsibilities*, both for doing their job well and in so doing, making a good marketing impression.

Gummesson observes that in industrial markets and in service businesses, the part-time marketers typically outnumber by several times the full-time marketers; that is, the specialists of the marketing and sales departments. Furthermore, he concludes that 'marketing and sales departments [the full-time marketers] are not able to handle more than a limited portion of the marketing *as its staff cannot be at the right place at the right time with the right customer contacts*' (Gummesson, 1990, p. 13). Hence, the part-time marketers not only outnumber the full-time marketers, the specialists; often they are the only marketers available at crucial moments (Normann, 1983), when the marketing impact is made and a basis for customer satisfaction is laid. Moreover, the marketing department cannot plan the job of the part-time marketers or in any way take responsibility for their attitude and performance. In the final analysis, the traditional marketing department stands in the way of spreading market orientation and an interest in the customer throughout the organization (Piercy, 1985; Grönroos, 1982, 1990).

Furthermore, the specialists in a marketing department may become alienated from the customers. Managing the marketing mix means relying on mass marketing. Customers become numbers for marketing specialists, whose actions, therefore, typically are based on surface information obtained from market research reports and market-share statistics. Frequently, such 'full-time' marketers may act without ever having encountered an actual customer. As we observed as early as 1982 in a study of service firms, traditional marketing departments may make a firm less customer oriented and make it more difficult to create interest in marketing among employees who do not belong to such departments (Grönroos, 1982).

Because marketing resources (i.e., part-time marketers) can be found throughout an organization, total marketing cannot be organized in the form of a traditional marketing department. Marketing responsibility must be spread organization-wide. Moreover, normally it is probably impossible for the head of a marketing department to be responsible for the marketing impact of part-time marketers and to have a decisive influence on investments in equipment and operational and administrative systems that also have a marketing impact on the customers. Only top management or the head of, for example, a regional organization or a division can take that responsibility.

Marketing specialists are, of course, still needed to perform such basic full-time marketing activities as market research, some advertising programs, and direct marketing. In addition, as specialists on their customers, they can assist top management as internal marketing facilitators; that is, as internal consultants. As Berry (1986) observes, 'service marketing directors not only must persuade customers to buy (for the first time), they must also persuade—and help—employees to perform' (p. 47). Marketing specialists can help making part-time marketers understand and accept their marketing responsibility through educating employees on managerial and nonmanagerial levels about the nature, purpose, and applications of part-time marketing, they can strive to support investments in tools and systems that make it easier for part-time marketers to perform, and they can be visible supporters of good quality in the organization (Berry and Parasuraman, 1991). *Internal marketing* becomes a critical issue in relationship marketing if the organization is to be well prepared for its new marketing tasks (Grönroos, 1990). In an article about relationship marketing, Bitner (1995) emphasizes the need for a firm to manage, not only the tasks of making and keeping promises, but also the task of enabling the fulfillment of promises, if marketing is to be successful.

If the group of marketing specialists in a firm becomes too big and becomes dominant, problems with market orientation and customer consciousness may follow. The part-time marketers may not understand or accept their responsibilities as marketers. Hence, we can formulate the third viewpoint about how to organize marketing and the fourth viewpoint about preparing the part-time marketers for their marketing duties.

> *Viewpoint 3:* In relationship marketing, marketing cannot be organized as a separate organizational unit, rather a marketing consciousness must be developed organization-wide. However, marketing specialists are needed for some traditional marketing activities and as internal

consultants to top management in order to help instill such a marketing consciousness.

Viewpoint 4: Because the implementation of relationship marketing relies upon the support of a host of part-time marketers, the firm must create an internal marketing process to ensure that part-time marketers understand and accept their marketing duties and learn the skills needed to perform in a customer-oriented manner.

Planning Marketing

Marketing planning is the process of planning and developing the activities of the marketing department and budgets for those activities. As long as almost all marketing activities are in the hands of the marketing department, traditional marketing planning is acceptable. However, in a situation where much or even most of the marketing impact is the result of activities that are not the responsibility of the marketing department, it does not make sense to plan the activities of that department separately and call this 'the marketing plan'. Such a plan includes, of course, part of what is needed to implement relationship marketing, but today so much more that is planned as parts of other plans should also be planned from the same customer perspective as the activities of the traditional marketing plan. Just preparing a 'marketing plan' within a marketing department does not mean that the firm's total marketing activities as perceived by its customers are planned. It can easily become a plan that counteracts what may be planned as part of human resource management, production and operations, for example, or is counteracted by those plans. *The result is not well-planned marketing.* What is called 'the marketing plan' may only cover those external marketing activities by which the firm *gives promises* to potential and existing customers. Interactive marketing activities and the performance, attitude, and behavior of the part-time marketers are not planned with a customer perspective in mind. Hence, how *promises are fulfilled* is not well planned from a marketing point of view. If top management, the marketers, and people from other departments internally believe in such a 'marketing plan', which they often seem to do, the marketing concept, that is, the notion that the interest of the customer should be kept in mind in the firm's planning processes, is unfulfilled.

Because marketing resources can be found throughout the organization, not only in the marketing department, marketing cannot be planned in the form of a traditional, separate marketing plan. Instead, the marketing impact of resources and activities that are planned elsewhere, such as in production and operations, human resources, or investment in systems and equipment, must be recognized.

All resources and activities that have such an impact must be integrated, regardless of in what department they may be. This can only be done in an overall corporate plan based, not only on establishing relationships, but also on a notion of relationship building and maintenance. As we concluded in an earlier study more than 15 years ago (Grönroos, 1982), a market orientation must be instilled in all plans through a market-oriented corporate plan. This plan would then serve as a governing *relationship plan*. Hence, we can formulate the fifth viewpoint about how to plan marketing from a relationship perspective.

> *Viewpoint 5:* Relationship marketing cannot be localized in the traditional marketing plans. Instead, a market orientation must be instilled in all plans and integrated through a market-oriented corporate plan as a governing relationship plan.

Individualizing the Customer Base

Market segmentation (Smith, 1956) is the process of identifying and evaluating subgroups of customers that are internally more homogeneous than the total market. As long as markets could be viewed as masses of anonymous customers, market segmentation served marketing well. However, when customers no longer want to be treated as numbers, but as individuals, the traditional notion of market segmentation becomes less helpful. Identifying groups of numbers that somehow look alike is, in many cases, still a valid approach to segmentation, but, it is often more important for the firm to identify its existing and potential customers as individuals representing households or organizations. *Individualizing* the market becomes more important for marketing than merely segmenting it. From a profitability point of view, getting a larger share of the purchases of such individuals may be better than getting a larger number of customers in a given market segment (Storbacka, 1997).

Because relationship marketing is based on the notion of relationship with identifiable customers who should not be treated as unknown persons but as individuals representing households or organizations, traditional segmentation is less appropriate. Instead of getting some of the business of a large segment, the firm should strive to get as much as possible of every individual customer's business (Peppers and Rogers, 1993). The basic idea behind market segmentation still holds true, of course. However, the nature of segmentation changes dramatically. It is no longer enough to distinguish between homogeneous groups of anonymous customers based on average measures. Much more detailed and individualized information in the form of, for example, customer information files (Vavra, 1994), or other types of databases must be compiled. Firms serving mass markets cannot, of course, develop as many individual and informative files as firms that have a limited number of customers. However, the basic principle should be the same in both situations. Hence, the sixth viewpoint about how to manage the customer base can be formulated.

> *Viewpoint 6:* In relationship marketing, marketing decisions and activities cannot be based on traditional market segmentation techniques. Choice of customers to serve and decisions about how to serve them must be based on individual customer information files and other types of databases.

Researching Customers and Monitoring Success

Market research and *market share statistics* are a way of finding out needs and expectations of customers, monitoring the level of satisfaction among the firm's customers, and evaluating the relative sales result of a firm as compared to that of the competition. When marketing is based on a notion of masses of anonymous customers, this is a practical way to monitor how well, on the average, the firm is doing. Far too often, however, market share alone is treated as a way of evaluating the success of the firm in satisfying the needs and expectations of its customers. The better the market share is maintained or increased, the healthier the customer base. Of course, this is not the case, but because frequently no other than at best ad hoc information about customer satisfaction or customer loyalty is available, good sales performance is easily taken as a measure of satisfied customers. This may, however, turn out to be a dangerous misunderstanding. Moreover, the closer natural contacts the firm has with its customers, the less justifiable it is to mix up market-share statistics with satisfaction and the health of the customer base.

Market research is often based on surveys, and because such data-gathering methods normally do not allow for obtaining in-depth information about the thoughts and intents of customers, only surface data are gathered. Such data may be useful, too, but, for example, information about customer satisfaction and about customer needs, desires, and expectations that employees who interact with customers are accumulating is neglected. The firm knows very little about the specific needs, desires, and expectations of individual customers, although the information technology available today makes it possible to develop customized databases (Vavra, 1994).

Measuring market share is an important way to monitor relative sales of a product when the product is marketed to a mass market of unknown customers. It is relatively easy to compile sales statistics. Studies of customer perceived quality and customer satisfaction measurements normally cannot be done on an equally regular basis. As a consequence, marketshare statistics are sometimes regarded as a proxy for customer satisfaction. Market share can be maintained, at least for sometime, even when customer satisfaction deteriorates. When a firm has direct contacts with its customers, information about the needs, desires, expectations, and future intentions of customers as well as about their quality and value perceptions and about satisfaction can be obtained directly in these contacts. This, however, requires an intelligent system for registering the bits of information many employees throughout the organization receive on a daily basis. This is vastly neglected today. However, only such direct management of the customer base gives management current and accurate information, not only about sales, but also about the needs, expectations, intentions, and level of satisfaction of its customers. Hence, we can formulate a seventh viewpoint about the need to manage the firm's customer base directly and not through market-share statistics and ad hoc customer studies alone.

> *Viewpoint 7:* In relationship marketing, the firm should manage its customer base directly through information obtained from the continuous interfaces between customers and employees, and only support this with market-share statistics and ad hoc studies of customers.

The Rebirth of Marketing: The Relationship Approach

The marketing mix management paradigm was developed to suit the requirements of marketing during the peak of the industrial society. Today it is helpful only in some types of businesses, such as many consumer goods industries, and even there it is being questioned (Rapp and Collins, 1990; McKenna, 1991). Relationship marketing, by going back to the roots of the marketing phenomenon, offers a new approach to managing market relationships. However, it is important to understand the paradigmatic nature of this perspective. It is foremost a philosophy that guides the planning and management of activities in the relationships between a firm and its customers, distributors, and other partners. The relationship philosophy relies on co-operation and a trusting relationship with customers (and other stakeholders and network partners) instead of an adversarial approach to customers, on collaboration within the company instead of specialization of functions and the division of labor, and on the notion of marketing as more of a market-oriented management approach with part-time marketers spread throughout the organisation than as a separate function for specialists only (Grönroos, 1996).

Common mistakes when discussing relationship marketing follow from a failure to understand this philosophical shift. We must realize that it is *a new paradigm, not just a new model,* that is emerging. Sometimes relationship marketing is used more or less as a synonym for direct marketing, database marketing, or for establishing customer clubs, and it becomes just another instrument in the marketing mix toolbox to be used to create transactions. In other situations, relationship marketing is used as a synonym for developing partnerships, alliances, and networks, or as part of marketing communications only. However, it is much more than all of these. It requires a totally new approach to some of the fundamental thoughts in marketing, as is implied by the seven propositions suggested in the previous section. The transition from transaction-oriented marketing mix-based practice of marketing to a relationship-oriented one is not an uncomplicated process. The old paradigm has deep roots in the minds of academics, as well as of marketers and nonmarketers in a company. Moreover, it still has a much easier-to-use toolbox of marketing instruments available than the emerging new paradigm can presently offer.

Hence, as illustrated in Figure 1, the transition toward a relationship-oriented marketing approach can be understood as a learning curve or a *transition curve* (Strandvik and Storbacka, 1996). In the beginning, firms that want to implement a relational approach to marketing remain very focused on products. Hence,

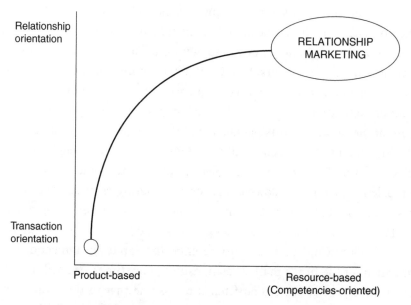

Figure 1 Relationship marketing: the transition curve

Source: Strandvik T and Storbacka K. Managing Relationship Quality. Proceedings from the QUIS 5 Quality in Services Conference, University of Karlstad, Sweden, 1996. Reproduced by permission of Tore Strandvik and Kaj Storbacka.

only easily developed relational activities are introduced. Typical examples are customized sales letters and information bulletins, customer clubs, and so forth. Such activities can easily backfire, especially if the customer is mistreated in other respects; for example, when using a service, in a recovery or complaints situation, or in just about any other interaction with the firm. Firms in this stage do not yet fully understand the philosophical nature of relationship marketing. Here, singular exchanges are still the basic focus of marketing. Today, most firms applying a relationship marketing approach are probably somewhere in this stage of the transition process. A true transition toward a relationship marketing strategy requires a focus on resources and competencies in the relationship. It is interesting that this changing demand from the market has had an impact on the strategy field that parallels the development of the relationship approach in marketing. Resources and core competencies are emphasised in the current strategy literature (Hamel and Prahalad, 1994).

In principle, the product is but one resource among others, although it is, of course, the necessary prerequisite for a successful relationship. The relationship itself becomes the focus of marketing.

However, as noted earlier, the roots of the old paradigm are very deep in the minds of most people, regardless of whether they are in managerial positions, or they are full-time marketers, or should consider themselves to be part-time marketers. Therefore, it may be difficult to instill a new philosophical approach in which marketing is practically every employee's business as part-time marketers or managers of part-time marketers. Getting the commitment of everyone to the new marketing philosophy and its consequences for marketing in practice may be difficult or even impossible. As we observed in another context (Grönroos, 1994), 'the use of the marketing mix paradigm and the 4 Ps has made it difficult for the marketing function to earn credibility' (p. 356). Far too many people feel uncomfortable with the thought of being involved in marketing. Some firms have solved this problem not only by downscaling or terminating their marketing departments altogether but also by *banning the use of the term marketing* (Grönroos, 1982, 1994). Such terms as 'customer contacts' and 'customer satisfaction' have been used instead of 'marketing' to describe the same phenomenon; i.e., the management of the firm's market relationships. Sometimes we need this kind of semantic nicety. It is not too far-fetched to assume that in the future this will occur in a growing number of cases. Therefore, an eighth, and final, viewpoint about relationship marketing as the rebirth of marketing is offered.

Viewpoint 8: To create an understanding of relationship marketing in an organization and to implement a culture of relationship marketing, it may be
necessary to replace the term 'marketing' with a psychologically more
readily accepted term to describe the task of managing the firm's
customer relationships.

Appendix

Eight Viewpoints about Relationship Marketing

Viewpoint 1: In relationship marketing, the firm cannot predetermine a set of
marketing variables. Instead, depending upon the stage and nature of the relationship
with any given existing or potential customer, it must use all resources and activities
that make a desired marketing impact by creating value and enhancing satisfaction,
regardless of where in the organization they are located.

Viewpoint 2: In relationship marketing, the firm cannot rely on a prefabricated product.
It must develop such resources as personnel, technology, know-how, the customer's
time, and the customer itself as a resource, as well as create a governing system that
manages these resources during the on-going relationship in such a manner that a
satisfactory total service offering emerges over time.

Viewpoint 3: In relationship marketing, marketing cannot be organized as a separate
organizational unit, rather a marketing consciousness must be developed
organization-wide. However, marketing specialists are needed for some traditional
marketing activities and as internal consultants to top management in order to help
instill such a marketing consciousness.

Viewpoint 4: Because the implementation of relationship marketing relies upon
the support of a host of part-time marketers, the firm must create an internal
marketing process to ensure that part-time marketers understand and accept their
marketing duties and learn the skills needed to perform in a customer-oriented
manner.

Viewpoint 5: Relationship marketing cannot be localized in the traditional marketing
plans. Instead, a market orientation must be instilled in all plans and integrated
through a market-oriented corporate plan as a governing relationship plan.

Viewpoint 6: In relationship marketing, marketing decisions and activities cannot be
based on traditional market segmentation techniques. Choice of customers to serve
and decisions about how to serve them must be based on individual customer
information files and other types of databases.

Viewpoint 7: In relationship marketing, the firm should manage its customer base
directly through information obtained from the continuous interfaces between
customers and employees, and only support this with market-share statistics and ad
hoc studies of customers.

Viewpoint 8: To create an understanding of relationship marketing in an organization
and to implement a culture of relationship marketing, it may be necessary to replace
the term 'marketing' with a psychologically more readily accepted term to describe
the task of managing the firm's customer relationships.

References

Bagozzi, R.P. (1975) Marketing as Exchange, *Journal of Marketing* 39 (October): 32–39.

Berry, Leonard L.: Relationship Marketing, in *Emerging Perspectives of Services Marketing*, Leonard L. Berry, G. Lynn Shostack, and G.D. Upah, eds., American Marketing Association, Chicago, IL. 1983, pp. 25–28.

Berry, Leonard L.: Big Ideas in Services Marketing. *Journal of Consumer Marketing* 3 (Spring 1986).

Berry, Leonard L, and Parasuraman, A.: Building a New Academic Field—The Case of Services Marketing. *Journal of Retailing* 69 (1991): 13–60.

Bitner, Mary Jo: Building Service Relationships: It's All About Promises. *Journal of the Academy of Marketing Science* 23 (1995): 246–251.

Blomqvist, Ralf, Dahl, Johan, and Haeger, Tomas: *Relationsmarknadsföring. Strategi och metod fö servicekonkurens* (Relationship Marketing. Strategy and Methods for Service Competition). IHM Förlag, Göteborg, Sweden. 1993.

Brodie, Roderick J.: From Transaction to Relationship Marketing: Propositions for Change, in *New and Evolving Paradigms: The Emerging Future of Marketing*, Tony Meenaghan, ed., The American Marketing Association Special Conferences, University College, Dublin, Ireland. 1997, pp. 615–616.

Brodie, Roderick J., Coviello, Nicole E., Brookes, Richard W., and Little, Victoria: Toward a Paradigm Shift in Marketing? An Examination of Current Marketing Practices. *Journal of Marketing Management* 13 (1997), pp. 383–406.

Calonius, Henrik: A Buying Process Model, in *Innovative Marketing—A European Perspective*, Proceedings of the XVIIth Annual Conference of the European Marketing Academy, Blois, Keith, and Parkinson, S., eds., University of Bradford, England, 1988.

Christopher, Martin, Payne, Adrian, and Ballantyne, David: *Relationship Marketing. Bringing Quality, Customer Service, and Marketing Together*, Butterworth, London 1992.

Dixon, Donald F., and Blois, Keith: *Some Limitations of the 4 Ps as a Paradigm for Marketing*, Marketing Education Group Annual Conference, Cranfield Institute of Technology, UK, July 1983.

Grönroos, Christian: *Strategic Management and Marketing in the Service Sector*. Swedish School of Economics and Business Administration, Helsingfors, Finland, 1982 (published in 1983 in the United States by Marketing Science Institute and in the UK by Studentliteratur/Chartwell-Bratt).

Grönroos, Christian: Defining Marketing: A Market-Oriented Approach. *European Journal of Marketing* 23 (1989): 52–60.

Grönroos, Christian: Relationship Approach to the Marketing Function in Service Contexts: The Marketing and Organizational Behavior Interface. *Journal of Business Research* 20 (1990): 3–12.

Grönroos, Christian: Quo Vadis, Marketing? Toward a Relationship Marketing Paradigm. *Journal of Marketing Management* 10 (1994): 347–360.

Grönroos, Christian: Relationship Marketing: The Strategy Continuum. *Journal of the Academy of Marketing Science* 23 (1995): 252–254.

Grönroos, Christian: The Relationship Marketing Logic. *Asia–Australia Marketing Journal* 4 (1996): 7–18.

Grönroos, Christian: Value-Driven Relational Marketing: From Products to Resources and Competencies. *Journal of Marketing Management* 13 (1997): 407–419.

Grönroos, Christian, and Gummesson, Evert: The Nordic School of Service Marketing, in *Service Marketing—Nordic School Perspectives*, Christian Grönroos, and Evert Gummesson, eds., Stockholm University, Stockholm, Sweden. 1985, pp. 6–11.

Gummesson, Evert: The New Marketing—Developing Long-Term Interactive Relationships. *Long-Range Planning* 20 (1987): 10–20.

Gummesson, Evert: *Relationsmarknadsföring. Från 4P till 30R* (Relationship marketing. From 4P to 30R). Liber-Hermods, Malmö, Sweden. 1995.

Håkansson, Håkan, ed.: *International Marketing and Purchasing of Industrial Goods*, Wiley, New York. 1982.

Håkansson, Håkan, and Snehota, Ivan: *Developing Relationships in Business Networks*, Routledge, London. 1995.

Hamel, Gary, and Prahalad, C.K.: *Competing For the Future. Breakthrough strategies for seizing control of your industry and creating the markets of tomorrow*, Harvard Business School Press, Boston, MA. 1994.

Holmlund, Maria: *A Theoretical Framework of Perceived Quality in Business Relationships*. Research report 36, CERS, Center for Relationship Marketing and Service Management, Swedish School of Economics and Business Administration, Helsinki, Finland. 1996.

Hunt, Shelby D., and Morgan, Robert M.: Relationship Marketing in the Era of Network Competition. *Marketing Management* 3 (1994): 19–30.

Kotler, Philip: It's Time for Total Marketing. *Business Week ADVANCE Executive Brief* 2 (1992).

Levitt, Theodore: *The Marketing Mode*, McGraw-Hill, New York. 1969.

McCarthy, E. Jerome: *Basic Marketing*, Irwin, Homewood, IL. 1960.

McKenna, Regis: *Relationship Marketing. Successful Strategies for the Age of the Customer*. Addison-Wesley, Reading, MA. 1991.

Normann, Richard: *Service Management*, Wiley, New York. 1993.

Peppers, D., and Rogers, Mary: *One-to-One Future: Building Relationships One Customer at a Time*. Currency/Doubleday, New York. 1993.

Piercy, Nigel: *Marketing Organisation. An Analysis of Information Processing, Power, and Politics*, George, Allen & Unwin, London. 1985.

Rapp, Stan, and Collins, Tom: *The Great Marketing Turnaround*, Prentice-Hall, Engelwood Cliffs, NJ. 1990.

Schultz, Don E.: The Inevitability of Integrated Communications. *Journal of Business Research* 37 (1996): 139–146.

Sheth, Jagdish N., and Parvatiyar, Atul, eds.: *Relationship Marketing: Theory, Methods, and Applications*, 1994. Research Conference Proceedings, Center for Relationship Marketing, Emory University, Atlanta, GA. June 1994.

Sheth, Jagdish N., and Parvatiyar, Atul: Relationship Marketing in Consumer Markets: Antecedents and Consequences. *Journal of the Academy of Marketing Science* 23 (1995): 255–271.

Smith, W.R.: Product Differentiation and Market Segmentation as Alternative Marketing Strategies. *Journal of Marketing* 21 (July 1956): 3–8.

Stewart, D.W.: Market-Back Approach to the Design of Integrated Communications Programs: A Change in Paradigm and a Focus on Determinants of Success. *Journal of Business Research* 37 (1996): 147–154.

Storbacka, Kaj: Segmentation Based on Customer Profitability—Retrospective Analysis of Retail Bank Customer Bases. *Journal of Marketing Management* 13 (1997): 479–492.

Strandvik, Tore, and Storbacka, Kaj: Managing Relationship Quality. Proceedings of The QUIS 5 Quality in Services Conference, University of Karlstad, Sweden. 1996.

Taylor, Frederick W.: *Scientific Management*, Harper & Row, London. 1947. (a volume of two papers originally published in 1903 and 1911 and written testimony for a Special House Committee in the United States in 1912).

Vavra, Terry G.: The Database Marketing Imperative. *Marketing Management* 1 (1994): 47–57.

Webster, Frederick E., Jr.: Executing the New Marketing Concept. *Marketing Management* 3 (1994): 9–18.

Wrange, Kim: *Customer Relationship Termination*. Research report, CERS, Center for Relationship Marketing and Service Management, Swedish School of Economics and Business Administration, Helsinki, Finland. 1997.

9

The Relationship Marketing Process: Communication, Interaction, Dialogue, Value

The objective of the article is to discuss a framework of central processes in relationship marketing. The framework includes an interaction process as the core, a planned communication process as the marketing communications support through distinct communications media, and a customer value process as the outcome of relationship marketing. If the interaction and planned communication processes are successfully integrated and geared towards customers' value processes, a relationship dialogue may emerge.

Introduction: the relationship marketing paradigm

The relationship marketing perspective is based on the notion that on top of the value of products and/or services that are exchanged, the existence of a relationship between two parties creates additional value for the customer and also for the supplier or service provider (Grönroos, 2000b; compare also Ravald and Grönroos, 1996). An on-going relationship may, for example, offer the customer security, a feeling of control and a sense of trust, minimized purchasing risks, and in the final analysis reduced costs of being a customer.

Grönroos, C. The Relationship Marketing Process: Communication, Interaction, Dialogue, Value. *Journal of Business & Industrial Marketing* 2004; **19**(2): 99–113. Reproduced by permission of Emerald Group Publishing Limited.

In a conference paper on service marketing, Berry (1983) first introduced the term relationship marketing, and a few years later Jackson (1985) used it in a business-to-business context. However, the phenomenon itself – a relationship approach to taking care of interactions with customers – is as old as the history of trade and commerce. The importance of relationships with customers was given less attention following the industrial revolution, when the middleman was introduced in the distribution chain (Sheth and Parvatiyar, 1995a). Even before the 1980s, Arndt (1979) observed a tendency of doing business in the form of long-term relationships, which he labelled 'domesticated markets'. He concluded that 'both business markets and consumer markets benefit from attention to conditions that foster relational bonds leading to reliable repeat business' (Arndt, 1979, p. 72). A few years later, Levitt (1983a, p. 111) used a marriage analogy in noting that 'the sale merely consummates the courtship . . . how good the marriage is depends on how well the relationship is managed by the seller'.

Before Berry and Jackson used the term 'relationship marketing', an explicit relationship perspective in marketing was inherent in the Nordic School of thought (see for example, Gummesson, 1983, 1987; Grönroos, 1980, 1983), even though the term was not taken into use until the end of the 1980s (Grönroos, 1989). The relationship notion was also an integral part of the interaction and network approach to industrial marketing of the IMP Group (Håkansson, 1982; Håkansson and Snehota, 1995). Similarities and differences between relationship marketing studies of these two schools of thought have been discussed by Mattsson (1997). The nature of relationship marketing as a contemporary marketing practice has been discussed by Coviello and Brodie (1998) and Coviello et al. (1997). Finally, it is noteworthy that although it was not explicitly expressed, a relationship notion was present also in the North American 7Ps model of service marketing of the early 1980s (Booms and Bitner, 1981).

Objective and perspective

The objective of this article is to analyze the nature and content of relationship marketing, seen as a process. The perspective of the article is predominantly that of the Nordic School of marketing thought, according to which understanding and managing services in the relationship is at the core of relationship building and maintenance, although relationship marketing also is supported by other factors, such as building networks (Håkansson and Snehota, 1995), creating strategic alliances and making partnership agreements (Hunt and Morgan, 1994), developing customer databases (Vavra, 1994) and managing relationship-oriented integrated marketing communications (Schultz *et al.*, 1992; Schultz, 1996; Duncan and Moriarty, 1997). Marketing is also seen more as market-oriented management than as a task for marketing specialists only, which means that marketing is viewed more as an overall process than as a separate function (Grönroos and Gummesson, 1985). In other approaches to relationship marketing, as in the network approach or in the strategic alliance and partnership approaches, other elements or phenomena are seen as the ground pillar. It all depends on the perspective of the researchers.

Services in relationship marketing

An integral part of service marketing is the fact that the consumption of a service is process consumption rather than outcome consumption (Grönroos, 1998). The consumer or user perceives the service production process as part of service consumption and not only the outcome of a process as in traditional consumer packaged goods marketing. Thus, service consumption and production have inter-faces that always are critical to the consumer's perception of the service and to his or her long-term purchasing behavior. In the services marketing literature the management of these interfaces is called interactive marketing, and this concept has been used in the relationship marketing literature as well (see Bitner, 1995). The service provider almost always has a direct contact with its customers. In these contacts relationships may easily start to develop and if the simultaneous consumption and production processes turn out well, an enduring relationship may follow.

When manufacturers of industrial goods and equipment turn their interest from single transactions with their customers to doing business on a long-term scale, the nature of consumption or usage changes from pure outcome consumption to an on-going process consumption or usage. In this process the customer uses the outcomes of the manufacturer's production processes (goods, equipment) that are exchanged between the parties in the relationship as well as a number of service processes that are produced and consumed or used before, during and in between the exchanges of outcomes. The nature of this process becomes very similar to the process consumption characteristic of services.

From a marketing point of view, when the outcomes (goods and equipment) constantly become more similar as competition increases, this change of the nature of consumption or usage is emphasized even more. In most cases even continuous product development alone does not lead to a sustainable competitive advantage anymore. Hence, only services, such as tailor-made design, deliveries and just-in-time logistics, installing equipment, customer training, documentation about how to install and use goods, maintenance and spare part service, customer-oriented invoicing, handling inquiries, service recovery and complaints management are left for the marketer to use. Customer service as discussed by Christopher *et al.* (1991) also becomes an important means of competition. If one does not want to use the price variable, which seldom creates a sustainable competitive advantage, only services are left for developing such an advantage.

Of course, transaction marketing may be justified in some cases (Jackson, 1985), but as the work by Reichheld and Sasser (1990), Reichheld (1993) and Storbacka (1994) demonstrates, long-term customer relationships often form a base for profitable business.

In order to implement relationship marketing a shift of focus is required. In this article three areas that are vital for the successful execution of a relationship strategy are discussed:

(1) An interaction process as the core of relationship marketing.
(2) A planned communication process supporting the development and enhancement of relationships.
(3) A value process as the output of relationship marketing.

The term planned communication process is used to indicate that in this process only communication through exclusive communication media, such as advertising, TV commercials, internet banners and sales calls, are included. Customers' interactions with products, service processes and with other aspects of the interaction process also include elements of communication. These communication effects follow as a by-product from the manner in which the various interactions are managed by the firm and perceived by the customers. However, as part of a total communications impact on customers these types of communication may very well be even more important than the planned communication efforts (Duncan and Moriarty, 1997).

Relationship marketing and service competition

Marketing from a relational perspective can been defined as the process of managing the firm's market relationships (Grönroos, 1996), or more explicitly as the process of identifying and establishing, maintaining, enhancing, and when necessary terminating relationships with customers and other stakeholders, at a profit, so that the objectives of all parties involved are met, where this is done by a mutual giving and fulfillment of promises (Grönroos, 1989, 2000a). This definition bears clear similarities with Berry's services marketing definition from a relationship perspective (Berry, 1983) and with more recently offered definitions by Hunt and Morgan (1994), Sheth and Parvatiyar (1994) and Christopher et al. (1991). Gummesson (1999) defines relationship marketing as marketing seen as interactions, relationships and networks, thus emphasizing three central phenomena in this marketing perspective.

As most definitions imply, relationship marketing is first and foremost a process. All activities that are used in marketing have to be geared towards the management of this process. Hence, no marketing variables are explicitly mentioned in these definitions. According to Grönroos' definition, the process moves from identifying potential customers to establishing a relationship with them, and then to maintaining the relationship that has been established and to enhance it so that more business as well as good references and favorable word of mouth are generated. Finally, sometimes relationships are terminated either by the supplier or by the customer (or by any other party in a network of relationships), or they just seem to fade away. Such situations must also be managed carefully by the supplier or service provider. As the Gummesson definition implies the relationship process includes interactions that form relationships which may be developing in networks of suppliers, distributors, and consumers or end users.

The focal relationship is the one between a supplier or provider of goods or services and buyers and users of these goods or services. Relationship marketing is first and foremost geared towards the management of this relationship. However, in order to facilitate this, other stakeholders in the process may have to be involved. If marketing is to be successful, other suppliers, partners, distributors, financing institutions, the customers' customers, and sometimes even political decision makers may have to be included in the management of the relationship in a network of relationships (Gummesson, 1999; compare also the six markets concepts in Christopher et al., 1991).

A shift of focus in marketing decision making from the transaction toward a process where a relationship is built and maintained has important effects on central marketing areas, such as organization, planning, organizational development and the measurement of success in the marketplace (Grönroos, 1999; Brodie et al., 1997). As this process becomes as important for the customer as the outcomes, for example, in the form of goods and equipment, the nature of the product concept changes. The product as the outcome of a production process is basically a transaction-oriented construct. In a relationship perspective physical goods and equipment (products) become a part of the process together with other elements such as a host of services. In the best case these services enhance the value of the products as with just-in-time deliveries, prompt service and maintenance and customer-oriented and timely service recovery. In the worst case, for example with delays in deliveries, or unsuccessful maintenance and unclear documentation about the use of equipment that has been bought, they damage or altogether destroy their value.

Customers do not only look for goods or services, they demand a much more holistic offering including everything from information about how to best and safest use a product to delivering, installing, repairing, maintaining and updating solutions they have bought. And they demand all this, and much more, in a friendly, trustworthy and timely manner. Moreover, the core product is less seldom than the elements surrounding the core the reason for dissatisfaction. As Webster (1994, p. 13) exemplifies, 'the automobile purchaser is unhappy with the car because of lousy service from the dealer; the insurance customer has problems with the agent, not with the policy'. What Levitt (1983b, pp. 9–10) concluded already in the early 1980s about what should accompany the sale of the mere product, 'having been offered these extras, the customer finds them beneficial and therefore prefers to doing business with the company that supplies them', is very much true today. By and large customers are more sophisticated and better informed than ever and therefore more demanding. Moreover, the increasing global competition offers customers more alternatives than ever before.

In a customer relationship that goes beyond a single transaction of a product, the outcomes themselves including goods, services outcomes or industrial equipment become just one element in the holistic, continuously developing service offering. For a manufacturer, the physical good is a core element of this service offering, of course, because it is a prerequisite for a successful offering. However, what counts beyond this prerequisite is the ability of the firm to manage the additional elements of the offering better than the competitors to create value for customers in their internal value-creating processes. The product becomes a process (compare Storbacka and Lehtinen, 2000), and the supplier has to truly serve its customers (Grönroos, 1996). For manufacturers this means that products must be turned into elements of a holistic service offering. They must be servicefied (Grönroos, 2000a).

The product seen as a process or a total service offering thus becomes a service including tangible elements such as physical goods and equipment and intangible elements such as a host of various types of services. In a long-term relationship, firms face a competitive situation for which we in another context have coined the term service competition (Grönroos, 1996). When service competition is the key to success practically for everybody and the product has to be defined as a service, every business is a service business (compare Webster, 1994).

The key processes of relationship marketing

Communication

In transaction marketing, marketing communication including sales is a central component. Marketing communication is predominantly mass marketing, however with a growing element of direct marketing. Sales are a directly interactive element of the communication process. In the field of marketing communication a new trend towards integrating communication elements such as advertising, direct marketing, sales promotion and public relations into a two-way integrated marketing communications perspective has emerged in North America during the 1990s (Schultz *et al.*, 1992; Schultz, 1996; Stewart, 1996). Integrated marketing communications is clearly influenced by the relationship perspective in marketing. 'As we are committed to two-way communication, we intend to get some response from those persons to whom the integrated marketing communications program has been directed. . . . We adapt the customer's or prospect's communication wants or needs and begin the cycle all over again. This is truly relationship marketing at its best' (Schultz *et al.*, 1992, p. 59).

Sometimes, communications researchers seem to treat integrated marketing communications using various means of communications in an integrated manner almost or totally as a synonym for relationship marketing. However, in transaction marketing effective marketing communication about a bad or inappropriate product does not lead to a good result. By the same token, if the customers' interactions with products and services and other elements in the contacts between buyers and sellers are bad and create a negative communication effect, effective integrated marketing communications as a purely communications program does not develop lasting relationships. Hence, integrated marketing communications is not the same as relationship marketing, but clearly, it is an important part of a relationship marketing strategy (Duncan and Moriarty, 1999). If relationship marketing is to be successful, an integration of all marketing communications messages is needed to support the establishment, maintenance and enhancement of relationships with customers (and other stakeholders).

Consequently, the integrated management of marketing communications activities, regardless of the source of communication messages, is required in relationship marketing.

Interaction

In a transaction-oriented approach to marketing, the product is the core of the marketing mix. There must be a product so that decisions can be made about how to distribute it, how to promote it, and how to price it. However, the product exists at one given point of time; it does not evolve in an on-going relationship. Hence, the product as the core construct has to be replaced with a long-term construct that fits the nature of relationship marketing. The relationship approach puts customer processes, or rather the internal value-generating processes of customers, not products, at the center of marketing. To be successful, the supplier or service provider has to align its resources, competencies and processes with the customer's value-generating processes. This being the case, interaction evolves as a concept which takes the place of the product concept. It has been developed as one key construct in services marketing and in the network approach to industrial marketing as well, and has been taken over by relationship marketing. Thus, as the exchange of a product is the core of transaction marketing, the management of an interaction process is the core of relationship marketing. In this process, a supplier of goods or a service firm represented by people, technology and systems, and know-how interact with its customer represented by everything from a single consumer to a group of buyers, users and decision makers in a business relationship. Sometimes, more parties in a network may be involved in the interactions (Gummesson, 1996).

Interactions may be prompted by planned communication messages and programs, but for a commercial relationship to develop successful interactions have to follow. A dialogue between the supplier or service firm and its customers only emerge from value-enhancing interactions. Only planned communication activities easily lead to parallel monologues, where the two parties never actually meet and get access to what is shared or common between them. A dialogue process is required for a sharing and even creation of knowledge among the parties to occur. We will return to this in a later section.

Value

One recent research stream in marketing is related to customer perception of value created in on-going relationships (Ravald and Grönroos, 1996). The importance of adding a relationship aspect in studies of customer value has also been demonstrated, for example, by Lapierre (1997), Payne and Holt (1999), Tzokas and Saren (1999), Collins (1999) and Wilson and Jantrania (1994). In the inter-action processes a value base is transferred to and also partly created together with customers, and in the final analysis, the ultimate perceived value for them is emerging in the customer processes. Thus, if the supplier or service provider manages to successfully align its resources (physical product elements, service elements, information and other resources of various kinds) and competencies with its customers' internal processes, in these processes this value base is turned into customer perceived value. This creation of value should be supported by marketing communication before and during the interaction process of the rela-tionship. Therefore, a value process is needed to demonstrate how the customer indeed perceives the creation of value over time. When all three processes are in place and well understood we have a good part of a theory of relationship marketing.

However, the value process has another aspect as well. Before the development of elements of the interaction process and of the dialogue process the marketer must develop an understanding of the customer's internal process which the solution provided by the seller should fit. The customer has some needs but also a process whereby the organizational customer fulfils these needs. Hence, it is not enough to understand the needs of customers, one must also know how they strive to achieve the results required to fulfill these needs. This can be labelled the customer's value-generating process (Grönroos, 2000a; compare also Storbacka and Lehtinen, 2000). Moreover, one must know the value systems of the customer that guide this internal need-fulfilling and value-generating process. Examples of such values are an interest in preserving the rain forests, in recycling waste, in minimizing stocks, in creating a manufacturing process with a minimum of ecologically harmful effects, and in keeping standstill costs at a minimum. If the firm does not understand this aspect of the customer's value systems and value-generating processes (this process could also be labeled the customer value chain), products, services, information and other elements of the interaction process cannot be developed and offered in a satisfactory way, and *value for the customer* cannot be created successfully.

The core: the interaction process of relationship marketing

As was noted in the previous section, successful marketing requires a good enough solution for the user. In transaction marketing, this solution is a product in the form of a physical good or a core service. In relationship marketing the solution is the relationship itself and how it functions and leads to value creation and need satisfaction for the customer. Customers' perceptions of relationships are holistic and cumulative. As we have concluded before, the exchange or transfer of products managed in a trustworthy and timely manner are part of the relationship, but in addition to that a host of service elements is required. Without them the products may be of limited value or without value for the customer. For example, delayed deliveries, late service calls, badly handled complaints, lack of information or unfriendly personnel may destroy an otherwise good solution.

The relationship proceeds in an interaction process where various types of contacts between the supplier or service firm and the customer occur over time. These contacts may be very different depending on the type of marketing situation. Some contacts are between people, some between people and machines and systems, and some contacts are between systems of the supplier and the customer, respectively.

In order to be able to understand and in practical marketing situations analyze and plan the interaction process one has to divide it into logical parts. In the context of services the interaction process has been studied in terms of acts, episodes and relationship (Liljander, 1994; Liljander and Strandvik, 1995; see also Storbacka, 1994; Strandvik and Storbacka, 1996; Stauss and Weinlich, 1995). According to Liljander and Strandvik (1995) an episode is, for example, a visit to a bank office to discuss a loan, whereas an act among other is the meeting with the loan officer during the visit. In the context of business relationships, IMP researchers have traditionally offered a two-level approach including short-term episodes including exchange of goods and services, information, financial and social aspects, and long-term processes leading to adaptation and institutionalization of roles and responsibilities (Håkansson, 1982; Möller and Wilson, 1995). In a more generic business relationship context, Holmlund (1996, 1997) has developed the understanding of the interaction process further, in order to achieve an extended analytical depth in the analysis of relationships. In Figure 1 the interaction process of the on-going relationship is divided into four levels of aggregation: the act[1], episode, sequence and relationship level.

Acts are the smallest unit of analysis in the interaction process, such as phone calls, plant visits, service calls and hotel registration. In the service management literature they are often called moments of truth (Normann, 1992). Acts may be related to any kind of interaction elements, physical goods, services, information, financial aspects or social contacts.

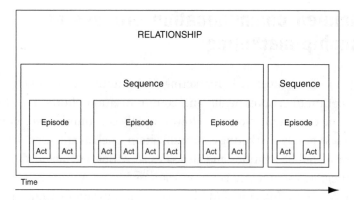

Figure 1 Interaction levels in a relationship
Source: Holmlund (1997, p. 96)

Interrelated acts form a minor natural entity in a relationship, an episode such as a negotiation, a shipment of goods and dinner at a hotel restaurant during a stay at that hotel. Every episode includes a series of acts. For example, 'a shipment may include such act(ion)s as the placement of an order by telephone, assembling and packing the products, transporting, . . . unpacking, making a complaint, and sending and paying an invoice'. (Holmlund, 1996, p. 49)

Interrelated episodes form the next level of analysis in the interaction process, a sequence. According to Holmlund (1996, pp. 49–50) sequences can be defined in terms of a time period, an offering, a campaign or a project, or a combination of these. 'This implies that the analysis of a sequence may contain all kind of interactions related to a particular year, when a particular project . . . has been carried out. Sequences may naturally overlap'. To take another type of example, in a restaurant context a sequence comprises everything that takes place during one visit to a particular restaurant.

The final and most aggregated level of analysis is the relationship. Several sequences form the relationship. Sequences may follow one another directly, may overlap or may follow with longer or shorter intervals depending, for example, on the type of business. This way of dividing the interaction process in several layers on different levels of aggregation gives the marketer, and the researcher, a detailed enough instrument to be used in the analysis of interactions between a supplier or service providers and their customers. In the formation of a relationship over time all different types of elements in the interaction process, goods and service outcomes, service processes, information, social contacts, financial activities etc., can be identified and put into their correct perspective.

The planned communication process of relationship marketing

According to the integrated marketing communications concept, various marketing communications media and communication efforts have to be integrated into one consistent message. However, only communicative activities that are more or less purely marketing communication, such as traditional advertising, direct response, public relations and also sales activities, are included (see the definition of integrated marketing communications by the American Association of Advertising Agencies' Integrated Marketing Communications Committee quoted in Reitman, 1994; see also Frischman, 1994). Other communications efforts are included only if they become transparent and merge with the marketing communications elements, as when distribution and communication might become the same in the case of direct response marketing (Stewart et al., 1996; Stewart, 1996).

The characteristic aspect of marketing communication in a relationship marketing context is an attempt to create a two-way or sometimes even a multi-way communication process. Not all activities are directly two-way communication, but all communication efforts should lead to a response of some sort that maintains and enhances the relationship. Any given effort, such as a sales meeting, direct mail letter or an information package, should be integrated into a planned on-going process. This planned communication process includes a variety of elements that, for example, can be divided into sales activities, mass communication activities, direct and interactive communication (other than sales efforts where a direct response is sought) and public relations. Any other number or type of categories could of course also be used, and the suggested groups naturally include a number of subgroups. Mass communication includes traditional advertising, brochures, sales letters where no immediate response is sought and other similar activities, whereas direct communication includes personally addressed letters including offers, information, recognition of interactions that have taken place, request of data about the customer etc. Here, a more direct response is sought in the form of feedback from previous interactions, request for more information or an offer, data about the customer, a purely social response, etc.

In Figure 2 the planned communication process is illustrated as a circle which parallels the interaction process, which in turn includes a number of episodes consisting of individual acts. For the sake of illustration, various types of communication efforts have been depicted throughout the on-going planned

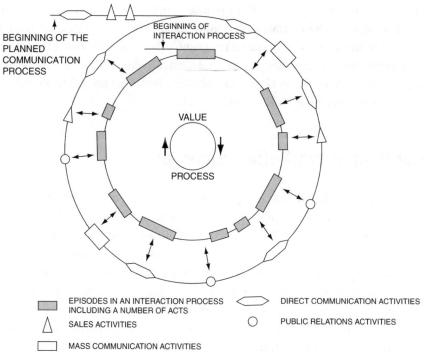

Figure 2   The interaction, planned communication and value processes
Source: Adapted from Grönroos (2000c, p. 107)

communication process. As can be seen this process often, but by no means always, starts before the interaction process. This is, of course, the stage where the relationship is established. From the point where the two processes go together the relationship is maintained and further enhanced. At some point the relationship may be broken or terminated. The interaction and planned communication processes indeed parallel one another, which means that they should support and not counteract one another. The two-way arrows between the two circles in Figure 2 indicate this. An activity in the planned communication process, a sales meeting or a personally addressed letter creates an expectation, and the interaction process must follow up on this expectation. If, for example, only the planned communication process is considered part of relationship marketing, negatively perceived acts or episodes in the interactions process easily destroy the initially good impression of a planned communication effort, and no relationship development takes place.

As a conclusion, although communication efforts such as sales negotiations and personally addressed letters may look relational, just planning and managing marketing communication through distinct communications media, even as a two-way process, is not relationship marketing. Only the integration of the planned communication and the interaction processes into one strategy that is systematically implemented creates relationship marketing. In such a case customers' perceived value of the relationship is developing favorably, as indicated by the value process circle in the middle of Figure 2.

Relationship marketing dialogue

Activities on both the interaction process and planned communication process send messages to customers about the firm and its way of serving its customers. Duncan and Moriarty (1997) divide the possible sources of messages into four groups, namely, planned marketing communication (i.e. messages sent as part of the planned communication process), product and service messages (i.e. messages created throughout the interaction process) and unplanned messages, where the first group can be expected to have the lowest credibility and the last group the highest credibility in the minds of customers. Planned marketing communication makes promises of how a solution to a customer's problems should function. Product messages include, for example, what the design, technical features, durability and distribution of product elements in a relationship communicate to customers. Service messages originate from interactions with an organization's customer service and other processes. Unplanned messages are communicated via news stories, employee gossip and word-of-mouth communication. In this context one should remember that absence of communication also sends distinct messages and therefore also contributes to the total communication process (Calonius, 1989). In Figure 3 these five sources of communication messages (including absence of communication) in on-going relationships are summarized and illustrated with examples.

Planned marketing communication takes place in the planned communication process in Figure 2. Product and service messages are created in the interaction process. Word-of-mouth referrals and other unplanned messages are a result of how customers and other individuals perceive these two processes and how they support or counteract one another. The various types of messages are developing in a continuous process, and in the minds of customers their effects are probably accumulating. This is illustrated in Figure 4 by the relationship communication globe. In the middle of the *globe* is the flow of interactions building up episodes, sequences of related episodes and eventually growing into a relationship (the interaction process zone of the globe). If the planned communication process with

PLANNED MESSAGES	PRODUCT MESSAGES	SERVICE MESSAGES	UNPLANNED MESSAGES	ABSENCE OF COMMUNICATION
Mass communication (e.g., advertising) Brochures Direct response Sales www-pages etc.	Usefeluness Design Appearance Rawmaterials Production processes etc.	Interactions with service processes Deliveries Invoicing Claims handling Product documentation Help centre services etc.	Word-of-mouth referrals References News stories Gossip Internet chatgroups etc.	Silence following a service breakdown Lack of information about the progress of service and manufact- uring processes etc.

Note: This figure is based on the discussion of communication messages in Duncan and Moriarty (1997). Duncan and Moriarty do not, however, discuss the communication impact of the fifth source of communication messages, i.e., *absence of communication*, a category of communication discussed in Calonius (1989)

Figure 3   Sources of communication messages in a relationship
Source: Grönroos (2000b)

its planned marketing communication (source 1 in the upper part of Figure 4) is supporting and supported by the product and service messages (sources 2 and 3) created in the flow of episodes of the interaction process, favorable unplanned communication (source 4) resulting in positive word-of-mouth communication will probably occur (Grönroos and Lindberg-Repo, 1998). Both the firm and the customer can be expected to be motivated to communicate with one another, which according to Dichter (1966) is a prerequisite for two parties to engage in a dialogue.

A dialogue can be seen as an interactive process of reasoning together (Ballantyne, 1999/2000), so a common knowledge platform is possible. If this knowledge plat- form enables the supplier to create additional value for the customer, relationship marketing is facilitated. Moreover, this should create extra value for the supplier as well. A connection between the firm and the customer has to be made, so that they find that they can trust one another in this dialogue or process of reasoning together. The intent of this process is to build shared meanings, and get insights in what the two parties can do together and for one another through access to a common meaning or shared field of knowledge (Schein, 1994; Bohm, 1996). Being involved in a dialogue means that one avails oneself of existing knowledge but also is involved in creating new knowledge (Gummesson, 1999), which, among other things, may lead to the development of better solutions for customers than otherwise would have been possible (Wikström and Normann, 1994).

Customers should feel that the firm which communicates with them shows a genuine interest in them and their needs, requirements and value systems and in a convincing way argues for products, services or other elements of the total

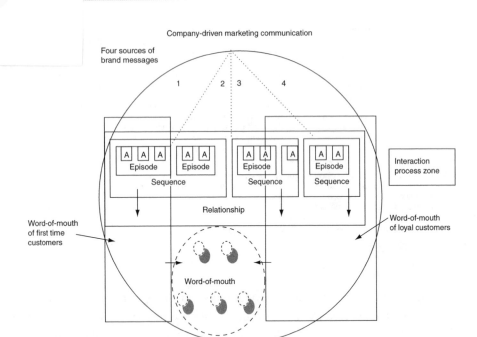

Figure 4 The relationship communication globe
Source: Adapted from Grönroos (1998, p. 10)

offering. Furthermore, they should see that the firm appreciates feedback and makes use of it. In such a situation the communication aspects of the interaction process of relationship marketing merge with the planned communication process into one single two-way communication process, i.e. the two processes merge into a relationship dialogue (Grönroos, 2000a, 2000b). The integration of planned communication messages with messages from the interaction process is required for dialogue to emerge. When a customer gets personal experiences of products, services, information etc., in the episodes of the interaction process, what Berlo (1960) calls connotative meaning might then be created. Through our personal experiences messages take on meaning[2] and a common knowledge platform of shared meanings has a chance to develop. However, for this to happen, all the parties involved have to be able to listen and respond to the other party's messages. In other words, planned communication messages do not lead to a dialogue. They may initiate a dialogue process, but interactions and interaction-based messages are required for one-way or even parallel monologues to develop into a dialogue. Finally, the nature and content of word-of-mouth referrals will probably differ depending how long the customer has been involved in the interaction process (Lindberg-Repo and Grönroos, 1999).

The value process of relationship marketing

Clearly, relationship marketing takes more efforts than transaction marketing. Therefore, a relationship marketing strategy must create more value for the customer or for some other party, such as a distributor, than the value of the mere transactions of goods or services in single episodes. The customer has to perceive and appreciate this value that is created in the on-going relationship. As a relationship is a process over time, value for customers is also emerging in a process over time. We call this a value process. If relationship marketing is to be successful and accepted as meaningful by the customer, there must be such a positive value process paralleling the planned communication and interaction processes that is appreciated by the customer.

Traditionally, value has been used in the marketing and consumer behavior literature as 'the value of customers for a firm'. Only to some extent has 'value for the customer' been discussed in the literature (for example, Peter and Olson, 1993; Zeithaml, 1988), and then it has more or less been in a transaction marketing context. For example, Zeithaml (1988) defines customer perceived value as the consumer's overall assessment of the utility of a product based on a perception of what is received and what is given. However, as Ravald and Grönroos (1996, p. 23) observe, 'the relational aspect as a constituent of the offering is not taken into account. . . . We suggest that the relationship itself might have a major effect on the total value perceived. In a close relationship the customer probably shifts the focus from evaluating separate offerings to evaluating the relationship as a whole. The core of the business, i.e. what the company is producing, is of course fundamental, but it may not be the ultimate reason for purchasing from a given supplier' (see Lapierre, 1997).

One can also imagine that even if the solution in terms of goods and services is not the best possible, if the relationship is considered valuable enough the parties involved may still find an agreement. 'Value is considered to be an important constituent of relationship marketing and the ability of a company to provide superior value to its customers is regarded as one of the most successful strategies . . .' (Ravald and Grönroos, 1996, p. 19; Heskett *et al.*, 1994; Nilson, 1992; Treacy and Wiersema, 1993).

When transactions are the foundation of marketing, the value for customers is more or less totally embedded in the exchange of a product for money in an episode. The perceived sacrifice equals the price paid for the product. However, when relationships are the base of marketing, the role of the product becomes blurred. In the case of industrial robots, for example, if the customer is to be satisfied with what has been bought, delivery, customer training, maintenance and spare part service, information and documentation about the use of a robot, claims handling and perhaps joint development of the final robots, and a number of other activities, are necessary additions to the core solution – the robot. If the additional services are missing or not good enough, it is easy to see how the value of the core of the offering becomes highly questionable. In a case like this the role of the core product to the value perception of customers is indeed very much blurred. Without the value-adding additional services it is highly questionable whether the core product, in this case the industrial robot, has any value at all.

In a relationship context the total offering includes both a core solution and additional services of various kinds (for instance, as demonstrated by the example of industrial robots). The sacrifice includes a price and also additional costs for the customer, owing to the fact that one is in relationship with another party. In a relationship context such additional sacrifice can be called relationship costs (Grönroos, 2000a). Such costs follow from the decision to go into a relationship with a supplier or service firm. Relationship costs may increase, if the customer, for example, has to keep larger inventories than necessary because of the delivery policy of the supplier (directly occurring relationship costs) or suffer from higher standstill costs than expected because of delayed repair and maintenance service or some other deviation from what has been agreed on (indirectly occurring relationship costs). Sometimes relationship costs are also purely psychological costs caused by the customer's feeling that he or she has lost control of the situation or cannot trust a supplier or service firm to perform according to plans.

Another way of looking at value for customers is to distinguish between a core value of an offering and an added value of additional elements in the relationship. Finally, the value for customer in a relationship can be seen as the sum of an episode value component and a value component that is embedded in the relationship itself. Hence, customer perceived value (CPV) in a relationship context can be described with the following three equations (Grönroos, 2000a):

$$CPV = \frac{\text{Core solution} + \text{additional services}}{\text{Price} + \text{relationship costs}} \tag{1}$$

$$CPV = \text{Core value} \pm \text{added value} \tag{2}$$

$$CPV = \text{Episode value} \pm \text{relationship value} \tag{3}$$

In a relationship customer perceived value is developing and perceived over time. In equation (1), the price has a short-term notion; in principle it is paid on delivery of the core product. However, relationship costs occur over time as the relationship develops, the usefulness of the core solution is perceived and the additional services are experienced in sequences of episodes and single acts. In equation (2), a long-term notion is also present. The added value component is experienced over time as the relationship develops. However, here it is important to observe the double signs. Often added value is treated as if something is always indeed added to a core value. This is clearly not the case, because the added value can also be negative. For example, a good core value of a machine can be decreased or even destroyed by untimely deliveries, delayed service, lack of necessary information, bad management of complaints handling, unclear or erroneous invoices, etc. The additional services do not add a positive value, instead by creating high and unexpected relationship costs they subtract from the basic core value, i.e. they provide a negative added value or cause value destruction.

In situations with negative added value, creating added value for customers does not necessarily require the addition of new services to the offering. Instead, in order to reduce or altogether eliminate the negative added value or rather value destruction effects, the firm must improve existing services in the relationship, such as deliveries, service and maintenance, invoicing, etc. Probably, this is a faster and more effective way of creating added value in most relationships than what the addition of new services is. When appropriate, new services, or physical product components, can of course be included in the offering. However, one should always remember that the value-enhancing effect of new services is counteracted and often offset by the value destruction of existing services that are perceived in a negative way.

Finally, as demonstrated by equation (3), on top of the value created by singular episodes (including the exchange of, for example, product elements, service elements, information or other kinds of resources), customer perceived value can be expected to include an explicit value component related to the mere fact that a relationship with a supplier or service provider exists (compare Sheth and Par vatiyar, 1995b; and Bagozzi, 1995). This value component includes, for example, a feeling of security, and a sense of trust, controlled relationship costs and minimized purchasing risks. This relationship value part of the equation should be positive, of course. However, if value destructors are present in the relationship, it can also be negative. In that case it is debatable whether the customer perceives that a relationship with the other party really exists. The customer may continue doing business with the same supplier only because of bonds related to, for example, price, location or technology. Theoretically, it seems important to keep the episode and relationship value components apart. Customers may, however, not always perceive them separately.

The core solutions and additional services provided in the sequences of episodes in the interaction process should create a perceived value for the customer on an on-going basis. The core value should not be counteracted by negative added value through badly or untimely handled services. Simultaneously, the communication activities in the planned communication process should support this value process and not counteract or destroy it.

In conclusion, a successful relationship marketing strategy requires that all three of the processes discussed be taken into account in relationship marketing planning. The interaction process is the core of relationship marketing, the planned communication process is the distinct communications aspect of relationship marketing, and the value process is the outcome of relationship marketing. When these processes are integrated a consistent total marketing communication impact is created. If this integration is successful, the interaction and planned communication processes may merge into a dialogue in an on-going relationship between a customer and a supplier or service provider.

If the progress of the customer value processes is not carefully analyzed, wrong or inadequate actions in the two other processes may easily be taken. In that case, owing to conflicting signals to customers and promises which are not fulfilled, the value process may easily take a negative turn. If any one of the three key processes is not analyzed and planned carefully, the implementation of relationship marketing may suffer.

Conclusions

In the literature relationship marketing is often offered as a solution for all customers in all situations where such a relationship approach is suitable. This is probably not the case. Some customers may be more willing to accept a relational contact with a firm, whereas others may want to have a transactional contact. Moreover, a person may in one situation be interested in a relationship and in other situations not. 'Thus, in a given marketing situation the consumer (or user in a business-to-business relationship) is either in a relational mode or in a transactional mode. Furthermore, consumers in a relational mode can be either in an active or passive relational mode. Consumers or users in an active mode seek contact, whereas consumers in a passive mode are satisfied with the understanding that if needed the firm will be there for them' (Grönroos, 1997, p. 409). There have been some suggestions in the literature why customers choose to enter a relational mode and react favorably to a relationship marketing approach (for example, Sheth and Parvatiyar, 1995b; Bagozzi, 1995), but so far there is almost no empirical research in this area. For example, we know far too little about the antecedents of an active or a passive relational mode, and about endogenous or exogenous factors that trigger a shift from a transactional mode to a relational mode or from a passive relational mode to an active one.

When the process of managing the firm's market relationships is approached from a relationship perspective, marketing is spread throughout the organization. Marketing resources, for example part-time marketers (Gummesson, 1991), are found all over the firm, and not only in a marketing department. Although specialists on traditional marketing areas such as market research, marketing communication and pricing still are needed, of course, marketing is no longer only or even predominantly a function of its own. It becomes part of many functions in the firm. In such a situation 'marketing cannot be organized. . . . Marketing can only be instilled in the organization' (Grönroos, 2000a, p. 311).

In business-to-business relationships the problems with traditional marketing mix approaches have long been recognized. In many firms the role of marketing as a separate function in customer relationships has often been minor. Marketing departments have frequently been preoccupied with planned marketing communication, however without integrating this very much with other elements of the relationships with the firm's customers. In business-to-business relationships the relationship perspective offers a comprehensive framework for integrating planned communication with the whole range of interactions with customers that take place. In that way marketing can truly be instilled in the organization and a true customer orientation be achieved.

The phenomenon 'marketing', i.e. managing the market relationships of an organization, is increasingly important, but the term 'marketing' may not always be the best possible anymore. Although in principle, people outside the group of marketing specialists, for example the part-time marketers and their supervisors and managers, may accept their role and responsibilities as part-time marketers, they do not necessarily want to associate themselves with something that is labelled marketing. For many of them the term marketing has a meaning which is colored by its transaction marketing history. Frequently marketing as practised by the marketing department has lost its credibility. 'To create an understanding of relationship marketing in an organization and to implement a culture of relationship marketing, it may be necessary to replace the term marketing with a psychologically more readily accepted term to describe the task of managing the firm's customer relationships' (Grönroos, 1999, p. 334). This notion offers interesting and challenging research opportunities. To some people, academics as well as practitioners, the idea of abolishing the term marketing may sound unnecessary, even heretic, but there are examples of firms that have renamed the process of managing their market relationships, and with successful results as far as the customer orientation of the organization as well as an increased acceptance of 'marketing' throughout the firm are concerned (see, for example, Grönroos, 2000a). We should also remember that the term 'marketing' is not more than a century old, whereas the phenomenon 'marketing' is as old as the history of trade and commerce. The term used for this phenomenon has been changed before.

A shift towards the adoption of a relationship marketing approach will demand a number of changes to old structures and attitudes. Substantial internal marketing (George, 1990; Ballantyne, 1997; Grönroos, 2000a; Voima, 2000) will be required. The traditional way of organizing the firm, the system for planning marketing, the methods and instruments for measuring success in the marketplace, the philosophy of market segmentation as a way of structuring the total market into a meaningful market platform, to mention a few only, have to be challenged, which we have done in another context (Grönroos, 1999). The need for such changes is really not very surprising. After all, most of the structures and attitudes that still are dominating marketing research and the practice of marketing alike are from the industrial era where a transactional approach to marketing did well for firms. However, today we live in a post-industrial society, sometimes labeled 'the new economy'. Marketing cannot live on untouched by the changes in the surrounding world.

Notes

1. Holmlund (1997) uses the term action, but here we use the term act, originally suggested by Liljander and Strandvik (1995) to describe the smallest unit of analysis.
2. As Gayeski (1993) argues, message and meaning are the two fundamental components of a communication process.

References

Arndt, J. (1979), 'Towards a concept of domesticated markets', *Journal of Marketing*, Vol. 43, Fall, pp. 69–75.
Bagozzi, R.P. (1995), 'Reflections on relationship marketing in consumer markets', *Journal of the Academy of Marketing Science*, Vol. 23 No. 1, pp. 272–7.

Ballantyne, D. (1997), 'Internal networks for internal marketing', *Journal of Marketing Management*, Vol. 13 No. 5, pp. 343–66.

Ballantyne, D. (2000), 'Dialogue and knowledge generation: two sides of the same coin in relationship marketing', paper presented at the 2nd WWW Conference on Relationship Marketing, November 1999–February 2000, Monash University and MCB University Press, available at: www.mcb.co.uk/services/conferen/nov99/rm/paper3. html

Berlo, D.K. (1960), *The Process of Communication*, Holt Rinehart & Winston, New York, NY.

Berry, L.L. (1983), 'Relationship marketing', in Berry, L.L., Shostack, G.L. and Upah, G.D. (Eds), *Emerging Perspectives on Services Marketing*, Proceedings Series, American Marketing Association, Chicago, IL.

Bitner, M.J. (1995), 'Building service relationships: it's all about promises', *Journal of the Academy of Marketing Science*, Vol. 23 No. 4, pp. 246–51.

Bohm, D. (1996), *On Dialogue*, Routledge, London.

Booms, B.H. and Bitner, M.J. (1981), 'Marketing strategies and organization structures for service firms', in Donnelly, J.H. and George, W.R. (Eds), *Marketing of Services*, Proceedings Series, American Marketing Association, Chicago. IL.

Brodie, R.J., Coviello, N.E., Brookes, R.W. and Little, V. (1997), 'Towards a paradigm shift in marketing? An examination of current marketing practices', *Journal of Marketing Management*, Vol. 13 No. 5, pp. 383–406.

Calonius, H. (1989), 'Market communication in service marketing', in Avlonitis, G.J., Papavasiliou, N.K. and Kouremeos, A.G. (Eds) *Marketing Thought and Practice in the 1990s, Proceedings from the XVIIIth Annual Conference of the European Marketing Academy*, Athens.

Christopher, M., Payne, A. and Ballantyne, D. (1991), *Relationship Marketing: Bringing Quality, Customer Service and Marketing Together*, Butterworth-Heinemann, Oxford.

Collins, B. (1999), 'Pairing relationship value and marketing', *Australasian Marketing Journal*, Vol. 7 No. 1, pp. 63–71.

Coviello, N.E. and Brodie, R.J. (1998), 'From transaction to relationship marketing: an investigation of managerial perceptions and practices', *Journal of Strategic Marketing*, Vol. 6 No. 3, pp. 171–86.

Coviello, N.E., Brodie, R.J., Brookes, R.W. and Collins, B. (1997), 'From transaction marketing to relationship marketing: an investigation of market perceptions and prac-tices', *Fifth International Colloquium in Relationship Marketing*, November, Cranfield University, Cranfield.

Dichter, E. (1966), 'How word-of-mouth advertising works', *Harvard Business Review*, Vol. 44 November-December, pp. 147–66.

Duncan, T. and Moriarty, S. (1997), *Driving Brand Value*, McGraw-Hill, New York, NY.

Duncan, T. and Moriarty, S. (1999), 'Commentary on relationship-based marketing communications', *Australasian Marketing Journal*, Vol. 7 No. 1, pp. 118–20.

Frischman, D.E. (1994), 'A voice of reality', in Faure, C. and Klein, L. (Eds), *Marketing Communications Strategies Today and Tomorrow: Integration, Allocation, and Inter-active Technologies*, Report 94–109, Marketing Science Institute, Cambridge, MA, pp. 35–6.

Gayeski, D. (1993), *Corporate Communication Management*, Focal Press, Boston, MA.

George, W.R. (1990), 'Internal marketing and organizational behavior: a partnership in developing customer-conscious employees at every level', *Journal of Business Research*, Vol. 20 No. 1, pp. 63–70.

Grönroos, C. (1980), 'Designing a long range marketing strategy for services', *Long Range Planning*, Vol. 13 April, pp. 36–42.

Grönroos, C. (1983), *Strategic Management and Marketing in the Service Sector*, Marketing Science Institute, Cambridge, MA (original published in 1982).

Grönroos, C. (1989), 'Defining marketing: a market-oriented approach', *European Journal of Marketing*, Vol. 23 No. 1, pp. 52–60.

Grönroos, C. (1996), 'Relationship marketing logic', *Asia-Australia Marketing Journal*, Vol. 4 No. 1, pp. 1–12.

Grönroos, C. (1997), 'Value-driven relational marketing: from products to resources and competencies', *Journal of Marketing Management*, Vol. 13 No. 5, pp. 407–20.

Grönroos, C. (1998), 'Marketing services: the case of the missing product', *Journal of Business and Industrial Marketing*, Vol. 13 No. 4/5, pp. 322–38.

Grönroos, C. (1999), 'Relationship marketing: challenges for the organization', *Journal of Business Research*, Vol. 46 No. 3, pp. 327–35.

Grönroos, C. (2000a), *Service Management and Marketing: A Customer Relationship Management Approach*, Wiley, New York, NY.

Grönroos, C. (2000b), 'Creating a relationship dialogue: communication, interaction, value', *Marketing Review*, Vol. 1 No. 1, pp. 5–14.

Grönroos, C. and Gummesson, E. (1985), 'The Nordic School of service marketing', in Grönroos, C. and Gummesson, E. (Eds), *Service Marketing – Nordic School Perspectives*, Stockholm University, Stockholm, pp. 6–11.

Grönroos, C. and Lindberg-Repo, K. (1998), 'Integrated marketing communications: the communications aspect of relationship marketing', *The IMC Research Journal*, Vol. 4 No. 1, pp. 3–11.

Gummesson, E. (1983), 'A new concept of marketing', *Proceedings of the European Marketing Academy (EMAC)*, Institut d'Etudes Commerciales de Grenoble, France, April.

Gummesson, E. (1987), 'The new marketing – developing long-term interactive relationships', *Long Range Planning*, Vol. 20 No. 4, pp. 10–20.

Gummesson, E. (1991), 'Marketing revisited: the crucial role of the part-time marketer', *European Journal of Marketing*, Vol. 25 No. 2, pp. 60–7.

Gummesson, E. (1996), 'Relationship marketing and imaginary organizations: a synthesis', *European Journal of Marketing*, Vol. 30 No. 2, pp. 31–44.

Gummesson, E. (1999), *Total Relationship Marketing. Rethinking Marketing Management: From 4 Ps to 30 Rs*, Butterworth-Heinemann, Oxford.

Håkansson, H. Ed. (1982), *International Marketing and Purchasing of Industrial Goods*, Wiley, New York, NY.

Håkansson, H. and Snehota, I. (1995), *Developing Relationships in Business Networks*, Routledge, London.

Heskett, J.L., Jones, T.O., Loveman, G.W., Sasser, W.E. and Schelsinger, L.A. (1994), 'Putting the service-profit chain to work', *Harvard Business Review*, Vol. 72, March-April, pp. 164–74.

Holmlund, M. (1996), *A Theoretical Framework of Perceived Quality in Business Relationships*, Hanken Swedish School of Economics Helsinki/CERS, Helsingfors.

Holmlund, M. (1997), *Perceived Quality in Business Relationships*, Hanken Swedish School of Economics Finland/CERS, Helsingfors.

Hunt, S.D. and Morgan, R.M. (1994), 'Relationship marketing in the era of network competition', *Marketing Management*, Vol. 3 No. 1, pp. 19–30.

Jackson, B.B. (1985), 'Build customer relationships that last', *Harvard Business Review*, Vol. 63, November–December, pp. 120–8.

Lapierre, J. (1997), 'What does value mean in business-to-business professional services?', *International Journal of Service Industry Management*, Vol. 8 No. 5, pp. 377–97.

Levitt, T. (1983a), *The Marketing Imagination*, Free Press, New York, NY.

Levitt, T. (1983b), 'After the sale is over', *Harvard Business Review*, Vol. 61, September-October, pp. 87–93.

Liljander, V. (1994), 'Introducing deserved service and equity into service quality models', in Kleinaltenkamp, M. (Ed.), *Dienstleistungsmarketing – Konzeptionen und Anwendungen*, Gabler Edition Wissenschaft, Berlin, pp. 1–30.

Liljander, V. and Strandvik, T. (1995), 'The nature of customer relationships in services', in Bowen, D., Brown, S.W. and Swartz, T.A. (Eds), *Advances in Services Marketing and Management*, Vol. 4, JAI Press, Greenwich, CT, pp. 141–67.

Lindberg-Repo, K. and Grönroos, C. (1999), 'Word-of-mouth referrals in the domain of relationship marketing', *Australasian Marketing Journal*, Vol. 7 No. 1, pp. 109–17.

Mattsson, L-G. (1997), 'Relationship marketing and the "market-as-networks" approach: a comparative analysis of two evolving streams of research', *Journal of Marketing Management*, Vol. 13 No. 5, pp. 447–61.

Möller, K. and Wilson, D. (1995), 'Business relationships: an interaction perspective', in Möller, K. and Wilson, D. (Eds), *Business Marketing: An Interaction and Network Perspective*, Kluwer Academic, Boston, MA, pp. 23–52.

Nilson, T.H. (1992), *Value-Added Marketing: Marketing for Superior Results*, McGaw-Hill, London.

Normann, R. (1992), *Service Management*, 2nd ed., Wiley, New York, NY.

Payne, A. and Holt, S. (1999), 'Review of the "Value" literature and implications for relationship marketing', *Australasian Marketing Journal*, Vol. 7 No. 1, pp. 41–51.

Peter, J.P. and Olson, J.C. (1993), *Consumer Behavior and Marketing Strategy*, 3rd ed., Irwin, Homewood, IL.

Ravald, A. and Grönroos, C. (1996), 'The value concept and relationship marketing', *European Journal of Marketing*, Vol. 30 No. 2, pp. 19–30.

Reichheld, F.E. (1993), 'Loyalty-based management', *Harvard Business Review*, Vol. 2, March-April, pp. 64–73.

Reichheld, F.E. and Sasser, W.E. Jr. (1990), 'Zero defections: quality comes to services', *Harvard Business Review*, Vol. 68, September-October, pp. 105–11.

Reitman, J. (1994), 'Integrated marketing: fantasy or the future?', in Faure, C. and Klein, L. (Eds), *Marketing Communications Strategies Today and Tomorrow: Integration, Allocation, and Interactive Technologies*, Report 94–109, Marketing Science Institute, Cambridge, MA, pp. 30–2.

Schein, E.H. (1994), 'The process of dialogue: creating effective communication', *The Systems Thinker*, Vol. 5 No. 5, pp. 1–4.

Schultz, D.E. (1996), 'The inevitability of integrated communications', *Journal of Business Research*, Vol. 37 No. 3, pp. 139–46.

Schultz, D.E., Tannenbaum, S.I. and Lauterborn, R.F. (1992), *Integrated Marketing Communications*, NTC Publishing, Lincolnwood, IL.

Sheth, J.N. and Parvatiyar, A. Eds. (1994), 'Relationship marketing: theory, methods, and applications', *Proceedings of the 1994 Relationship Marketing Research Conference*, Center for Relationship Marketing, Emory University, Atlanta, GA, June.

Sheth, J.N. and Parvatiyar, A. (1995a), 'The evolution of relationship marketing', *International Business Review*, Vol. 4 No. 4, pp. 397–418.

Sheth, J.N. and Parvatiyar, A. (1995b), 'Relationship marketing in consumer markets', *Journal of the Academy of Marketing Science*, Vol. 23 No. 4, pp. 255–71.

Stauss, B. and Weinlich, B. (1995), 'Process-oriented measurement of service quality by applying the sequential incident technique', paper presented at the Fifth Workshop on Quality Management in Services, EIASM, Tilburg.

Stewart, D.W. (1996), 'Market-back approach to the design of integrated communications programs: a change in paradigm and a focus on determinants of success', *Journal of Business Research*, Vol. 37 No. 3, pp. 147–54.

Stewart, D.W., Frazier, G. and Martin, I. (1996), 'Integrated channel management: merging the communications and distributions functions of the firm', in Thorson, E. and Moore, J. (Eds), *Integrated Marketing and Consumer Psychology*, Lawrence Erlbaum Associates, Hillsdale, NJ.

Storbacka, K. (1994), *The Nature of Customer Relationship Profitability: Analyses of Relationships and Customer Bases in Retail Banking*, Swedish School of Economics and Business Administration, Helsingfors.

Storbacka, K. and Lehtinen, J.R. (2000), *Customer Relationship Management* (in Swedish), Liber Ekonomi, Malmö.

Strandvik, T. and Storbacka, K. (1996), 'Managing relationship quality', paper presented at the QUIS 5 Quality in Services Conference, University of Karlstad, Karlstad.

Treacy, M. and Wiersema, F. (1993), 'Customer intimacy and other value disciplines', *Harvard Business Review*, January-February, pp. 84–93.

Tzokas, N. and Saren, M. (1999), 'Value transformation in relationship marketing', *Australasian Journal of Marketing*, Vol. 7 No. 1, pp. 52–62.

Vavra, T.G. (1994), 'The database marketing imperative', *Marketing Management*, Vol. 2 No. 1, pp. 47–57.

Voima, P. (2000), 'Internal relationship management – broadening the scope of internal marketing', in Varey, R.J. and Lewis, B.R. (Eds), *Internal Marketing: Directions for Management*, Routledge, London.

Webster, F.E. Jr (1994), 'Executing the new marketing concept', *Marketing Management*, Vol. 3 No. 1, pp. 9–18.

Wikstrom, S. and Normann, R. Eds. (1994), *Knowledge and Value: A New Perspective on Corporate Transformation*, Routledge, London.

Wilson, D.T. and Jantrania, S. (1994), 'Understanding the value of a relationship', *Asia-Australia Marketing Journal*, Vol. 2 No. 1, pp. 55–66.

Zeithaml, V.A. (1988), 'Consumer perceptions of price, quality and value: a means-end model and a synthesis of evidence', *Journal of Marketing*, Vol. 52, July, pp. 2–22.

Further reading

Dixon, N. (1998), *Dialogue at Work*, Lemos and Crane, London.

Grönroos, C. (2000c), 'Relationship marketing: the Nordic School perspective', in Sheth, J.N. and Parvatiyar, A. (Eds), *Handbook of Relationship Marketing*, Sage, Thousand Oaks, CA, pp. 95–118.

Part Three
A New Logic for Marketing

Adopting a Service Logic for Marketing

Following the article by Vargo and Lusch (2004) the use of a service-dominant logic has become an international topic for discussion. In the present article, following the research tradition of the Nordic School the contribution of service marketing to marketing at large is discussed. In this article a service logic is compared to a goods logic. It is concluded that a service logic fits best the context of most goods producing businesses today. These conclusions are similar to those proposed by Vargo and Lusch (2004). However, there are differences as well, as the approach of the Nordic School is to study services directly in their marketing context and report on how changing marketing contexts influence the logic required for effective marketing.

Introduction

Although there are some earlier service marketing publications, the development of service-oriented concepts and models started in the 1970s. However, it was Lynn Shostack's (1977) article in the *Journal of Marketing* that really promoted service marketing as an interesting and acceptable field of research, albeit one that has since developed separately from mainstream goods-based marketing.

Reprinted by permission of Sage Publications Ltd from: Grönroos, C. Adapting a Service Logic for Marketing. *Marketing Theory*, 2006; **6**(3): 317–333.

Likewise, the *Journal of Marketing* article by Stephen Vargo and Robert Lusch (2004) discussing a new service-dominant logic (S-D logic) for marketing has fuelled a truly international discussion about the potential of a service logic to change the mainstream, goods-based logic. The authors conclude that 'perhaps the central implication of a service-centered dominant logic is the general change in perspective' (Vargo and Lusch, 2004:12). However, between the years 1977 and 2004 there is an abundance of research in service marketing and relationship marketing where service-based concepts and models have been developed, and in quite a few cases, the potential for a service logic to impact mainstream marketing has been discussed.

In Europe, two internationally recognised schools of service marketing research started to develop in the early 1970s (Berry and Parasuraman, 1993), one based in the Nordic countries (see Grönroos and Gummesson, 1985) and the other in France (Eiglier and Langeard, 1976; Langeard and Eiglier, 1987). Both these schools of thought took the standpoint that a new marketing perspective was needed. For example, Grönroos (1978, 1982) and Gummesson (1979, 1991), representing the Nordic School, argued that marketing must not remain a business function on its own and be the responsibility of a marketing department. They also demonstrated that customer preferences were influenced by a number of resources and interactions – employees as well as physical resources and systems – outside the scope and responsibility of a marketing department. Customers were also found to be a 'resource' participating as co-producers in the service production process (Grönroos, 1978; Gummesson, 1979; Lehtinen, 1983; Eiglier and Langeard, 1976). Moreover, as an extension of this view of the customer as participant in the service process, Grönroos noted that *'the consumers are actively taking part in shaping the service offering, i.e., in product development. . . .* The consumer himself can be considered part of the service he buys and consumes' (Grönroos,1978: 596; emphasis in original) and 'the *consumer influence* on the service offering is twofold. The consumer himself takes part in the production process and, consequently, has an impact on what he gets in return. On the other hand, the other customers simultaneously buying or consuming a service also influence the service offering' (Grönroos, 1982:38–39).

To understand the development of the Nordic School view of service marketing it is also important that one keeps in mind another factor. Contrary to a mainstream approach to service marketing research, where the starting point was existing, goods-based marketing models, the researchers took the *phenomenon* of service in its marketing context as a starting point, and asked themselves, 'How should marketing look like to fit this phenomenon?'. In this way existing marketing models that had been developed based on a different logic did not become a straitjacket for the development of service marketing.

The *purpose* of this article, mainly drawing on the Nordic School research tradition, is to discuss marketing based on a *service logic* and to analyse if and how this perspective fits the marketing of goods as well. Although there are some differences between the Nordic School perspective and the service-dominant logic of Vargo and Lusch (2004), there are many features in common. According to the Nordic School view, because the customer contacts of goods marketers include more and more service elements, a marketing orientation based on the logic of service as has been developed over the past three decades, may also fit the marketing of goods. A point of difference is that with Vargo and Lusch (2004), goods are seen as transmitters of service, as distribution mechanisms for customers achieving value-in-use. Mostly the difference stems from the fact that the Nordic School view is based on studies of services in their marketing context, whereas the service-dominant logic as presented by Vargo and Lusch is derived from an analysis of the service concept based on an extensive analysis of how this concept has been side-lined in classic economic theory (Vargo and Lusch, 2004: 6–8; also Vargo and Morgan, 2005).

Penetrating the black box of consumption

Within the research tradition of the Nordic School of service marketing it was early established that the only aspect of services that clearly distinguishes them from physical goods is their *process* nature. Services emerge in 'open' processes where the customers participate as co-producers and hence can be directly influenced by the progress of these processes. Traditionally physical goods are produced in 'closed' production processes where the customer only perceives the goods as outcomes of the process.

Traditional goods-based marketing models do not provide the marketer with any means of entering the consumption process in an interactive way. Only the good as the product variable in the marketing mix is perceived by the customer, perhaps supported by some information provided by marketing communication. However, the goods are not interactive and the marketer does not know what the customer is doing with the goods. Therefore, consumption is a *black box* for the goods marketer.

Given the processual nature of services, it follows that the consumption and production of services are at least partly simultaneous processes, and that the service provider at least partly enters the consumption sphere. The production of services is an 'open system' for the consumer, but likewise the consumption of services is an open system for the service provider (see for example, Grönroos, 1978; Gummesson 1979; Lehtinen, 1983). According to goods marketing models the goods are delivered to customers but the consumption of goods is a 'closed system' for the firm and the process of consuming goods is treated as a black box. These two characteristics of services – their process nature and the fact that customers consume the service while it is produced and hence are involved in the service production process – have had a profound impact on the concepts and models of service marketing that have been developed by Nordic School researchers. Although some of the four characteristics of services invariably listed in service marketing publications (see Fisk, Brown and Bitner, 1993) – intangibility, heterogeneity, inseparability, perishability – sometimes are mentioned, they have never been emphasised very much (see also the criticism of them in Lovelock and Gummesson, 2005).

The process nature and observation that customers at the same time are both co-producers and consumers of a service made Nordic School researchers focus on the role and effects of the consumption process on marketing. The most important contribution to marketing by service marketing research is that the black box of consumption in goods-based marketing models was penetrated and explored (Grönroos, 2006). Previous marketing models that revolve around the marketing mix metaphor and the view of marketing as one separate function have been geared towards pushing products, goods or services, albeit in the best case as suggested by the marketing concept, based on what customers in specific target groups really are looking for.

As *exchange* has been viewed as the subject matter of marketing research (Bagozzi, 1975) and facilitating exchange has been considered the objective of marketing, mainstream models have become focused on transactions and on creating and facilitating transactions. In other words, marketing had been preoccupied with persuading customers to buy, i.e., to engage in transactions, and mainstream marketing is still preoccupied with that. What happens after the purchase during the consumption process has been outside the scope of marketing. Hence, to use a *promise* metaphor (Calonius, 1986), goods-based marketing models have been and still are geared towards making promises, whereas the fulfilment of the expectations created by these promises by means other than a pre-produced product is essentially outside the scope of marketing and the realm of the firm's marketers.

Service marketing research changed all this. Already in the 1970s in the Nordic School research, a marketing approach geared toward facilitating *interactions* with customers during their consumption process rather than the exchange itself was developed (Gummesson, 1979 and Grönroos, 1978). In France the foundations for incorporating consumption within the scope of services marketing were laid. This was the system-model labelled *servuction* (Eiglier and Langeard, 1976; Langeard and Eiglier, 1987). Also in North America there was interest in 'selling' jobs to employees (Sasser and Arbeit, 1976) and in *internal marketing* (Berry, 1981). As well, there was interest in incorporating additional service-oriented ingredients into an augmented marketing mix for services (Booms and Bitner, 1982), and the observation made that without being integrated with human resource management and operations, marketing in service organisations cannot be successfully implemented (see for example, Lovelock, 1984). All these demonstrate a desire to make the management of the consumption process part of service marketing.

However, the established view of marketing as a separate function and the use of the marketer-as-a-mixer-of-ingredients metaphor (Culliton, 1948; Borden, 1964) really do not make it possible to enjoin in marketing activities those people and activities from functions other than the marketing function. This, in turn, has restricted the development of service marketing and made it difficult to incorporate these observations in an integrated service marketing body of knowledge.

The Nordic School research took another approach. Because services were seen as a phenomenon in the marketing context, no existing marketing perspectives, models and concepts were taken as the starting point for research. It became quite obvious that without including the *interactions* between the service provider and the customer during the consumption process as an integrated part of marketing, successful marketing could not be implemented and realistic marketing models could not be developed. Therefore, exchange and facilitating transactions never became a focus of research, nor a starting point for the development of marketing models. Instead facilitating interactions and the management of interactions between the firm and the customer became a more productive focal point. Much of the Nordic School research has been geared towards this view. Although at some point the consumption of a service and therefore also the production of that service has come to an end and the customer has paid money for it, it is successful management of interactions that makes this possible. A first exchange may occur, but without successful interactions, continuous exchanges will not take place. Moreover, as services are processes, rather than objects for transactional exchange, it is impossible to assess at which *point in time* an exchange would have taken place. Money can be transferred to the service provider either before the service process or after the process or continuously on a regular basis over time. However, as Ballantyne and Varey conclude (2006:228), 'interactions over time are enactments of the exchange process', and thus exchange is seen here as a higher order concept. Although one can argue theoretically that exchanges take place in services, exchange is a too fuzzy and elusive phenomenon to be used as the focal point of marketing research. As a construct, *exchange*, and *relational exchange*, points at *transactions* and draws the researcher's and practitioner's attention away from what is essential for service marketing, namely *process* and *interaction*. In a relationship marketing context Sheth and Parvatiyar (2000) came to a similar conclusion, namely that exchange theory perhaps should be given up.

Focus on interactions instead of exchange

A focus on interactions by Nordic School researchers has lead to a new and different perspective on marketing. It was noticed that marketing is not one function but several functions: a *traditional external function*, involving typically specialist activities such as advertising, market research and direct mail, and an *interactive marketing function*, drawing on resources from functions other than the marketing specialist function. *Interactive marketing* is what takes place during the interactions when the simultaneous production and consumption occur (Grönroos, 1982). Following the observation of the importance of interactive marketing to overall marketing success the concept of *part-time marketers* was introduced (Gummesson, 1987; 1991). During these simultaneous production and consumption processes, no representative of a separate specialist marketing function is present. In the *moments of truth* concept (Normann, 1983), successful service marketing becomes the responsibility of the part-time marketer for making customers satisfied. How well this happens is dependent on the knowledge, skills and motivation of the part-time marketers to handle interactions with customers in a marketing fashion. Bitner (1992) has shown with the *servicescape* model that much more than the impact of employees influence customer perceptions (see also, for example, the *servuction* model in Langeard and Eiglier, 1976:11; the *interactive marketing* resource model in Grönroos, 1982:36; and the *service style/consuming style* model in Lehtinen, 1983). Of course, frequently the service employees are in a pivotal position. Of all employees whose work and behaviour one way or another impacts on customers, the part-time marketers normally outnumber the marketers of the marketing department several times. Moreover, as Gummesson (1991) concludes, the marketing specialists of the marketing department are seldom at the right place at the right time with the right customer contacts.

Also, the concept of *perceived service quality*, where quality perception takes place during the consumption process, was developed and introduced to help understand the consumption of services (Grönroos, 1982:33–34, 1984; see also Edvardsson, 2005, on the role of service quality and the service experience when consuming services). Perceived service quality was picked up by researchers in North America (first and predominantly by Berry, Parasuraman and Zeithaml). The perceived service quality model was extended to the *gap model* (Parasuraman, Zeithaml and Berry, 1985; see also a comparison between the Nordic School and American approaches to service quality and for an extension of such models in Brady and Cronin, 2001), also to the *Servqual* measurement instrument (Parasuraman, Zeithaml and Berry, 1988), to *Servperf* (Cronin and Taylor, 1992; see also Liljander, 1995), and subsequently extended to include the notion of *tolerance zones* (Berry and Parasuraman, 1991; see also Strandvik, 1994).

However, it is interesting to note that service quality studies have been positioned as just that, as studies of how the quality of services is perceived. Publications where service quality and marketing are clearly integrated are exceptional (for a noteworthy exception see Christopher, Payne and Ballantyne, 1991). Even though service quality studies have been presented at marketing conferences and published in service marketing journals, studies of service quality have, if at all, only vaguely and indirectly through the *customer expectations* variable been related to marketing and to understanding the consumption process and to how to facilitate the interactions with customers as part of marketing. The reason for this is probably that the specialist marketing function alone cannot manage the perception of quality, and accordingly, the mainstream perspective of marketing is restricted to what it can functionally do. To manage service quality a customer consciousness has to permeate all business functions. An interest in customers must be extended to everyone – and every system and physical resource as well – who has a direct or indirect impact on the customers' perception of quality. One way or another, a customer focus has to be present throughout the firm and not be restricted to the marketing department. In service marketing the concept of internal marketing was developed to help firms create customer consciousness and motivation for interactive marketing throughout the organisation (Berry 1981; Grönroos, 1982:40; see also Ballantyne, 2003, for a relationship-oriented development of internal marketing, and Lings and Greenley, 2005, for a development of an internal market orientation instrument).

In conclusion, although part of service marketing research has been hampered by the mainstream marketing paradigm, research into service marketing has broken new ground for marketing. It has opened up the black box of consumption and created a marketing perspective, concepts and models that are potentially useful for understanding the marketing of products other than services. We shall return to this in a later section.

Services as activities and service as a marketing logic

Especially during the 1980s, how to define a service was discussed extensively. Yet so far, there is no common definition in the literature. Based on the Nordic School view, services can be defined as *processes that consist of a set of activities which take place in interactions between a customer and people, goods and other physical resources, systems and/or infrastructures representing the service provider and possibly involving other customers, which aim at solving customers' problems* (developed from Grönroos, 2000:46).

This and other definitions are based on *what a service is*, i.e., based on the service activity. However, as Edvardsson, Gustafsson and Roos (2005:118) conclude, in a recent study based on the views of eleven academic experts in the service marketing field: 'Service is a perspective on value creation rather than a category of market offerings'. In their analysis, perspective seems to mean a way of thinking, or a 'logic'. Hence, another starting point for defining a service is to consider *what a service should do for the customer*, i.e. service as a marketing logic. Following the growing interest in value for customers a logical starting point for developing such a definition could be that a service should support customers in a value-generating way. Supporting customers in a value-generating way means that with the service as support provided by the firm the customers should perceive that they are better off in some way than before or as compared to the expected support of another firm. Traditionally value is viewed in the literature as embedded in a product that is exchanged, the *value-in-exchange* notion. When exchange is considered the central concept in marketing, the value for customers has inevitably to be embedded in what is exchanged, i.e., in the product itself.

According to a more recent view in the literature of how value for customers emerges, value is created when products, goods or services, are used by customers. This is the *value-in-use* notion (Woodruff and Gardial, 1996). As Vargo and Lusch (2004:6–7) show, the view that value for customers is embedded in the product seems to be due to competing logics within economic theory and misunderstandings arising when the dominating value concept from economics was transferred to management and marketing. It is of course only logical to assume that the value really emerges for customers when goods and services do something for them. Before this happens, only potential value exists. Although the expression *value-in-use* is not always used in the contemporary management and marketing literature, this notion of value creation seems likely to become the dominant view (see for example, Normann, 2001; Storbacka and Lehtinen, 2001; Grönroos, 2000; Gummesson, 2002; Ravald and Grönroos, 1996; Wikström, 1996; Vandermerwe, 1996; Woodruff and Gardial, 1996; Jüttner and Wehrli, 1994; Normann and Ramirez, 1993).

According to the value-in-use view, suppliers and service providers do not create value in their planning, designing and production processes. The customers do it themselves in their *value-generating processes*, i.e., in their daily activities when products are needed by them for them to perform activities. *'Value for customers is created throughout the relationship by the customer, partly in interactions between the customer and the supplier or service provider*. The focus is not on products but on customers' *value-creating processes* where value emerges for customers' (Grönroos, 2000:24–25; emphasis in original). This view is echoed by Vargo and Lusch: 'A service-centered dominant logic implies that value is defined by and cocreated with the consumer rather than embedded in the product' (2004:6).

Suppliers only create the resources or means required to make it possible for customers to create value for themselves. In this sense at least, when suppliers and customers interact, they are engaged in co-creation of value (compare Prahalad and Ramaswamy, 2004; Wikström, 1996). However, customers are also sole-creators of value, for example when using a shirt that recently has been washed at a laundry. Goods are resources like other physical objects such as credit cards and airline seats: the firm makes them available for money so that customers in their *own* processes will be able to use them in a way that creates value for them, as individuals, households or organisations. Such customer processes are by way of examples, cooking dinner, cleaning a house, transportation by car, producing paper, etc.

Service logic vs. goods logic

A *goods logic* means that *the firm makes goods as resources available for customers* so that they can manage their own processes in a value-generating way. The supplier firm is sole producer of these goods, whereas in adopting a value-in-use view, the customer is the sole creator of value. Consequently, goods marketing is to make customers buy goods as resources to be used in their value-generating processes, i.e., as *resources that support* customers' value generation.

Services, on the other hand, are processes where a set of company resources interact with the customers so that value is created or emerges in the customers' processes. Hence, unlike goods that are value-supporting *resources*, services are value-supporting *processes*. In the Nordic School reckoning, *service logic* means that *the firm facilitates processes that support customers' value creation*. Due to the customers' involvement in these interactive processes, firms and customers are co-producers of the service and co-creators of value. As was pointed out earlier, at some point the customer may be a sole creator of value as well. Following this service logic, *a service as an activity* can be defined *as a process where a set of resources interact with each other and with the customer aiming at supporting the customer's processes in a value-generating way*. Service marketing, therefore, is to invite customers to use the service processes by making promises about value that can be expected to be captured from the service, and to implement these processes in a way that allows customers to perceive that value is created in their processes (promise keeping through value fulfilment).

Following the Nordic School tradition to focus on consumption Korkman (2006) discusses a service logic based on the impact of services on the consumption process as a *practice*. According to *practice theory*, consumption can be understood as a practice – a person's daily activities – and as a consumer this person becomes a carrier of practices. If allowed, a service provider can join a person's practice in a supporting manner (e.g., Shove and Pantzar, 2005). Drawing on practice theory Korkman (2006) suggests that one could understand a service logic 'as a way of empowering consumption as a practice' so that value emerges for the customer from that practice. According to Korkman value is not created, it *emerges* for the consumer from a well-supported practice.

According to a goods logic, goods are resources in customers' sole creation of value. However, according to a service logic and due to the firm-customer interactions that occur, the goods components in the service process are part of the service provider's process of co-creating value with the customer. In this case goods are resources in the co-creation of value for customers. In both cases, resources other than goods are needed as well. When consuming goods, customers need at least information about how to use the goods and how to create value with them, and other goods may perhaps also be needed. For example, a piece of meat bought from the butcher is not enough to cook dinner. When services as processes are consumed, goods components in the service process have to be accompanied by other resources as well. In a restaurant, for example, the steak has to be accompanied by other ingredients as well as by waiters who take the order and serve the meal. Vargo and Lusch (2004:8–9) consider goods transmitters of service and 'distribution mechanisms for service provision'. However, in the Nordic School view it is not the goods alone that transmit services. Goods are seen as one type of resource alongside others, such as people, systems, infrastructures and information (see, for example, Grönroos 1982, 1996, 2006). The service is the process where these resources function together with each other and interact with the customer in his or her capacity as a consumer and as a co-producing resource. Depending on how this process functions and on its outcome, more or less value emerges for the customer. Service as a process supports customers' value creation. As a resource alongside others in this process goods *contribute* to the service that supports customers' value creation.

Goods become service-like

Traditionally, in the service literature, services have been described with goods as the defining marketing logic. For some time already it has been claimed that the differences between goods and services may not be that important. Some goods are also perceived as intangible, and modular production processes make it possible for customers, using for example cad/cam techniques, to interact with the manufacturing firm and participate in at least part of the production process. Also mass customisation is a way of bringing customers into part of the production process. Because goods, for example, are produced in new ways using techniques that allow customers to participate in the production process, the goods logic is under pressure to change. The goods logic and the goods-based marketing models may not provide the same dominating guidelines for goods marketing as they used to do. Instead the service logic and the service-based marketing models may provide more general guidelines.

What has happened is this. Because of the opening up of goods manufacturing systems for customers, and due to the extension of the range and content of customer contacts following a growing interest in relationship marketing (Grönroos, 1999), the number of touch-points between the producer and the customer has increased beyond the specific requirements needed to support the goods themselves. In other words, the customer interface has grown. In this process a number of new interactions between the firm and its customers have been introduced. In businesses such as consumer durables, business-to-business and even fast moving consumer goods, the content of the firm-customer contacts often includes information services, call centre advice, repair and maintenance and other service activities. The point is that gradually the customer contacts and contact points in many businesses today have grown to include more interactive content than what a goods logic would imply.

Within the Nordic School thinking, a distinguishing characteristic of services is the simultaneous production and consumption process, which includes a varying number of interactions and different kinds of resources. Customer contacts in goods-dominant industries are certainly becoming more *service-like*, including continuing processes and interactions between the customer and the firm and its resources, and its sets of activities. To support the customers' value creation processes it is not a matter of providing a physical product only. Instead, this product becomes but one resource in a bundle of resources – other physical products, people, information, etc., – that customers interact with. 'This bundle of resources, in which the goods are nothing but one resource among others, is required to support the customers' processes so that value is created in those processes' (Grönroos, 2006:362). If customer contacts for goods are becoming more like services it is questionable whether a goods logic provides a useful guideline for goods marketing anymore. This is one reason why a service logic may be more productive for traditionally goods-based businesses.

An extended consumption concept

Traditionally production is related to the process where an object is produced. This production concept emanates from a goods-oriented literature. On the other hand consumption is the process where customers consume goods, whatever the purpose. As has been discussed previously, in the service literature another view of the relation between production and consumption has emerged. According to this view production and consumption are partly simultaneously occurring processes, and hence, the customers participate in the production process and assume the role of co-producers, thereby influencing the nature of the service that is produced and consumed, and likewise the value customers create from the service experience.

If consumption is defined differently, from a value-creating point of view based on the value-in-use notion, instead of being understood as customers' usage of an object, the consumption concept widens. Instead of including only the use of the marketed product itself, consumption also encompasses all elements, physical objects such as goods, information, people-to-people encounters, encounters with systems and infrastructures and possible interactions with other customers that together have an impact on customers' value creation. This is how consumption is viewed, for example, in the Nordic School literature on service marketing and in the vast literature on service quality. However, to make the marketing consequences of this visible, consumption must no longer be viewed as a black box.

The goods logic tends to ignore the value support of the wide range of elements of the customer contacts and firm-customer interactions. Instead it connects the *core value* and sometimes all value on offer for customers with the physical product and the price paid for it alone. Because of this, marketing is geared towards creating and communicating the value for customers that goods may stand for. The service logic on the other hand is geared towards supporting the customers' processes and daily activities in such a way that value is created for the customers. Hence, following this logic, from a marketing standpoint this means that the firm does not only need resources to make promises about value for customers through, for example, product development, pricing and marketing communication. It also has to *mobilise such resources as well as such knowledge and leadership that are needed to develop, manage and implement chains of processes, interactions and outcomes which makes this value support possible.* Hence, following a service logic marketing means not only making promises about value but also facilitating value fulfilment as an integral part of marketing (compare the service marketing triangle in Grönroos, 2000:55). This has consequences for the *value proposition* concept frequently used in marketing. A value proposition should be a proposition, a suggestion, which has to be followed up by an offering that fulfils the expectations created by this proposition or suggestion. According to Vargo and Lusch's (2004:5) discussion of a service-dominant logic, firms can *only* make value propositions. This seems, however, like a conclusion based on a goods logic, according to which the firm cannot be actively involved in the consumption process. The goods are consumed by the customer alone and they cannot be changed during consumption. Value is captured by the customer from the consumption of the physical product. However, in service consumption, co-production and co-creation of value takes place during the consumption process. Both the customer and the firm can be active. For example, part-time marketers involved in interactive marketing can and should influence the value that customers capture from the consumption of a service. Hence, suggesting or *proposing value* – making a value proposition or suggestion about the *future value* to be expected by the customer – and being actively involved in *value fulfilment* through interactive marketing efforts (keeping promises), are conceptually different aspects of value creation. Also from a marketing point of view they have to be kept apart.

The goods-oriented marketing literature is based on the idea of a marketing mix managed within a marketing function by full-time marketers, where the product variable represents more or less standardised physical goods. Through market research the products are supposed to meet the requirements of targeted customers. More than that, mainstream marketing models are not penetrating the consumption process. The research into services has brought marketing and the consumption process into the same arena. For example, the concepts of interactive marketing and part-time marketers of the Nordic School and international research into service quality have provided marketers with structures, concepts and models for understanding consumption as part of marketing models.

An important Nordic School aspect of service marketing is recognition of the widened consumption concept, where not only customers' interactions with physical objects take place, such as when goods have been bought for consumption (or tangible things offered in service processes), but the customers' perception of all elements of any sort that they interact with during the consumption and production processes are included. In this way all aspects of consumption, all content in the firm-customer interactions that has an impact on customers' perception of quality and support their value creation, can be taken into account and handled as part of marketing. These interactions make customers' co-creation of value possible and at the same time they enable active marketing efforts directly during the consumption process. This is what in the Nordic School approach is labelled interactive marketing.

Service logic as a dominant logic

In goods contexts where the customer interface includes more content than standardised goods only, such as home deliveries, installation, documentation and other types of information, call centre advice, repair and maintenance, complaints handling and correction of quality problems and service failures, invoices and invoicing systems, etc., or only one or a few of these activities, the consumption process is much more elaborate than a goods only focus would imply. Many more elements other than the goods alone impact the consumption process. How the firm handles all these elements influences the customers' value-generating processes, some of which take place during the simultaneous production and consumption process, some of which afterwards. Customer value is not created by one element alone but by the total experience of all elements.

The more content there is in the customer interface, the more complicated it probably is for the firm to manage the whole value-generating process. However, taking a value-in-use perspective the marketer has to try to carefully design and manage as many elements of the interface as possible. Some elements are more critical to the customer than others and have to be managed accordingly. Even if the goods support the customers' processes perfectly well, this potential support value may be destroyed by something being absent, or some other part of the extended consumption process not functioning in a value-supporting way. For example, late deliveries of a Christmas present bought on the Internet or a lacking corkscrew to open a bottle of good wine are such examples. Deliveries can probably be influenced directly by the marketer, whereas the existence of a corkscrew can only be managed indirectly by the seller of wine.

Hence, the marketer should not market the physical objects and goods only, but they should market them as part of overall services in the same way as, for example, restaurants use meat as part of the total restaurant service process. In other words, when the total customer interface is taken into account the goods should not be marketed solely as goods, but as services. However, when the customer contact only includes a physical product without any service support, from a marketing point of view is this a goods context or a service context? If one argues that both goods and services are used by the customer to capture value-in-use from them, it is a service context and a service logic can be used to explain consumption (see the arguments in Vargo and Lusch, 2004:6–7). From this perspective a service-dominant logic offers a truly dominant logic for marketing. On the other hand, does a service logic always lead to more effective marketing? If the customer contact only includes a physical product and the marketer does not, and has no way to interact with the customer in any way during consumption, does a marketing approach based on service logic fit? It does: as an overall philosophy mainly based on an analysis of consumption, according to which 'it is . . . reasonable to consider both goods and services to be bought by consumers in order to give some service or value satisfaction' (Grönroos, 1979:59), and if customers 'buy offerings (including goods or services) which render service which create value' (Gummesson, 1995:250; see also Levitt, 1974; and for an explanation from within economic theory, see Becker, 1965). However, from a marketing point of view, in situations like the one mentioned above where there are no ways for the marketer to intervene with the customer's interactions with the product, marketing models based on a traditional goods-based logic may be helpful. As Stauss (2005) points out, when moving towards a service-dominant logic, goods-based concepts and models may still be useful in some situations. It should be observed, though, that goods-based marketing models developed using a goods logic are only useful in those special cases where the customer contact is stripped from everything else other than the physical product. As this is the extreme situation, a residual, not the norm, goods marketing can be considered a special case of marketing, where service marketing is the norm.

Conclusions

When taking a widened view of the consumption process, and bringing marketing and consumption into the same arena and viewing them from a value creation perspective, one can see how customers in many varied contexts other than what traditionally are considered service interfaces in reality are involved in service-like processes. Service-based marketing concepts and models fit such situations better than using models based on a goods logic. This conclusion is similar to the one communicated by the service-dominant logic presented by Vargo and Lusch (2004). However, according to the Nordic School view, goods do not render services as such, and customers do not consume goods as services. Instead goods are one of several types of resources functioning in a service-like process, and it is this *process* that is the service that customers consume. A customer does not consume a drill as a service, but the process of using the drill together with, for example, information about the drill and knowledge about drilling in order to make a hole in the wall. This process is the service. The drill is not a transmitter of service, rather it is one resource needed to make a service process possible.

In addition to what normally is treated as services, at least consumer durables and industrial products in business-to-business contexts can be treated as services. In these situations the customer interfaces fulfil the characteristics of services more than they fulfil characteristics for goods. A service logic describes better than a goods logic these types of situations. If elements are added to the customer interface of fast moving consumer goods, such as call centre advice, websites with suggestions about how to use goods and frequently asked questions, etc., these customer interfaces, too, are becoming more service-like. When enough additional elements are included, a service logic provides better guidelines for how to market a physical product than a goods logic does.

Because part-time marketers who are not part of a marketing specialist function and activities and processes performed by other functions influence customers' value creation, marketing as a separate functional approach does not make sense anymore (Grönroos, 1982; 1999). Although marketing is the only or dominant focus of full-time marketers, the part-time marketers' focus on the customer is not the only area of importance to them. We must not draw the conclusion from this that marketing is more important than other business functions. Finance, human resource management, manufacturing and operations, accounting, technology and goods and service development, etc., are equally important to the success of a firm. However, the focus on customers is not less important than the others.

The arguments put forward in this article demonstrate that a service marketing context and a service logic rather than a goods marketing context and a goods logic are the norm and not a special case. When the customer interface is stripped of most of its content and simplified to include a physical product only, goods marketing and applying a goods logic in marketing may very well work. However, this is a special case, with service-based marketing as the norm, which might occur when the context of the customer interface has become limited enough to warrant the use of a goods logic and goods-based marketing models. In a competitive situation it may be important for the firm to find ways of extending the customer contacts and thus moving into a marketing context where a service logic applies.

However, when developing and applying models based on a service logic it is important to remember that one must not neglect the power of concepts developed as part of goods-based models. For example, pricing and marketing communication using various types of media as well as segmentation and targeting are, of course, still important marketing variables. And the other way round, when applied in goods contexts the power of service marketing concepts and models must not be diluted (see Stauss, 2005).

References

Bagozzi, R.P. (1975) 'Marketing as Exchange', *Journal of Marketing* 39 (October):32–39.
Ballantyne, D. (2003) 'A Relationship-Mediated Theory of Internal Marketing', *European Journal of Marketing* 37(9):1242–1260.
Ballantyne, D. and Varey, R.J. (2006) 'Introducing a Dialogical Orientation to the Service-Dominant Logic of Marketing', in Lusch, R.F. and Vargo, S.L. (eds.) *The Service-Dominant Logic of Marketing: Dialog, Debate, and Directions*, pp. 224–235. Armonk, NY: M.E. Sharpe.
Becker, Gary S. (1965) 'A Theory of Allocation of Time', *The Economic Journal*, 75, 299 (September): 493–517.
Berry, L.L. (1981) 'The Employee as Customer', *Journal of Retailing* 3 (March):33–40.
Berry, L.L. and Parasuraman, A. (1991) *Marketing Services: Competing through Quality*. New York: The Free Press.
Berry, L.L. and Parasuraman, A. (1993) 'Building a New Academic Field – The Case of Service Marketing', *Journal of Retailing*, 69(1):13–60.

Bitner, M.J. (1992) 'Servicescapes: The Impact of Physical Surroundings on Customers and Employees', *Journal of Marketing* 56 (April):57–71.

Booms, Bernard, H. & MaryJo Bitner (1982): Marketing Structures and Organization Structures for Service Firms. In Donnelly, John H. & William R. George, eds., Marketing of Services. Chicago, IL: American Marketing Association, 47–51.

Borden, N.H. (1964) 'The Concept of The Marketing Mix', *Journal of Advertising Research*, 4 (June): 2–7.

Brady, M.K. and Cronin, Jr., J.J. (2001) 'Some Thoughts on Conceptualizing Perceived Service Quality: A Hierarchical Approach', *Journal of Marketing* 65 (July):34–49.

Calonius, H. (1986) 'A Market Behaviour Framework', in K. Möller and M. Paltschik (eds.) *Contemporary Research in Marketing*. Proceedings from the XV Annual Conference of the European Marketing Academy, pp. 515–524. Helsinki: Helsinki School of Economics and Hanken Swedish School of Economics, Finland,

Christopher, M., Payne, A. and Ballantyne, D. (1991) *Relationship Marketing: Bringing Quality, Customer Service and Marketing Together*. Oxford: Butterworth Heinemann.

Cronin, Jr., J.J. and Taylor, S.A. (1992) 'Measuring Service Quality: A Re-Examination and Extension', *Journal of Marketing* 56 (July):55–68.

Culliton, J. (1948) *The Management of Marketing Costs*. Boston, MA: Graduate School of Business Administration, Research Division, Harvard University.

Edvardsson, B. (2005) 'Service Quality: Beyond Cognitive Assessment', *Managing Service Quality* (15)2:127–131.

Edvardsson, B., Gustafsson, A. and Roos, I. (2005) 'Service Portraits in Service Research: A Critical Review', *International Journal of Service Industry Management* 16(1):107–121.

Eiglier, P. and Langeard, E. (1976) 'Principe de Politique Marketing Pour les Enterprises de Service', working paper of the *Institut d'Administration des Enterprises Université d'Aix-Marseille*.

Fisk, R.P., Brown, S.W. and Bitner, M.J. (1993) 'Tracking the Evolution of the Services Marketing Literature', *Journal of Retailing* 69 (Spring):61–103.

Grönroos, C. (1978) 'A Service-Oriented Approach to Marketing of Services', *European Journal of Marketing* 12(8):588–601.

Grönroos, C. (1982) 'An Applied Service Marketing Theory', *European Journal of Marketing* 16(7):30–41.

Grönroos, C. (1984) 'A Service Quality Model and its Marketing Implications', *European Journal of Marketing* 18(4):36–44.

Grönroos, C. (1996) 'Relationship Marketing Logic', *The Asia-Australia Marketing Journal*. 4 (1):7–18.

Grönroos, C. (1999) 'Relationship Marketing: Challenges for the Organization', *Journal of Business Research* 46(3):327–335.

Grönroos, C. (2000) *Service Management and Marketing: A Customer Relationship Approach*. Chichester: John Wiley.

Grönroos, C. (2006) 'What Can a Service Logic Offer Marketing Theory?' in Lusch, R.F. and Vargo, S.L. (eds.) *The Service-Dominant Logic of Marketing: Dialog, Debate, and Directions*, pp. 354–364. Armonk, NY: M.E. Sharpe.

Grönroos, C. and Gummesson, E. (1985) 'The Nordic School of Services - An Introduction', in C. Grönroos, C. and Gummesson, E. (eds.) *Service Marketing - Nordic School Perspectives*, Series R2, pp. 6–11. Stockholm: University of Stockholm.

Gummesson, E. (1979) 'The Marketing of Professional Services – An Organizational Dilemma', *European Journal of Marketing* 13(5):308–318.

Gummesson, E. (1987) 'The New Marketing – Developing Long-Term Interactive Relationships', *Long Range Planning* 20(4):10–20.

Gummesson, E. (1991) 'Marketing Revisited: The Crucial Role of the Part-Time Marketer', *European Journal of Marketing* 25(2):60–67.

Gummesson, E. (1995) 'Relationship Marketing: Its Role in the Service Economy', in W.J. Glynn and J.G. Barnes (eds.) *Understanding Services Management*, pp. 244–268. New York: Wiley.

Gummesson, E. (2002) 'Relationship Marketing and the New Economy: It's Time for Deprogramming', *Journal of Services Marketing* 16(7):585–589.

Jüttner, U. and Wehrli, H.P. (1994) 'Relationship Marketing from a Value Perspective', *International Journal of Service Industry Management*, 5(5):54–73.

Korkman, O. (2006) *Customer Value Formation in Practice: A Practice-Theoretical Approach*. Report A155. Helsinki: Hanken Swedish School of Economics Finland.

Langeard, E. and Eiglier, P. (1987) *Servuction: Le Marketing des Services*. Paris: Wiley.

Lehtinen, J.R. (1983) *Asiakasohjautuva Palveluyritys* (In Finnish: The Customer-Oriented Service Firm). Espoo, Finland: Weilin+Göös.

Levitt, T. (1974) *Marketing for Business Growth*. New York: McGraw-Hill.

Liljander, V. (1995) *Comparison Standards in Perceived Service Quality'*. Report A62. Helsinki: Hanken Swedish School of Economics Finland.

Lings, I.N. and Greenley, G.E. (2005) 'Measuring Internal Market Orientation', *Journal of Service Research* 7(3):290–305.

Lovelock, C.H. (1984) *Services Marketing*. Englewood Cliffs, NJ: Prentice-Hall.

Lovelock, C.H. and Gummesson, E. (2004) 'Whither Service Marketing? In Search of a New Paradigm and Fresh Perspectives', *Journal of Service Research* 7(1):20–41.

Normann, R. (1983) *Service Management*. New York: Wiley.

Normann, R. (2001) *Reframing Business: When the Map Changes the Landscape*. Chichester: Wiley.

Normann, R. and Ramirez, R. (1993) 'From Value Chain to Value Constellation: Designing Interactive Strategy', *Harvard Business Review* 71 (July–August):65–77.

Parasuraman, A., Zeithaml, V.A. and Berry, L.L. (1985) 'A Conceptual Model of Service Quality and its Implications for Future Research', *Journal of Marketing* 49 (Fall):41–50.

Parasuraman, A., Zeithaml, V.A. and Berry, L.L. (1988) 'SERVQUAL: A Multi-Item Scale for Measuring Consumer Perceptions of Service Quality', *Journal of Retailing* 64(1):12–40.

Prahalad, C.K. and Ramaswamy, V. (2004) *The Future of Competition: Co-Creating Unique Value with Customers*. Boston, MA: Harvard Business School Press.

Ravald, A. and Grönroos, C. (1996) 'The Value Concept and Relationship Marketing', *European Journal of Marketing* 30(2):19–30.

Sasser, W.E. and Arbeit, S.P. (1976) 'Selling Jobs in the Service Sector', *Business Horizons*, 19 (June):61–65.

Sheth, J.N. and Parvatiyar. A. (2000) 'Relationship Marketing In Consumer Markets: Antecedents and Consequences', in Sheth, J.N. and Parvatiyar, A. (eds.) *Handbook of Relationship Marketing*, pp. 171–208. Thousand Oaks, CA: Sage.

Shostack, G.L. (1977) 'Breaking Free from Product Marketing', *Journal of Marketing* 41 (April):73–80.

Shove, E. and Pantzar, M. (2005) 'Consumers, Producers and Practices: Understanding the Invention and Reinvention of Nordic Walking', *Journal of Consumer Culture* 5(1):43–64.

Stauss, B. (2005) 'A Phyrric Victory: The Implication of an Unlimited Broadening of the Concept of Service', *Managing Service Quality* 15(3):219–229.

Storbacka, K. and Lehtinen, J.R. (2001) *Customer Relationship Management*. Singapore: McGraw-Hill.

Strandvik, T. (1994) *Tolerance Zones and Perceived Service Quality*. Report A58. Helsinki: Hanken Swedish School of Economics Finland.

Vandermerwe, S. (1996) 'Becoming a Customer "Owning" Company', *Long Range Planning* 29(6):770–782.

Vargo, S.L. and Lusch, R.F. (2004) 'Evolving To a New Dominant Logic for Marketing', *Journal of Marketing* 68 (January):1–17.

Vargo, S.L. and Morgan, F.W. (2005) 'Services in Society and Academic Thought: An Historical Analysis', *Journal of Macromarketing* 25(1):42–53.

Wikström, S. (1996) 'Value Creation by Company-Consumer Interaction', *Journal of Marketing Management* 12: 359–374.

Woodruff, R.B. and Gardial, S. (1996) *Know your Customers – New Approaches to Understanding Customer Value and Satisfaction*. Oxford: Blackwell.

Conclusion
Towards a Contemporary Marketing Theory

The nine articles in this volume include thirty years of development of service and relationship marketing frameworks, models and concepts. The scientific approach has constantly been that of what internationally has been called the Nordic School of thought. In this concluding chapter, I will discuss the logic of service and relationship marketing and its potential for a logic for marketing and for the development of a contemporary marketing theory. With the growing interest in a service-dominant logic, it is only natural to analyse whether the logic of service and relationship marketing can provide a useful foundation for a contemporary marketing theory. For natural reasons this logic is compared with the marketing mix management logic that still dominates marketing research and practice and forms the mainstream.

What Should Be Achieved by Marketing?

According to a traditional approach to marketing, achieving sales and acquiring customers are considered the main objectives. This has been called *transaction marketing*. During the past twenty years or so, research into *relationship marketing* has pointed out the importance of retaining customers. Marketing should aim not only at acquiring customers but also, and in most cases probably more so, to keep and further develop the customer contacts that have been established. Hence, three levels of marketing objectives can be identified: (1) *get customers*; (2) *keep customers*; and (3) *grow customers into a customer relationship*. The objectives of marketing on these three levels and the commitment of customers sought are summarized in Table 1.

Transactional marketing aims at achieving the first level. Even if customers have bought from the same provider previously, they are still approached by activities aiming at customer acquisition, such as advertising campaigns, price offers or sales calls. For the marketer, each new purchase is like a trial purchase.

Table 1 Marketing objectives and levels of customer commitment

Level	Marketing objective	Customer commitment
Level 1: Get customers	To make customers choose the firm's offerings (goods, services) over those of the competitors	Trial purchase
Level 2: Keep customers	To make customers satisfied with what they bought so that they decide to buy again	'share of the customer's wallet'
Level 3: Grow customers into customer relationships	Create a trusting relationship and an emotional connection with the customers so that they feel committed to the firm and continuously patronize it	In addition, a 'share of the customer's heart and mind'

Source: Grönroos (2007)

In situations where the firm and its customers interact on a continuous or in some other way regular basis, the firm can attempt to develop its customer contacts during service processes in a way that influences the customers favourably and encourages them to continue purchasing. This requires that a customer focus is extended to all employees and other resources where there is the customer's interface. In this way, the firm can capture a continuous share of these customers' purchases in a certain category ('a share of the customer's wallet').

Here it is important to realize that even though these customers seem to be in a relational mode, a real relationship does not necessarily exist. Due to their continuous purchasing behaviour, these customers look relational, but in fact they may only be *bonded* to the firm in a non-committal way (Arantola 2002). The reason for their behaviour may be a lack of alternatives. A retailer may be the only one that for the time being is conveniently located or a supplier of equipment may be the only one that for the time being has the required technology or offer, and so on. As soon as an alternative with a better or equal location, or offering a better price or an improved or perhaps only acceptable technology is available, the customer will go.

To develop a true relationship with a customer, the firm has to strive to reach the third level, where the customer feels emotionally committed to the firm, which then also has managed to capture 'a share of the heart and mind' of such a customer (Storbacka and Lehtinen 2001). Here a real customer relationship has developed. This does not mean that this customer could not stop patronizing a given firm at some stage, but it makes the customer less prone to shop around. To achieve this third level, the firm has to take a relational approach in its marketing.

Three Basic Marketing Guidelines

Before discussing how marketing can be developed to fit the changing circumstances, three basic assumptions about marketing need to be emphasized. These are basic guidelines for the development of marketing that are almost axiomatic (compare Grönroos 2006a and 2007):

1. Resources and activities of a firm that influence a customer's preferences and behaviours are marketing resources and activities.
2. The marketing resources and activities of a firm have to be present and function in situations where the customer can perceive them and they can influence the customer.
3. The customers of a firm, not the firm nor its marketers, decide which of the firm's resources and activities are marketing resources and activities.

These assumptions seem self-evident, but nevertheless they are seldom, if ever explicitly pointed out in the marketing literature. They are somehow disguised behind the marketing concept, according to which the needs and wants of the customer should be the starting point for a firm's decision-making. The basic idea of marketing is to relate a firm to its existing and potential customers. What pursues these objectives has to be marketing, regardless of existing organizational planning, and budgeting structures.

Moreover, to be effective, what is planned and implemented under the rubric of marketing has to be perceived by customers and has to influence them. In the final analysis only customers can decide what has an impact on them and which of a firm's resources and activities influence their preferences. What has an impact on customers will vary from situation to situation, customer to customer and even from time to time.

How Do Customers Capture Value from Goods and Services: Value-in-Exchange or Value-in-Use?

Customers do not buy goods or services, they buy the value they can capture from offerings in order to reach a state of satisfaction (Levitt 1972). Traditionally a *value-in-exchange* view has been used in marketing and this view of where and how value for customers is created is reflected in the tenets of mainstream marketing and therefore also in the role and scope of marketing. According to the value-in-exchange concept, value for customers is created in the supplier's design and production processes and then transferred to customers for their use in the form of goods or services. Hence, value is considered to be embedded in the product (a good or a service). If this is the case, the role of the marketer is to create programmes and activities that aim to persuade customers to buy this ready-made value. Because the value for customers is embedded in the product and known to the firm, the marketer does not have to create interactions with customers during the consumption/usage processes. This notion, combined with the customer response mechanism inherited from economic theory, according to which the market, not the individual customer, demonstrates whether customers collectively accept the value or not by either buying or not buying, has made marketing models blind to what goes on in the customers' consumption processes. Marketing's active responsibility ends with sales and a preferably positive purchasing decision.

The value-in-exchange view of how customers capture value from products is, however, a misconception. As Vargo and Lusch (2004) have shown, this misunderstanding seems to have occurred when a value concept in macroeconomics was transferred to microeconomics and from there borrowed by management and marketing. Although the old value concept still dominates the literature, in the past fifteen years or so, an alternative view of how value is created for customers has emerged in the management and marketing literature. This view has been called *value-in-use* (see Woodruff and Gardial 1996; Vargo and Lusch 2004; see also Holbrook 1994). According to this value concept that is gaining ground in management and marketing, value for customers is not created in the producer's space but in the consumer's space (Vandermerwe 1996; see also Ravald and Grönroos 1996 and Normann 2001). Value is created in customers' everyday activities and processes or *value-creating processes* (Grönroos 2007), i.e., when customers use the products they have bought. This is, of course, a much more realistic description of how a consumer captures value from any type of solution, for example, physical goods, services, information, and combinations of these and other elements.

The value-in-use concept has paramount consequences for marketing theory. If value is captured by customers in their daily life and in their everyday activities and processes, ready-made value embedded in products (value-in-exchange) does not exist. At that stage, *only a promise about value* exists. To make sure that customers indeed capture a wanted value from goods and services, the firm has to develop ways of entering the consumption process and create interactions with the customers during that process. Marketing must not end with sales. Instead it has to extend its area of interest beyond creating sales and a positive purchasing decision and become directly and actively involved with consumption and usage.

To a large extent, research into service marketing and also relationship marketing, especially, but of course not only, along the lines of the Nordic School of thought, is founded on the observation that, in services, production and consumption are partly simultaneous processes and that the firm and the customer interact with each other during the consumption process, and therefore, marketing has to be and can be extended to the consumption process as *interactive marketing*. Because of this, when exploring new avenues for marketing theory it seems only natural to take service and relationship marketing as the point of departure.

The Service Logic: From an Odd Exception to the Norm

In the ninth article on adapting a service logic for marketing a *service logic* was described to mean that *a firm facilitates processes that support customers' value creation* (Grönroos 2006b). This was contrasted to a goods logic which was described as providing customers with value-supporting resources for their use. When goods can be described as *value-supporting resources*, services were defined as *value-supporting processes* (Grönroos 2006b). Using a goods logic, the firm cannot enter the consumption or usage process of goods and cannot influence it. The goods must stand up for themselves, and the consumers have to make use to the best of their knowledge of what the goods can do for them. Hence, value for customers has to be embedded in the goods themselves. This is very much in line with the traditional *value-in-exchange* concept that management and marketing borrowed from economics.

Following the value-in-use concept but adapting a goods logic, the consumption and usage of goods can be described as customers' *sole creation* of value. The customers have to combine a physical good with other resources, for example, with other goods and knowledge about how to use them, in order to capture value from them in the consumption process. The supplier can no longer interfere.

On the other hand, service as value-supporting processes that go into customers' consumption means that the firm does not meet the customers during the purchasing phase only but continues *interacting* with the customers during the consumption process. Hence, following the value-in-use notion, the firm has an opportunity to influence customers' value creation. And as service marketing research has claimed for about thirty years already, the customer participates as co-producer in the service process (often also called service production/service delivery) and influences the flow of the process and its outcome and therefore also the perceived quality of the service. Consequently, service marketing and later relationship marketing have always considered the customer a co-producer and therefore also a co-creator of value. The other way round, the firm is not only a co-producer of services, but due to the interactions with customers, during simultaneous production and consumption processes, also a co-creator of value-in-use. Later, management literature also picked up this notion of customer co-production and co-creation of value (Normann and Ramirez 1993; Wikström 1996; Prahalad and Ramaswamy 2004).

When accepting that *value-in-use* is a more accurate way of describing how customers capture value from goods for themselves than value-in-exchange, marketers of physical goods need to find ways of entering the customers' consumption and usage processes. Only by creating interactive contacts with customers at that stage can firms influence the consumption process beyond the goods' capability of doing so. Many firms are indeed striving to do so by adding call centre and e-mail advice, frequently asked questions on an Internet website, delivery, maintenance and repair services, etc. What firms are doing is, first of all, adding more resources to the goods themselves to support customers' use of the goods. In other words, instead of providing customers with a good alone as a value-supporting resource, it now provides the customer with a number of different resources – goods, service activities, information and access to advice – in a value-supporting process. This of course means that the goods-marketing firm has moved away from a goods logic and adopted a service logic. In other words, the goods have been turned into services for customers.

Increasingly, customer interfaces include more and more elements beyond the goods themselves. To stay competitive, firms in consumer and business markets alike have had to add various types of elements as illustrated in the previous paragraph. The competition drives firms to do so and this trend makes the firms' offerings more service-like. Hence, there are at least two reasons for services to become the marketing norm: (1) adapting a value-in-use view of how customers capture value requires the firm to find ways of interacting with its customers during their consumption and usage processes, and thus, to develop opportunities for the firm to become co-creators of value during those processes; (2) the competitive situation forces firms to grow their customer interfaces far beyond the goods themselves and add a variety of elements to the consumption and usage processes, which also makes co-creation of value together with the customers possible.

Both the above-mentioned reasons turn the offerings of a goods-marketing firm into services. Service becomes the norm for marketing, and therefore, mainstream marketing needs to renew itself so that it can capture this development. However, when extending the customer interface and interactions with customers during consumption beyond the goods, another change in the marketing approach is called for as well. As the number of customer touchpoints increase, a time dimension has to be included. For the firm it is not a matter of achieving sales only, as in transaction marketing, but being able to handle post-purchase interactions with the customers. This means that, at least potentially, it becomes important to recognize relationships. A customer contact during a purchasing and consumption process is a latent relationship, and it may cover only one consumption episode or the first such episode may lead to another and subsequently into continuous contacts between the firm and a customer. Latent relationships may turn into what could be called true relationships, where the customer starts to feel a certain degree of emotional attraction to the firm.

The Focal Point: Exchange or Interaction

For the past decades *exchange* has been viewed as the subject matter of marketing research (Bagozzi 1975; Hunt 1976) and facilitating exchange has been considered the true aim of marketing. Therefore, mainstream models have become focused on transactions and on creating and facilitating transactions. In other words, marketing has been preoccupied with persuading customers to engage in transactions, i.e., to make a favourable purchasing decision. What happens after the purchase during the consumption process has been outside the scope of marketing. According to marketing's roots in economics, the market reaction, i.e., continuous sales achieved or not, shows whether the customers liked what they bought or did not like it. The exchange paradigm has effects for marketing that do not fit the contemporary marketing environment. First of all, it makes marketing transaction-oriented. Second, it makes the marketer lose sight of the individual customer and possible enduring relationships with that individual. Finally, and most fatally, because facilitating exchange relates to a process that ends with sales and the purchasing decision, it draws the marketers' attention away from what is essential today, namely the interactions with customers during the use of products (e.g., good services information).

Of course, exchange of products for money still takes place, but especially in an on-going customer relationship it is difficult to say when it exactly took place. Due to traditional external marketing efforts, a first exchange may take place, but for continuous exchanges to occur, the interactions with customers have to be handled successfully. The focal concept is *interaction*.

As Ballantyne and Varey conclude, 'interactions over time are enactments of the exchange process' (2006, p. 228), and thus exchange can be seen as a higher-order concept. Although one can argue theoretically that exchanges take place in all commercial contexts, exchange is a too fuzzy and elusive phenomenon to be used as the focal point of marketing research. As already was concluded, *exchange*, and *relational exchange*, point towards *transactions* and draw the researcher's and practitioner's attention away from marketing as a *process including the customers* and *interaction*. In a relationship marketing context, Sheth and Parvatiyar (2000) came to a similar conclusion, namely that exchange theory perhaps should be given up. In a relationship marketing context, Evert Gummesson argues that marketing consists of 'interactions, relationships and networks' (Gummesson 2002). He does not include exchange as a focal concept either. Of his three concepts, interaction seems to be the basic one, where relationships are developing from successfully managed interactions and this may take place in various types of networks (Gummesson 2005).

Hence, because interactions enable the firm to enter the consumption and usage processes in a direct and active way, when developing marketing theory, *the focal construct should be interaction rather than exchange*.

Managing Customer Relationship or Customer Management

Relationship marketing and IT-based so-called customer relationship management tools have created an interest in managing the customer relationship. Clearly, managing customer relationships is at the heart of relationship marketing. However, what is its role in a more generic marketing theory?

The literature on relationship marketing and studies of relationship marketing in practice show a variety of different views on the subject. Managing customer relationships is considered to be anything from creating a mutual commitment and understanding of the supplier and the customer and a win-win situation (see Grönroos 1989; Morgan and Hunt 1994; Håkansson and Snehota 1995; Sheth and Parvatiyar 1995; Gummesson 2002) as a basis for marketing, to having customers who show repetitive buying behaviour (see Liljander and Strandvik 1995), to managing relationship marketing instruments such as loyalty programmes and direct mailings (Verhoef 2003), and relationship marketing tactics (Leong and Qing 2006) and relationships as yet another variable in the marketing mix toolbox used to manipulate customers (see the criticism of relationship marketing in practice in Fournier, Dobscha and Mick 1998).

Moreover, because the costs of retaining customers may be higher than the benefits to be gained from such a strategy, a relationship marketing approach with the goal of increasing customer retention may not always be a profitable strategy (Reinartz and Kumar 2002; Ryals 2005). In addition, the research on 'contemporary marketing practices' demonstrates that firms across cultures seem to use a variety of marketing approaches, some of which can be described as relational, some of which cannot (see, for example, Coviello, Brodie, Danaher and Johnston 2002).

In marketing and management jargon, the term 'customer relationship' is also used in a multitude of ways. For some, it means customers with whom a behavioural *and* emotional connection and a mutual sense of connectedness (Lindberg-Repo and Grönroos 2004) have been developed. In addition to repetitive purchasing behaviour (a behavioural component), a larger share of *the customers' heart and mind* is also required (an emotional or attitudinal component) (Storbacka and Lehtinen 2001). For others, every customer who has shown up at least twice or even every customer, regardless of their purchasing behaviour, is called a customer relationship.

Only customers can decide whether they have, or want to have, a relationship with a firm, i.e., whether a customer relationship exists or not. It seems quite obvious that all customers do not want to be in a relationship with firms whose products they are using. Customers can be in *transactional modes* as well as in *relational modes*, and the same customer may probably shift from one mode to another depending on type of products, or firms, or even situation. There is no research yet that would demonstrate when a customer recognizes a relationship exists, wants a relationship to exist or shifts from a transactional to a relational mode. There is not much knowledge about customers' interests in relational behaviour and about their reactions to relationship marketing approaches.

Latent relationships always exist, but neither the firm nor the customer may always want to develop them into true relationships and use such relationships as a foundation for marketing. Hence, it is wiser to use the more neutral term *customer management* and to develop a marketing theory *which does not require relationships with the customer to exist, but when firms and customers do want this, it allows relationships to be developed.*

Mixing Ingredients or Managing Promises

Since the 1950s, after Neil Borden's introduction of the marketing mix notion (Borden 1964), this metaphor has been the central guideline for the management of marketing efforts and programmes. It sets the limits for which of a firm's resources and activities are part of marketing and consequently which are not. Borden based his notion of the marketers' task on Culliton's view of the marketer as a mixer of ingredients, which he expressed in a report published in 1948 (Culliton 1948). Eventually McCarthy (1960) synthesized the marketing mix ingredients into four categories which became known as the 4 Ps (product, price, place, and promotion). This framework quickly grew into a cemented model, totally overshadowing other suggested ways of systematizing marketing (e.g., Hansen 1956, the first textbook organized around a P-like structure; see Frey 1961; Lazer and Kelley 1962; Staudt and Taylor 1965; Lipson and Darling 1974) as well as other, European approaches to understanding marketing and customer-influencing activities, such as *parameter theory* (Rasmussen 1955; Mickwitz 1959) and its earlier economics-founded *action parameter* approaches (Frisch 1933; von Stackelberg 1939). It is interesting to note that these tablets-of-stone commandments (Kent 1986) for marketing academics and practitioners alike actually violate one of the central views of the marketing mix metaphor as expressed by Borden. His list of marketing ingredients included twelve variables and he explicitly claimed that its content must not be considered a final once-and-for-all list of marketing variables. Instead, he said, it must constantly be reconsidered and redeveloped for every specific marketing situation. However, this turned out to be wishful thinking.

Although the 4 Ps of the marketing mix put customers in the centre of the framework, the model is oriented towards structure and makes marketing an inside-out managerial activity that easily alienates marketing from the customer. The model has drawn the marketers' interest away from process and directed it towards an easily manageable structural decision-making framework.[1] It has

---

[1] By and large, the renewed marketing definition launched in 2004 is still based on an inside-out marketing mix management approach, where marketing is defined as one organizational function. The vague references to value to customers and management of customer relationships that are added do not make the definition any clearer. Compare the critical analysis of the underpinning logic of this definition in Grönroos, C. (2006b) 'On defining marketing: finding a new logic for marketing'. *Marketing Theory*, 6(4): 395–417.

also made marketing overly tactical. Moreover, the beauty of the simplicity of the framework has led academics, professors and students alike, to embrace it as an easily taught, understood and used model. For almost fifty years now, it has been so easy to use that it has seduced proponents of mainstream marketing into neglecting questioning the realism of the marketing mix metaphor in a changing environment. As marketing is a process, a model which predominantly is a list of marketing variables contradicts the inner meaning of marketing. And a list inevitably becomes obsolete, including structural elements that still are important but excluding elements that over time have become essential to manage with a customer focus. Such a list is potentially dangerous to use.

Because the mixer-of-ingredients metaphor, the marketing mix and the 4 Ps of mainstream marketing were developed during an era with growing markets and surplus demand that waits to be met by goods and services, they are mainly oriented towards customer acquisition and creating sales and do not include possibilities to enter the customers' consumption and usage processes other than with a pre-produced and standardized product. Today the marketing environment and consequently the challenges for the firms are different. Getting customers is still important of course, but in a constantly growing number of markets, being able to keep customers and to grow their involvement with the firm towards a relationship-type of connectedness is the key to marketing success. To use the promise concept, *mainstream marketing is preoccupied with making promises, but neglects promise keeping.* The disturbing fact of the matter today is, as Brown observes in his discussions with top management members from large companies, 'the keeping of promises and building customer loyalty is typically considered the responsibility of others [than the marketers] in the enterprise' (Brown 2005, p. 3).

In service and relationship marketing research, another foundation for marketing than the marketer-as-a-mixer-of-ingredients metaphor has been introduced and used on a slowly increasing number of occasions. This is the *promise concept*. It was originally introduced in the marketing literature by Henrik Calonius in the mid-1980s (Calonius 1983, 1986, 1988). Since then it has been used in relation-ship marketing (e.g., Grönroos 1989, 1996, 2006b; Berry 1995) and in service marketing (e.g., Grönroos 1984, 2007; Bitner 1995). Berry (1995) claims that the fulfilment of promises made to customers is the foundation for retaining customers. Although Grönroos discusses relationship marketing in general and Berry and Bitner service relationships, obviously the conclusions regarding the role of promises have to be true for any types of products in any context.

Calonius' promise concept is partly founded on an observation by Levitt (1981): 'When prospective customers can't experience the product in advance, they are asked to buy what are essentially promises – promises of satisfaction. Even tangible, testable, feelable, smellable products are, before they are bought, largely just promises' (p. 96). Calonius (1986) defines promises as 'a more or less explicitly expressed conditional declaration or assurance made to another party, or to oneself, with respect to the future, stating that one will do or refrain from some specific act, or that one will give or bestow some specific thing' (p. 518).

Some marketing activities and processes, such as communicating and pricing, aim at *making promises*, whereas others are *promise keeping*. The latter category of activities and processes includes, for example, deliveries, usage of goods and other types of solutions, information about how to use products, repair and maintenance, recovery of problems and mistakes and call centre advice.

The promise concept adds another new dimension to marketing as well. Promises cannot be expected to be successfully kept unless the organization is prepared to do so (Bitner 1995). *Enabling promises* is, therefore, an integral part of making and keeping promises. Employees involved in the fulfilment of promises, regardless of the organizational function they belong to and of their position in the organization, have to take a customer focus. This demonstrates the need to include *internal marketing* as an integral part of marketing. Internal marketing as a concept was developed in service marketing (e.g., Eiglier and Langeard 1976; Berry 1981; Grönroos 1978, 1981) and has also become a part of relationship marketing (e.g. Dunne and Barnes 2000; Ballantyne 2003).

In conclusion, making promises involves traditional external marketing activities, such as marketing communication and pricing, which aim at communicating value propositions to prospective customers. Fulfilling promises means that expectations created by promises made about value propositions are supported in a value-creating manner. Enabling promises again means that prerequisites for promise making and promise keeping are created. In Figure 1, the marketing game plan is illustrated around the promise and value-in-use concepts.

The full-time marketers, possibly organized in a marketing department, are responsible for making promises through *external marketing* activities. The target customer may be part of a mass market or can be approached as an individual. With the firm's value-supporting resources – goods and other tangible elements, employees, information, systems and technologies – expectations created by promises made should be met. Such expectations can be explicitly or implicitly

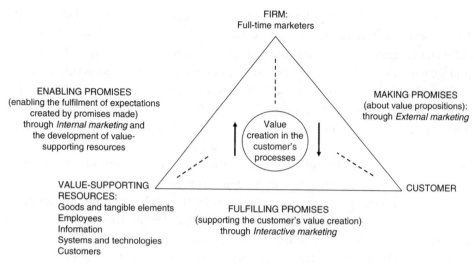

Figure 1 The marketing game plan

perceived or they can even be fuzzy and become explicitly perceived only during consumption (Ojasalo 1999). In the interactions with customers that occur, the customer performs as a co-producer and a co-creator of value. Hence, in this process the customer is a resource as well, and is not only a consumer. In that way the promises are fulfilled and the customer's value-creating processes are supported. Because this part of the total marketing process always involves inter- actions between the customer and the various resources of the firm – e.g., inter- actions with goods, with people, with systems – the term *interactive marketing* developed in service marketing fits well as a label for the process of keeping promises. One should note that this original interactive marketing term has nothing to do with the much younger interactive marketing and interactive media notions in marketing communications. Finally, *internal marketing* is the process of enabling the fulfilment of expectations created by promises made. Internal marketing aims at ensuring that the firm has employees who are customer-focused and motivated and knowledgeable to perform as part-time marketers. However, in addition, systems and technologies as well as goods and other physical resources have to be developed in a customer-focused manner as well.

Marketing: A Function or a Multi-Functional Process

Research into service marketing and relationship marketing and especially the Nordic School research clearly demonstrate that when customer interfaces grow beyond a more or less standardized product to include additional elements and touchpoints, customer management cannot be successfully implemented by the full-time specialists of the marketing department without the support of people and systems that are part of other organizational functions (in addition to Nordic School references, see also, for example, Lovelock 2000; Brown 2005; Brown and Bitner 2006). Because they cannot always be at the right place at the right time with the customer contacts, the marketing and sales representatives, the full-time marketers, cannot handle more than a limited portion of marketing, and moreover, they are outnumbered several times by people from other functions who handle customer contacts and influence the customers' preferences, i.e., by the firm's part-time marketers (Gummesson 1991). And even more importantly, 'the part-time marketers do not only outnumber the full-time marketers, the specialists; *often they are the only marketers around'* (Grönroos 1994, p. 352; emphasis in the original). The organizational purpose of marketing should be to relate the firm to its customers.

Marketing, together with sales, should be all about customer management. Nevertheless, for the past fifty years the American Marketing Association, the world's leading authority on how to define mainstream marketing, has always maintained that marketing is one organizational function alongside other functions. Even the 2004 updated definition claims that marketing is an organizational function. In the marketing literature, the shortcomings of this view have been addressed in various ways, for example, by offering marketing as the most important function or even as an integrative function (Kotler 1994). In practice, none of these suggestions have ever been an effective solution to the problem. People in every organizational function are professionals in their own areas, and all functions are needed for successful business operations.

Proponents of mainstream marketing do not seem to have drawn the obvious conclusion, as has been done in service and relationship marketing research as well as in the IMP (industrial marketing and purchasing) research into business-to-business marketing (see, for example, Håkansson and Snehota 1995), namely, that marketing cannot be managed, planned and implemented as one organizational function. From this conclusion it follows that structurally marketing cannot be totally organized as one department responsible for marketing. *It is no longer a matter of marketing management, but market-oriented, customer-focused management above the departmental level and throughout the organization,* wherever the undertakings of people and the ways systems function directly or indirectly impact customers' value creation and their preferences and willingness to continue doing business with the firm.

Towards a New Logic for Marketing

As the articles in this volume and the discussion in this concluding chapter have demonstrated, increasingly every firm is becoming a service business (e.g., Grönroos 1990; Webster 1992, 1994). Already in the 1970s Levitt (1972) noted that there are no goods or service businesses but businesses with more or less service components in their offerings. Gummesson states that 'customers do not buy goods or services: they buy offerings which render services which create value. . . . The traditional division between goods and services is long outdated' (1995, pp. 250–251). 'Thus it seems inevitable that understanding service processes is becoming an imperative for all types of businesses, not just for what used to be called service businesses' (Grönroos 1998, p. 336). Levitt's (1974) classical example about customers who do not buy quarter-inch drills but quarter-inch holes implies the same thing, namely, customers buy services that create value in their everyday activities. Customers look for services and if they choose to do so, firms can develop their offerings into service offerings and perform as service businesses.

For the development of a contemporary marketing theory the obvious conclusion is that the underpinning logic of such a theory has to be geared towards the marketing reality of service businesses. As services are inherently relational, the tenets of relationship marketing also, alongside service marketing, form a foundation for such a marketing theory.

Because of the transaction-focused traditions of mainstream marketing, this still dominating marketing perspective includes a number of shortcomings for the development of a contemporary marketing theory. In Table 2 the shortcomings of mainstream marketing and the requirements of a service and relationship based foundation for marketing are summarized.

- *Diffusion of customer-management activities, i.e., of marketing.* Successful customer management, where expectations created by promises about value propositions made are fulfilled, requires that a customer focus exists throughout the organization and tasks that directly or indirectly influence customers are performed and managed as part of the total marketing process. Part-time marketers often outnumber the full-time marketers.
- *Dedication to a customer management and customer-focused performance, i.e., to marketing.* The motivation for and interest in customer-focused behaviour and part-time marketing performance must exist throughout the organization. If those who are in a part-time marketer position do not have

Table 2 Consequences for marketing in service competition of its transaction-related traditions and requirements of a service and relationship-focused perspective

Aspect of marketing	Consequences of transaction-related traditions	Requirements of a service and relationship-focused perspective
Diffusion of customer management activities (marketing)	A customer focus normally exists only in some of these places where customers interact with the firm	A customer focus has to be present throughout the organization, wherever external or internal customers are present
Dedication to customer management (marketing)	Only a limited part of the organization is engaged in customer-focused behaviour and have a customer-focused attitude	In addition to full-time marketers and sales people, a major part of the organization must be committed to customer-focused attitudes and behaviour
Organizing for customer management (marketing)	Marketing is normally a hostage of marketing and sales departments. Marketing is normally organized in marketing departments consisting of full-time marketers only	All marketing cannot be organized in a traditional sense. Only full-time marketing can be organized in a specialized department. In part-time marketers a customer-focused (marketing) attitude can only be instilled
Planning and preparing budgets for customer management (marketing)	Plans and budgets for customer-focused performance (sales and marketing) are normally plans of sales and marketing departments only	Planning and preparing budgets for customer-focused performance must be part of all plans and budgets of a firm and co-ordinated in the business plan
Commitment to internal marketing	All marketing and sales people are considered professionals. Hence, no internal marketing is needed.	Part-time marketers outnumber full-time marketers several times. Hence, internal marketing is of strategic importance
The term used for customer management (marketing)	For appr. a century marketing has been used as the term for a firm's customer-focused performance	Marketing as a term may relate too much to customer acquisition only. Moreover, part-time marketers often do not accept to be involved in something called marketing. Hence, this term may be outdated and psychologically wrong and therefore not useful as an overall label for customer management and customer-focused attitudes and behaviours

Source: Grönroos (2007)

customer-focused attitudes and know how to and want to perform in a customer-oriented manner, promises made by external marketing efforts will not be fulfilled and the appropriate support for the customers' value creation will be missing.

- *Organizing for customer-management, i.e., for marketing.* The full-time marketing specialists can be organized in a department of their own, but the part-time marketers who are spread throughout the organization in different functions, processes and departments cannot. They are part of other departments, to which their main duties belong. One must remember that the part-time marketers' responsibility for customers is on top of their main duty, be that driving a delivery truck, repairing a production machine, handling a complaint, or negotiating a loan with a bank customer. Hence, marketing cannot be organized in a traditional structural manner. Only the full-time marketers can be organized in a group of their own, but other than that *marketing can only be instilled in the organization as a customer-focused attitude of mind.*

- *Planning and preparing budgets for customer-management, i.e., for marketing.* Traditional marketing plans and budgets are plans for the firm's marketing department. However, a customer focus must be present in all plans and in preparing all budgets where the performance guided by these plans and budgets influence customers either directly or indirectly.

- *Commitment to internal marketing.* In mainstream marketing where customer management is the responsibility of marketing specialists only, no programmes that aim at developing a marketing attitude among the marketers are needed. However, when a customer focus is required throughout the organization, favourable attitudes towards marketing and an understanding of what taking a customer focus really means cannot be taken for granted. Therefore, the firm has to have a strong commitment to internal marketing and top management must see internal marketing as a strategic issue and not only as a tactical personnel training task.

- *The term used for customer-management, i.e., for marketing.* Marketing as a term has not been used for more than about a century. However, the marketing phenomenon, i.e., customer management, is as old as the history of trade and commerce. There are really no traditions that would require us to stick to this term. It often turns out that marketing is an awkward term that easily creates resistance among employees who should accept a role as part-time marketers. Moreover, for most of its century-old history, the term 'marketing' has been used for customer acquisition and the term is heavily loaded with such connotations. In contemporary marketing, getting out onto the market and acquiring customers is still important, of course, but increasingly, keeping and growing customers and staying in the market is even more important.

As no generally applicable term that would fit the contemporary marketing environment seems to have been developed, the traditional term 'marketing' is still used in this concluding chapter. My hypothesis is, however, that a growing number of firms will follow what some firms already have done and use other labels for customer management and that eventually the marketing literature will find a more appropriate term to use in the new environment of customer management (see Grönroos 1994, 1999).

Propositions for the Development of a Contemporary Marketing Theory

In the following four propositions, including eleven sub-propositions, the guiding principles for the development of a contemporary marketing theory are listed. These propositions follow on from the articles included in this volume as well as from the arguments in this final chapter. They have been more thoroughly developed in 'On Defining Marketing. Finding a New Roadmap for Marketing' (Grönroos 2006b).

The propositions are as follows:

Proposition 1a: Value is not delivered by a firm to customers but created in customer processes through support to those processes and through co-creation in interactions with customers (value-in-use).
Proposition 1b: The role of marketing is, on one hand, to develop and communicate value propositions to customers and, on the other hand, to support customers' value creation through goods, services, information and other resources as well as through interactions where co-creation of value can take place.

Proposition 2a: Customers can be in relational as well as non-relational modes, thus they do not always appreciate being approached in a relational manner by firms, nor is a relational strategy always profitable for firms, and hence, even though managing customers as relationships often may be effective, it cannot be considered a generic approach to relating a customer to the firm.
Proposition 2b: Managing customer relationships cannot be considered a generic guiding principle for the development of marketing. In an implicit way,

marketing must allow both for relational and non-relational marketing strategies and activities.

Proposition 3a: Marketing cannot be implemented by one organizational function of marketing specialists, the full-time marketers, only.
Proposition 3b: Marketing needs a customer focus throughout the organization, thus involving both full-time marketers, totally or predominantly trained to take a customer focus, and part-time marketers, who when performing their tasks from the outset are not at all or only partly trained to take a customer focus.
Proposition 3c: To be effective, marketing also requires that technologies, information systems and other systems are designed and function in a customer-focused manner.

Proposition 4a: Customers have explicit as well as implicit and fuzzy expectations and these expectations should be fulfilled by the performance of the firm.
Proposition 4b: Fulfilment of promises in a customer-focused manner requires internal marketing efforts as promise enablers.
Proposition 4c: Customer-focused technologies, information systems and other systems as well as appropriate leadership are also required to support a customer-focused performance by part-time marketers.
Proposition 4d: Making promises, supported by internal activities, such as internal marketing geared towards the fulfilment of expectations created by promises made, as well as technology, systems and leadership support, and fulfiling expectations created by promises made, form a firm's marketing process.

The propositions represent the logic of a service and relationship perspective on customer management. Based on this logic the following marketing definition can be derived (Grönroos 2006b):

> Marketing is a customer focus that permeates organizational functions and processes and is geared towards making promises through value proposition, enabling the fulfilment of individual expectations created by such promises and fulfilling such expectations through support to customers' value-creating processes, thereby supporting value creation in the firm's as well as its customers' and other stakeholders' processes.

This definition could be labelled a *promises management definition*. Its backbone is the process of making promises and enabling and fulfilling expectations created by promises made (compare Figure 1). Making promises includes activities such as developing, pricing and communicating value propositions. Promises are enabled through internal marketing programmes and activities and through the development of customer-focused goods, technologies, service processes, information systems and other systems as well as appropriate leadership. Expectations created by promises are fulfilled by supporting customers' value creation. This is done by providing customers with resources and processes – goods, services, information and people, systems, infrastructures, physical resources – and interactions between the customer and these resources and processes as well as by mobilizing customers as a resource in the purchasing and consumption and usage processes.

This logic is based on the value-in-use notion, according to which value for customers is created in customers' value-creating processes. With a set of resources, processes and interactions, firms support customers' value creation.

In the contemporary business environment, longer-term relationships with customers are often a basis for profitable business. However, customers cannot always be expected to want to engage in a relational contact with firms and firms do not always consider creating relationships with customers as the foundation of business to be the best possible strategy. Therefore, this definition only implicitly includes the potential for developing customer relationships. Providing customers with products that successfully support value creation and doing so in a way that meets individual expectations created by promises that have been made will increase the likelihood that customers who are in a *relational mode* will want to do repeat purchasing and even develop an emotional connection with the firm. It may also make customers relationship prone (De Wulf, Odekerken-Schröder and Iacobucci 2001; Odekerken-Schröder, De Wulf and Schumacher 2003). In these cases relationships will develop.

Furthermore, several organizational functions have to be customer-focused and take a responsibility for marketing. What according to mainstream marketing is called the marketing function, including, for example, market research, advertising and other means of marketing communication, as well as sales, will be 100 per cent focused on the customer, whereas other functions such as R&D, product and service development, manufacturing and service operations, logistics, procurement, repair and maintenance, call centre activities, service recovery and complaints handling wherever they are located in the organization, and human resource management and finance will have to be part-time focused on customers. Hence, marketing as a customer focus is one dimension among others of the planning and implementing of the tasks of these functions.

This definition is not based on a list of variables that are *the* decision-making areas of marketing. Such lists can never be conclusive and can easily become obsolete. Moreover, various types of situations will require different lists. It is impossible to prepare a list of decision-making areas that would fit the demands of all possible marketing situations. Therefore, the promises management definition includes in marketing anything that supports value formation in customers' processes by making promises, enabling these processes, and fulfilling expectations created by them. Enabling promises is explicitly included in the definition. If this internal support is missing or mismanaged, supporting customers' value-creating processes well will be difficult.

Finally, the role of expectations (Miller 1977) and expectancy disconfirmation (see, for example, Oliver 1980) is taken into account in an explicit way. Communicating value propositions and making promises set expectations, and the way such expectations are met by the value support provided has a decisive impact on the success of marketing. Based on promises made, customers develop expectations and therefore it is not the promises as such that are met but rather the customers' individual expectations created by these promises.

Some Concluding Thoughts

The mainstream marketing framework with its focus on one function, exchange of pre-produced value and a structure, a set of marketing variables, rather than process, does not fit the contemporary marketing situation well, at least not for other types of products than standardized consumer goods. It has become just as much a straitjacket for marketing practice as for marketing research. The service and relationship-based logic for marketing with its process nature helps academics and practitioners alike locate all the firm's marketing resources and activities and it helps planning and budgeting procedures to include all these resources and activities and not only what the marketing department is doing. Then marketing becomes more relevant again for the firm's customers. If this is the case, marketing also becomes more relevant for top management, and in the final analysis for the firm's shareholders as well.

Following mainstream marketing's structural approach, it has been comparatively uncomplicated to understand marketing, and to organize, plan and execute marketing programmes. The marketing mix management metaphor has served as a pedagogically straightforward and easily understood and replicable marketing formula. It has been easy for professors to teach marketing and for marketers to practice marketing. The new marketing logic and the promises management definition with its process view of marketing and focus on enabling, making and fulfilling promises offer far more complicated guidelines. It will be less straightforward to define which marketing resources and variables to use in a given situation and it will be impossible to determine for a longer period of time what is included in marketing and what is not. For example, with changes in the customer base, in customer preferences and purchasing and usage behaviour, in the competitive situations and actions by competitors, and in the business environment, the resources and activities that should be included in the marketing process will change. Such changes may be slow or they may occur almost overnight.

Finally, one should, of course, ask whether this service and relationship-based logic and the customer-focused promises management definition will provide a better foundation for a contemporary marketing theory than mainstream marketing. Or is there another better alternative? Of course, the latter question cannot be answered categorically. However, in my opinion, thirty years of service and relationship marketing research have demonstrated that the development of marketing thought within these fields and the parallel development of the business environments for a growing number of industries merge. Service and relationship marketing seem to provide a logic for marketing which well meets today's challenges for marketing theory and practice. In view of this, the promise-based and process-oriented definition of marketing has the potential to be a generic definition and the underpinning logic potential for a contemporary marketing theory. For marketing subfields specialized definitions geared to the characteristics of those fields can probably be derived, much as, for example, relationship marketing has developed its own definitions.

References

Arantola, H. (2002) *Relationship Drivers in Provider-Consumer Relationships. Empirical Studies of Customer Loyalty Programs*. Helsinki: Hanken Swedish School of Economics, Finland.

Bagozzi, R.P. (1975) 'Marketing as Exchange', *Journal of Marketing*, 39(October): 32–39.

Ballantyne, D. (2003) 'A Relationship-Mediated Theory of Internal Marketing', *European Journal of Marketing*, 37(9): 1242–1260.

Ballantyne, D. and Varey, R.J. (2006) 'Introducing a Dialogical Orientation to the Service-Dominant Logic of Marketing', in Lusch, R.F. and Vargo, S.L. (eds) *The Service-Dominant Logic of Marketing: Dialog, Debate, and Directions*. Armonk, NY: M.E. Sharpe, pp. 224–235.

Berry, L.L. (1981) 'The Employee as Customer', *Journal of Retailing*, 3(March): 33–40.

Berry, L.L. (1995) 'Relationship Marketing of Services: Growing Interest, Emerging Perspectives', *Journal of the Academy of Marketing Science*, 23(4): 236–245.

Bitner, M.J. (1995) 'Building Service Relationships: It's All About Promises', *Journal of the Academy of Marketing Science*. 23(4): 246–251.

Borden, N.H. (1964) 'The Concept of the Marketing Mix', *Journal of Advertising Research*, 4 (June): 2–7.

Brown, S.W. (2005) 'When Executives Speak, We Should Listen and Act Differently', *Journal of Marketing* 69(October): 2–4.

Brown, S.W. and Bitner, M.J. (2006) 'Mandating a Service Revolution for Marketing', in Lusch, R.F. and Vargo, S.L. (eds) *The Service-Dominant Logic of Marketing: Dialog, Debate, and Directions*. Armonk, NY: M.E. Sharpe, pp. 393–405.

Calonius, H. (1983) 'On the Promise Concept', unpublished discussion paper. Helsinki: Hanken Swedish School of Economics, Finland.

Calonius, H. (1986) 'A Market Behaviour Framework', in Möller, K. and Paltschik, M. (eds) *Contemporary Research in Marketing*. Proceedings from the XV Annual Conference of the European Marketing Academy. Helsinki School of Economics and Hanken Swedish School of Economics, Finland, pp. 515–524 (also published in *Marketing Theory* 6(4), 2006, pp. 419–428).

Calonius, H. (1988) 'A Buying Process Model', in Blois, K. and Parkinson, S. (eds) *Innovative Marketing: A European Perspective*. Proceedings from the XVIIth Annual Conference of the European Marketing Academy. University of Bradford, pp. 86–103.

Coviello, N.E., Brodie, R.J., Danaher, P.J. and Johnston, W.J. (2002) 'How Firms Relate to Their Markets: An Empirical Examination of Contemporary Marketing Practice', *Journal of Marketing*, 66 (July): 33–46.

Culliton, J. (1948) *The Management of Marketing Costs*. Graduate School of Business Administration, Harvard University, Boston.

De Wulf, K., Odekerken-Schröder, G.J. and Iacobucci. D. (2001) 'Investments in Consumer Relationships: A Cross-Country and Cross-Industry Exploration', *Journal of Marketing*, 65(1): 33–50.

Dunne, P.A. and Barnes, J.G. (2000) 'Internal Marketing: A Relationships and Value Creation View', in Varey, R. and Lewis, B. (eds) *Internal Marketing: Directions for Management*. London: Routledge, pp. 192–220.

Eiglier, P. and Langeard, E. (1976) *Principe de politique marketing pour les enterprises de service*, Working Paper. Institut d'Administration des Enterprises, Université d'Aix-Marseille.

Fournier, S., Dobscha, S. and Mick, D.G. (1998) 'Preventing the Premature Death of Relationship Marketing', *Harvard Business Review*, 76 (January–February): 42–51.

Frey, A. (1961) *Advertising*, 3rd edn, New York: Ronald Press.

Frisch, R. (1933) Monopole-Polypole – le notion de la force l'économie. *Nationalekonomisk Tidskrift*, Denmark, pp. 241–259.

Grönroos, C. (1978) 'A Service-Orientated Approach to the Marketing of Services', *European Journal of Marketing*, 12(8): 588–601.

Grönroos, C. (1981) 'Internal Marketing – An Integral Part of Marketing Theory', in Donnelly, J.H. and George, W.R. (eds) *Marketing of Services*. Chicago, Ill.: American Marketing Association, pp. 238–238.

Grönroos, C. (1984) 'A Service Quality Model and Its Marketing Implications', *European Journal of Marketing*, 18(4): 36–44.

Grönroos, C. (1989) 'Defining Marketing: A Market-Oriented Approach', *European Journal of Marketing*, 23(1): 52–60.

Grönroos, C. (1990) *Service Management and Marketing. Managing the Moments of Truth in Service Competition*. Lexington, MA: Lexington Books.

Grönroos, C. (1994) 'Quo Vadis, Marketing? Toward a Relationship Marketing Paradigm', *Journal of Marketing Management*, 10(5): 347–360.

Grönroos, C. (1996) 'Relationship Marketing Logic', *The Asia-Australia Marketing Journal,* 4(1): 7–18.

Grönroos, C. (1998) 'Marketing Services: The Case of a Missing Product', *Journal of Business & Industrial Marketing,* 13(4/5): 332–338.

Grönroos, C. (1999) 'Relationship Marketing: Challenges for the Organization', *Journal of Business Research,* 46(3): 327–335.

Grönroos, C. (2006a) 'What Can a Service Logic Offer Marketing Theory', In Lusch, R.F. and Vargo, S.L. (eds) *The Service-Dominant Logic of Marketing: Dialog, Debate, and Directions,* Armonk, NY: M.E. Sharpe, pp. 354–364.

Grönroos, C. (2006b) 'On Defining Marketing: Finding a New Roadmap for Marketing', *Marketing Theory,* pp. 6(4).

Grönroos, C. (2007) *Service Management and Marketing: Customer Management in Service Competition.* Chichester: John Wiley & Sons, Ltd.

Gummesson, E. (1991) 'Marketing Revisited: The Crucial Role of the Part-Time Marketer', *European Journal of Marketing,* 25(2): 60–67.

Gummesson, E. (1995) 'Relationship Marketing: Its Role in the Service Economy', in Glynn, W.J. and Barnes, J.G. (eds) *Understand Services Management.* New York: John Wiley & Sons, pp. 244–268.

Gummesson, E. (2002) *Total Relationship Marketing: Rethinking Marketing Management: From 4Ps to 30Rs.* London: Butterworth Heinemann.

Gummesson, E. (2005) *Many-to-Many marknadsföring (Many-to-many marketing).* In Swedish. Malmö: Liber.

Håkansson, H. and Snehota, I. (1995) *Developing Relationships in Business Networks:* London: Routledge.

Hansen, H.L. (1956) *Marketing: Text, Cases, and Readings.* Homewood, IL: Richard D. Irwin.

Holbrook, M.B. (1994) 'The Nature of Customer Value: An Axiology of Service in the Customer Experience', in Rust, R.T. and Oliver, R.L. (eds.) *Service Quality: New Directions in Theory and Practice,* Thousand Oaks, CA: Sage pp. 21–71.

Hunt, S.D. (1976) 'The Nature and Scope of Marketing', *Journal of Marketing,* 40(July): 17–28.

Kent, R.A. (1986) 'Faith in Four Ps: an Alternative', *Journal of Marketing Management,* 2(2): 145–154.

Kotler, P. (1994) *Marketing Management.* Englewood Cliffs, NJ: Prentice-Hall.

Lazer, W. and Kelley, E.J. (1962) *Managerial Marketing: Perspectives and Viewpoints.* Homewood, IL: Richard D. Irwin.

Leong Yow Peng and Quing Wang (2006) 'Impact of Relationship Marketing Tactics (RMTs) on Switchers and Stayers in a Competitive Service Industry', *Journal of Marketing Management,* 22(1–2): 25–59.

Levitt, T. (1972) 'Product-line Approach to Service', *Harvard Business Review,* 50(September-October): pp. 41–52.

Levitt, T. (1974): *Marketing for Business Growth.* New York: McGraw-Hill.

Levitt, T. (1981) 'Marketing Intangible Products and Product Intangibles', *Harvard Business Review,* 59 (May-June): 94–102.

Levitt, T. (1986) *The Marketing Imagination.* New York: The Free Press.

Liljander, V. and Strandvik, T. (1995) 'The Nature of Customer Relationships in Services', in Swartz, T.A., Bowen D.E. and Brown, S.W. (eds.) *Advances in Services Marketing and Management,* 4, Greenwich, CT: JAI Press, pp. 141–167.

Lindberg-Repo, K. and Grönroos, C. (2004) 'Conceptualising Communications Strategy from a Relational Perspective', *Industrial Marketing Management,* 33: 229–239.

Lipson, H.A. and Darling, J.R. (1974) *Marketing Fundamentals: Text and Cases*. New York: John Wiley & Sons.

Lovelock, C.H. (2000) 'Functional Integration in Services: Understanding the Links Between Marketing, Operations, and Human Resources', in Swartz, T.A. and Iacobucci, D. (eds) *Handbook of Services Marketing and Management*. Thousand Oaks, CA: Sage, pp. 421–437.

'Marketing Renaissance: Opportunities and Imperatives for Improving Marketing Thought, Practice, and Infrastructure' (2005) *Journal of Marketing*, 69 (October): 1–25.

McCarthy, E.J. (1960) *Basic Marketing: A Managerial Approach*. Homewood, IL: Irwin.

McGovern, G.J., Court, D., Quelch, J.A. and Crawford, B. (2003) 'Bringing Customers into the Boardroom', *Harvard Business Review*, 82 (November): 70–80.

Mickwitz, G. (1959) *Marketing and Competition*. Helsingfors, Finland: Societas Scientarium Fennica.

Miller, J.A. (1977) 'Studying Satisfaction, Modifying Models, Eliciting Expectations, Posing Problems and Making Meaningful Measurements', in Junt, H.K. (ed.) *Conceptualization and Measurement of Consumer Satisfaction and Dissatisfaction*. Cambridge, MA: Marketing Science Institute, pp. 72–91.

Morgan, R.M. and Hunt, S.D. (1994) 'The Commitment-Trust Theory of Relationship Marketing', *Journal of Marketing*, 58(January): 20–38.

Normann, R. (2001) *Reframing Business: When the Map Changes the Landscape*. Chichester: John Wiley & Sons, Ltd.

Normann, R. and Ramirez, R. (1993) 'From Value Chain to Value Constellation: Designing Interactive Strategy', *Harvard Business Review*, 71(July–August): 65–77.

Odekerken-Schröder, G.J., De Wulf, K. and Schumacher, P. (2003) Strengthening Outcomes of Retailer-Consumer Relationships: The Dual Impact of Relationship Marketing Tactics and Consumer Personality, *Journal of Business Research*, 56(3): 177–190.

Ojasalo, J. (1999) *Quality Dynamics in Professional Services*. Helsinki: Hanken Swedish School of Economics, Finland.

Oliver, R.L. (1980) 'A Cognitive Model of the Antecedents and Consequences of Satisfaction Decisions', *Journal of Marketing Research*, 17 (November): 460–469.

Prahalad, C.K. and Ramaswamy, V. (2004) *The Future of Competition: Co-Creating Unique Value with Customers*. Boston, MA: Harvard Business School Press.

Rasmussen, A. (1955) *Pristeori eller parameterteori? Studier omkring virksomhedens avsaetning* (Price Theory or Parameter Theory? Studies of the Sales of a Firm). Copenhagen: Erhvervsekonomisk forlag.

Ravald, A. and Grönroos, C. (1996) 'The Value Concept and Relationship Marketing', *European Journal of Marketing*, 30(2): 19–30.

Reinartz, W. and Kumar, V. (2002) 'The Mismanagement of Customer Loyalty', *Harvard Business Review*, 80 (July–September): 4–12.

Ryals, L. (2005) 'Making Customer Relationship Mangement Work: The Measurement and Profitable Management of Customer Relationships', *Journal of Marketing*, 69 (October): 252–261.

Sheth, J.N. and Parvatiyar, A. (1995) 'The Evolution of Relationship Marketing', *International Business Review*, 4(4): 397–418.

Sheth, J.N. and Parvatiyar. A. (2000) 'Relationship Marketing in Consumer Markets: Antecedents and Consequences', in Sheth, J.N. and Parvatiyar, A. (eds) *Handbook of Relationship Marketing*. Thousand Oaks, CA: Sage, pp. 171–208.

Stackelberg, H. von (1939) Theorie der Vertriebspolitik und der Qualitätsvariation. *Schmollers Jahrbuch*, 63(1) 73–85.

Staudt, T.A. and Taylor, D.A. (1965) *Marketing: A Managerial Approach*. Homewood, IL: Richard D. Irwin.

Storbacka, K. and Lehtinen, J.R. (2001) *Customer Relationship Management*. Singapore: McGraw-Hill.

Vandermerwe, S. (1996) 'Becoming a Customer "Owning" Company', *Long Range Planning*, 29(6): 770–782.

Vargo, S.L. and Lusch, R.F. (2004) 'Evolving to a New Dominant Logic for Marketing', *Journal of Marketing*, 68(January): 1–17.

Verhoef, P.C. (2003) 'Understanding the Effect of Customer Relationship Management Efforts on Customer Retention and Customer Share Development', *Journal of Marketing*, 67(October): 30–45.

Webster Jr., F.E. (1992) 'The Changing Role of Marketing in the Corporation', *Journal of Marketing*, 56(October): 1–17.

Webster, Jr., F.E. (1994) 'Executing the New Marketing Concept', *Marketing Management*, 3(1): 9–18.

Webster Jr., F.E., Malter, A.J. and Ganesan, S. (2005) 'The Decline and Dispersion of Marketing Competence', *MIT Sloan Management Review*, 46(4): 35–43.

Wikström, S. (1996) 'Value Creation by Company-Consumer Interaction', *Journal of Marketing Management*, 12: 359–374.

Woodruff, R.B. and Gardial, S. (1996) *Know Your Customers: New Approaches to Understanding Customer Value and Satisfaction*. Oxford: Blackwell Publishers

Index